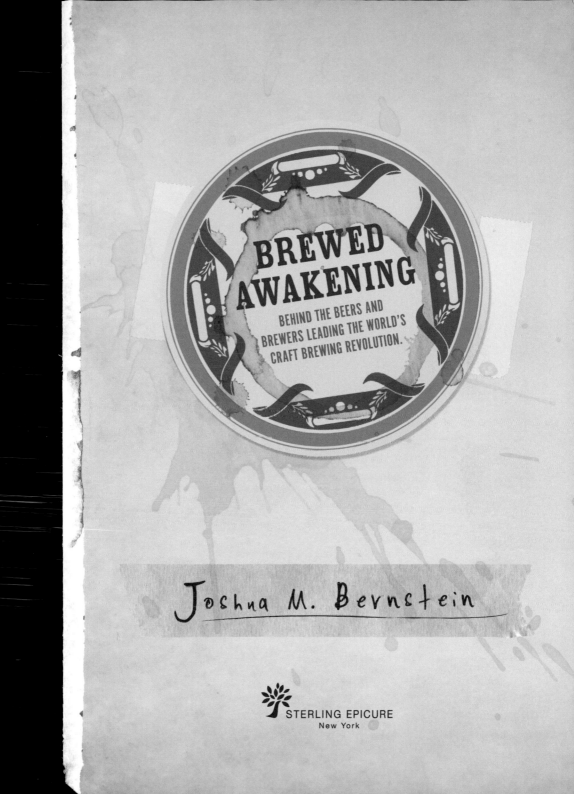

BREWED AWAKENING

BEHIND THE BEERS AND BREWERS LEADING THE WORLD'S CRAFT BREWING REVOLUTION.

Joshua M. Bernstein

STERLING EPICURE

New York

STERLING EPICURE
New York

An Imprint of Sterling Publishing
387 Park Avenue South
New York, NY 10016

© 2011 by Joshua M. Bernstein
Photo Credits are on pages 280–281
Book design by Rachel Maloney

ISBN 978-1-4027-7864-3 (hardcover)

Library of Congress Cataloging-in-Publication Data

Bernstein, Joshua M.
  Brewed awakening : behind the beers and brewers leading the world's craft brewing revolution /
Joshua M. Bernstein.
    p. cm.
  Includes bibliographical references and index.
  ISBN 978-1-4027-7864-3 (alk. paper)
  1. Beer. 2. Brewing. I. Title.
  TP570.B47 2011
  663'.42–dc22

                      2011003196

Distributed in Canada by Sterling Publishing
^c/o Canadian Manda Group, 165 Dufferin Street
Toronto, Ontario, Canada M6K 3H6
Distributed in the United Kingdom by GMC Distribution Services
Castle Place, 166 High Street, Lewes, East Sussex, England BN7 1XU
Distributed in Australia by Capricorn Link (Australia) Pty. Ltd.
P.O. Box 704, Windsor, NSW 2756, Australia

For information about custom editions, special sales, and premium and corporate purchases,
please contact Sterling Special Sales at 800-805-5489 or specialsales@sterlingpublishing.com.

Manufactured in China

6 8 10 9 7 5

www.sterlingpublishing.com

Some of the selections were previously published in slightly different forms as follows: Parts of
"Hop to It" were published as "Flavor of the Month" in *Imbibe*. "Rye Rising" was published as
"Against the Grain" in *Imbibe*. Parts of "Falling in Flavor," "Ancient Ales," "Going Green Has Never
Tasted So Good," "Barrel-Aged Brews," and "Pre-Prohibition Lagers" were adapted from "Blast
from the Past" in *Imbibe*. "Cask Ales" was published as "A Living Tradition" in *Imbibe*. "What a Pair:
Beer and Food" was published as "Look Who's Coming to Dinner" in *Imbibe*. "Of a Certain Age" was
published as "Time in a Bottle" in *Imbibe*. "Berliner Weisse," "California Common," "Kölsch," and
"Saison" were adapted from "Unsung Heroes" in *Imbibe*. "International Spotlight: Norway's Nøgne
Ø" was published as "Hey Nøgne Nøgne" in *New York Press*. Parts of "Gose" were published as "So
the Story Gose" in *Imbibe*.

For my parents, Jenene, and all the brewers making the world a more delicious place.

Contents

Acknowledgments

MY LONG, CARBONATED JOURNEY FROM PINT GLASS to print would have been far less enjoyable without the endless support of friends who patiently listened as I babbled on about brewing minutiae and helped me conduct endless "research." Thanks for never telling me that another beer was a bad idea.

For my parents, Jack and Maryann, and siblings, Becky and Jon, for believing that beer bottles could lead to a book.

Thanks to all my encouraging editors, especially Karen Foley and the crew at *Imbibe* and Adam Rathe and Jerry Portwood at the *New York Press*, for allowing me to write at length about a subject I adore.

To all the brewers, bar owners, barkeeps, cellarmen, photographers, farmers, festival organizers, fellow journalists, historians, and beer lovers, thanks for taking the time to tipple and talk.

Thanks to Carlo DeVito, Diane Abrams, and the Sterling Publishing gang, especially my tireless editor, Pam Hoenig. Kudos for navigating the sea of ABVs and IBUs and, once and for all, answering the question: Is it *pilsner* or *pilsener*?

Last, and most important, thanks to my dear Jenene for her unwavering love, even when I was a complaint-filled cranky pants. I couldn't have written this without your support.

The Making of a Beer Geek

WHEN I WAS IN HIGH SCHOOL, I WAS IN LOVE WITH Busch Light. Since I was just seventeen, I kept this affair secret. Busch and I met only on weekends, long after my parents were deep in their sugarplum dreams.

Long past the witching hour, my band of suburban Ohio miscreants would congregate in my backyard. As moonlight bathed our pimply bodies, we would climb into my parents' hot tub armed with a frosty 30-pack of Busch Light purchased at a lenient beer-and-wine drive-through and watch Geoff assemble his latest invention. Geoff was an engineering whiz who, these days, maintains the navy's nuclear submarines. His smarts were paired with a deviant streak. During high school, that meant constructing things like flame-powered potato guns and, more pertinent to this story, colossal beer bongs.

For the enlightenment of those who did not attend public college or join a frat, a beer bong is a funnel attached to plastic tubing. Though it recalls a torture tool, something that the boys at Gitmo might have dreamed up, we would fight to insert the tube betwixt our jaws. On the count of three, a Busch can was cracked and dumped into the funnel. Gravity sent the foamy brew racing down our gullets like a burst dam. If you finished the funnel, we cheered. If you vomited, we cheered—quietly, lest my parents rustle. When we were seventeen, the beer bong was a portal into an adult universe. We pretended to be mature by pounding Busch.

That early conditioning, combined with a healthy dose of advertising, convinced my taste buds that Busch Light was

America's best beer. My belief endured through my undergrad days at Ohio University, when I'd occasionally flirt with wincing Natural Ice—Natty to those in the know. And when it came to beer, I knew no better. My peers cared about quantity, not quality. Me too. Why spend $10 on a six-pack when the same money could purchase 24 cans of inebriation? Or perhaps a half dozen 40-ouncers of Phat Boy, the malt liquor made with ginseng?

My Tastes Improve with Age

I graduated in 2000 with a journalism degree as worthless as a week-old newspaper. Nursing a case of wanderlust, I embarked on a cross-country road trip with my platonic pal Bari. She and I steered west, across Kansas and Nevada and up California's coast-hugging Highway 1. The scenery was as rugged as our fights were fierce. Bari and I were polarized magnets, drawn apart by proximity. By the time we reached Great Falls, Montana, we made like bananas and split. "Just drop me off at the Greyhound station!" I screamed, gathering my belongings. "Where are you going?" she asked. "I don't know!" She screeched off in a cloud of dust, just like they do in the movies.

At the bus station, I sat on a bench and pondered my future. I had a pack of smokes. I had total freedom. I had nowhere to go. On a payphone, I called a friend in Boulder, Colorado, and pled my plight. "Come on down. We'll drink some beer." Twenty bumpy, sleepless hours later, I arrived at my friend's home. I was greeted with hugs and a trip to the megastore Liquor Mart. Wandering the aisles stuffed with six-packs bearing then-foreign monikers such as Avery and New Belgium and Boulder, I felt as clueless as a newborn lamb. My friend bought a sixer of Avery IPA, and we headed home.

"What is that?" I asked my host, cradling the bottle as if it were a rare talisman.

"It's from Colorado," my pal said. "It's a nice, bitter India pale ale."

I took a sip. My taste buds were pummeled with citrus and sweet caramel, with an aroma of resinous pine needles. This was Fourth of July fireworks compared to the wan sparklers to which I'd become accustomed. I sought out other local elixirs, such as Boulder Brewing's hoppy, unfiltered Hazed & Infused and Flying Dog's floral pale ale. Though I was in the land of Coors, I thirsted for more flavor than the Silver Bullet could offer.

After a wasted week, my friend Aaron called. "What are you doing out there?" he asked. "Drinking." "Well, do you want to come get a drink in New York City?" Aaron and his then girlfriend Emily had just moved into an apartment in heavily Greek Astoria, Queens. They had a free bedroom. Did I want it? My other option was returning to Ohio to split a bunk bed with my younger brother. New York, here I come.

Big Apple, Big Beers

Unlike the average New York transplant, I had no dreams of conquering the Big Apple. I wanted only to drink good beer, hit dive bars, eat dumplings, and pay my meager rent. By day, I toiled as a temp receptionist at financial firms, learning to answer phones with a polished, honeyed "Hello, how can I help you?" By night I hit bars downtown, searching out great microbrews such as Victory's bracing and bitter HopDevil and crisp Brooklyn Pennant Ale. These were heady, hop-filled times, where every cooler contained another six-pack portal to a new, ever-more-delicious drinking world.

After several increasingly disillusioned years of temping—and thousands of dropped calls—I dusted off my journalism degree. I began writing about the alehouses I uncovered and the beers I consumed. The alternative weekly *New York Press* hired me to pen a column on my nighttime ramblings. I wrote beer articles for *Time Out New York* and *New York* magazines. Then beverage magazine *Imbibe* asked me to start writing beer-focused features, followed by a gig at the dearly departed *Gourmet* as its online beer columnist. This led me to consume more delicious beer than most livers process in a lifetime. One evening, it would be a stout aged in bourbon barrels. The next, a sour ale spiked with virulent yeasts. Each beer was wilder, weirder, and tastier than the next. Like any good junkie, I always wanted more.

I flew to Portland, Oregon, to partake in the Oregon Brewers Festival, then checked out the English-style ales of Portland, Maine. San Francisco, Philadelphia, Austin, Asheville—I navigated the nation in search of the finest brews and brewers. I traveled light so I could pack beer into my luggage. Pint by pint, I was sampling a liquid revolution. And every revolution needs an intrepid chronicler.

However, *Brewed Awakening* does not begin in 1965, when Fritz Maytag bought what became the Anchor Brewing Company. It also doesn't kick off with Ken Grossman hand-delivering clattering cases of Sierra Nevada Pale Ale. And sorry, Jim Koch, but I'm not rehashing Sam Adams rolling off the bottling line. While this book could not have existed without their tireless efforts, *Brewed Awakening* looks to now.

The Revolution Has Arrived

Concerning beer, the last decade has witnessed more seismic changes than any time since Prohibition. There are more than 1,700 craft breweries in America, from community-based nanobreweries to the new breed of national brands such as Dogfish Head and Stone. Untethered from stodgy tradition and driven by unbridled creativity, American brewers are leading a boundaryless charge into the global future of beer.

In the United States, the bitter India pale ale has birthed the burly, super-aromatic double IPA. Alcohol percentages have climbed above 10 percent, on par with wine—and now join pinot noir at dinner tables and on tony restaurants' drink lists. Wild yeasts have been harnessed and are used to inoculate beers that, in the best way possible, taste like a barnyard. Naturally carbonated cask ales have now achieved cult status. And brewmasters have begun aging their creations in wooden casks that once contained bourbon, brandy, chardonnay, and even tequila, reviving techniques last seen more than a century earlier.

But it's not all happening in America. *Brewed Awakening* explores the creative fringes of craft brewing, touching down in Nebraska, Norway, New Zealand, and everywhere that better—or stranger—beer is being made. I dig into the oddball hops making beer taste like white wine or tropical fruit, and how IPAs have turned to the dark side and brewers are acting an awful lot like farmers. I find beer styles, like salty gose and tart Berliner weisse, that have been saved from extinction. I walk the blurry line separating amateur and professional brewers, and uncover pint-size breweries popping up in basements and garages. I interview brewers taking beers to extremes, wresting out wild flavors seemingly designed in a mad scientist's lab. Salt and coriander in beer? Why not? How about low-alcohol beers as flavorful as suds that are twice as strong? Or a brew made without barley or wheat? No problem, thanks to the world's *Brewed Awakening*.

You've already cracked this book. Now crack a beer. Next round's on me.

Best,

ONE

INGREDIENTS OF SUCCESS:

Meet the Malts, Hops, and Yeasts Leading Craft Beer to a Flavorful New Frontier

WHEN GROCERY SHOPPING, YOU'VE LIKELY EYEBALLED the ingredients on the labels of packaged goods and scratched your skull. What's maltodextrin, and what's it doing in Doritos? Beer is simpler. Hops, grain, yeast, and water are the four essential ingredients, with occasional aid from supporting adjuncts. And like strings on a guitar, those flavor notes can spin off in countless tangents. Sour, bitter, sweet, chocolaty, spicy—dream it, do it, drink it. But why do these ingredients cause beers to taste so different? Let's dig beneath the hood and discover brewers' new tools for crafting delicious beer.

Hop to It

If you watched sporting events in the early 1990s, you caught commercials for Keystone Light. In the ads, guys swilled "bitter beer" that caused their faces to scrunch up, lower lips covering noses. "Eww, bitter-beer face!" pretty gals would shout, aghast. To save the day, a dude would deliver a cooler of cold Keystone Light. "Don't grab a bitter beer . . . grab a better beer!" the announcer said, as drinkers' faces sprung back to normal.

What a difference a couple of decades makes. For today's craft-beer drinkers, making the bitter-beer face is a point of pride. Bars are packed with lip-pursing India pale ales, double IPAs, and other styles proudly boasting elevated IBUs—international bittering units, a measurement of a beer's hop bitterness. However, all hops breeds are not created equal. Some strains are better suited for providing astringent bitterness, while others are used for their aromas of citrus or even pine.

You've probably savored a piney, citric beer. That's because "brewers often follow fashions in hops," says Garrett Oliver, Brooklyn Brewery's head brewer. "For a while, it seemed like every American craft beer tasted like Cascade"—a flowery, fragrant hop—"then Amarillo," which is citrusy, verging on orange.

No longer. Each year, in the lush hop fields of the Pacific Northwest, dozens of experimental breeds are planted, most identified only by a string of numbers like a shadowy government project. These fledgling varieties are often the result of crossing existing strains in hopes of, say, increasing mildew resistance, amping yields, or devising unique flavors. Annually, large craft breweries such as Sierra Nevada examine dozens of numbered hop breeds not yet in the marketplace. The researchers are hoping to answer a single question: Will this help create a great new beer?

"Many hops taste really bad," says Sierra's communications coordinator, Bill Manley. "Some taste like cabbage or cat piss." But every once in a while, a hop shows serious promise. Perhaps it imparts an alluring flavor that evokes lychee or green tea. The hop is named, and it graduates from lab to brew kettle.

The years-in-development Citra hop gives Sierra Nevada's Torpedo Extra IPA a tropical twist. Elsewhere, the buttery, lemony Sorachi Ace drives Brooklyn Brewery's summery saison (which takes its name from the hop variety), while New Zealand's Nelson Sauvin contributes a white-wine profile for BrewDog's Punk IPA. Elsewhere, brewers are building DIY equipment to wring out hops' flavors, while others are taking hops to the dark side by creating black IPAs that, despite their roasty profile, remain refreshingly bitter. Here's a toast to the new frontier of hops and beer.

Harvested hops from Silverton, Oregon's Goschie Farms.

GET HIP TO HOPS

KNOW YOUR CASCADE FROM YOUR CHINOOK? THIS LIST OF THE MOST COMMONLY USED HOPS WILL TELL YOU WHY YOUR BEER SMELLS LIKE A PINE TREE, TASTES LIKE AN ORANGE, AND IS AS BITTER AS AN OLD MAN. NOTE: NOBLE HOPS ARE EUROPEAN HOP VARIETIES THAT ARE AROMATIC AND LESS BITTER.

AHTANUM

FAIRLY GRAPEFRUITY AND FLORAL, ALONGSIDE NOTES OF PINE AND EARTH. ITS BITTERNESS IS RELATIVELY LOW.

USAGE: AROMA AND FLAVOR

AMARILLO

SEMISWEET AND SUPER-CITRUSY, VERGING ON ORANGES. CONSIDER IT CASCADE ON STEROIDS.

USAGE: FLAVOR AND AROMA

APOLLO

THIS POTENT VARIETY CONTRIBUTES NOTES OF RESIN, SPICE, AND CITRUS— MAINLY ORANGE.

USAGE: BITTERING

BREWER'S GOLD

A COMPLEX, PUNGENT VARIETY WITH A SPICY AROMA AND FLAVOR, AS WELL AS A FRUITY CURRENT OF BLACK CURRANT.

USAGE: BITTERING

CASCADE

POPULAR IN AMERICAN PALE ALES AND IPAS, THIS FLORAL HOP SMELLS STRONGLY OF CITRUS, SOMETIMES GRAPEFRUIT.

USAGE: FLAVOR, AROMA, BITTERING

CENTENNIAL

OFFERS OVER-THE-TOP CITRUS FLAVOR AND AROMA, WITH A RELATIVELY RESTRAINED FLORAL NOSE.

USAGE: FLAVOR, AROMA, BITTERING

CHALLENGER

THE ROBUST AROMA OFFERS A POLISHED, SPICY PROFILE THAT CAN VERGE ON FRUITY; THE BITTERNESS IS CLEAN AND PRESENT.

USAGE: FLAVOR, AROMA, BITTERING

CHINOOK

AN HERBAL, EARTHY, SMOKY, PINEY CHARACTER, WITH SOME CITRUS THROWN IN FOR FUN.

USAGE: AROMA, BITTERING

CITRA

A HEAVY TROPICAL AROMA OF LYCHEE, MANGO, PAPAYA, AND PINEAPPLE. A FULL-ON FRUIT ATTACK.

USAGE: AROMA

COLUMBUS (ALSO KNOWN BY THE TRADE NAME TOMAHAWK)

EARTHY AND MILDLY SPICY, WITH SUBTLE FLAVORS OF CITRUS; VERY SIMILAR TO THE ZEUS HOP.

USAGE: AROMA, BITTERING

CRYSTAL

FLORAL AND SPICY, SOMEWHAT
REMINISCENT OF CINNAMON AND
BLACK PEPPER.
USAGE: FLAVOR, AROMA

DELTA

THE BOUQUET IS A BLEND OF FRUIT,
EARTH, AND GRASS—FLAVOR-WISE,
SUBDUED CITRUS WITH AN
HERBAL EDGE.
USAGE: FLAVOR, AROMA

FUGGLES

TRADITIONALLY USED IN ENGLISH-
STYLE ALES, THIS HOP IS EARTHY,
FRUITY, AND VEGETAL.
USAGE: FLAVOR, AROMA, BITTERING

GALENA

PROVIDES CLEAN, PUNGENT
BITTERNESS THAT PLAY'S WELL
WITH OTHER HOP VARIETIES.
USAGE: BITTERING

GLACIER

A MELLOW HOP WITH AN AGREEABLE
FRAGRANCE THAT FLITS BETWEEN
GENTLE CITRUS AND EARTH.
USAGE: AROMA

GOLDINGS

THE TRADITIONAL ENGLISH HOP'S
FLAVOR IS SMOOTH AND SOMEWHAT
SWEET; IT'S CALLED "EAST KENT" IF
GROWN IN THAT REGION.
USAGE: FLAVOR, AROMA, BITTERING

HALLERTAUER

PRESENTS A MILD, AGREEABLE
PERFUME THAT'S FLORAL AND EARTHY,
WITH A SPICY, FRUITY COMPONENT.
ONE OF GERMANY'S FAMED NOBLE
HOPS. HALLERTAUER ENCOMPASSES
SEVERAL VARIETIES; "HALLERTAU"
OFTEN SIGNIFIES HOPS GROWN
IN AMERICA.
USAGE: FLAVOR, AROMA

HERSBRUCKER

ITS PLEASANT, REFRESHING SCENT
OFFERS HINTS OF GRASS AND HAY.
A NOBLE HOP.
USAGE: AROMA

HORIZON

OFFERS A TIDY, UNCLUTTERED
PROFILE THAT'S EQUAL PARTS CITRIC
AND FLORAL; ITS BITTERNESS IS
SMOOTH, NOT ABRASIVE.
USAGE: FLAVOR, BITTERING

LIBERTY

PRESENTS A MILD, DIGNIFIED AROMA
OF HERBS AND EARTH.
USAGE: FLAVOR, AROMA

MAGNUM

THE ACUTELY SPICY AROMA RECALLS
BLACK PEPPER AND PERHAPS
NUTMEG; THERE'S A TOUCH OF
CITRUS TOO.
USAGE: BITTERING

MT. HOOD

EARTHY AND FRESH, THIS HOP
OFFERS A RESTRAINED SPICY NOSE
REMINISCENT OF NOBLE HOPS.
USAGE: AROMA

MT. RAINIER

THE HOP'S NOSE PULLS A NEAT TRICK:
BLACK LICORICE CUT WITH A KISS
OF CITRUS.
USAGE: AROMA, BITTERING

NELSON SAUVIN

PARTLY NAMED AFTER THE SAUVIGNON
BLANC GRAPE, NEW ZEALAND'S
NELSON IS BRIGHT, JUICY, AND PACKED
WITH THE FLAVOR OF PASSION FRUIT.
USAGE: FLAVOR, BITTERING, AROMA

NORTHERN BREWER

THIS MULTIPURPOSE HOP'S FRAGRANT
AROMA LEANS TOWARD EARTHY,
WOODY, AND RUSTIC—MAYBE SOME
MINT, TOO.
USAGE: AROMA, BITTERING

NUGGET

THIS WAY-BITTER HOP HAS A HEAVY
HERBAL BOUQUET.
USAGE: BITTERING

PACIFIC GEM

A WOODY HOP THAT PROVIDES A BRISK,
CLEAN BITTERNESS AND SUBTLE
NOTES OF BLACKBERRY.
USAGE: BITTERING

PERLE

THIS ALL-PURPOSE VARIETY HAS A
CLEAN, GREEN BITTERNESS, VERGING
ON MINT; IT'S SOMEWHAT SPICY AND
FLORAL AS WELL.
USAGE: FLAVOR, AROMA, BITTERING

PRIDE OF RINGWOOD

USED IN MANY AUSTRALIAN BEERS,
IT PRESENTS A FORTHRIGHT EARTHY,
HERBAL, WOODY SCENT.
USAGE: BITTERING

SAAZ

THIS NOBLE HOP HAS A DISTINCTLY
CLEAN, CINNAMON-SPICY BOUQUET
AND IS TYPICALLY USED IN PILSNERS.
USAGE: FLAVOR, AROMA

SIMCOE

PINE, WOOD, AND CITRUS DRIVE THIS
BITTERING HOP'S PROFILE.
USAGE: AROMA, BITTERING

SORACHI ACE

THE JAPAN-BRED HOP HAS A STRONG LEMONY
AROMA; IT CAN ALSO TASTE BUTTERY.
USAGE: AROMA

SPALT

A SPICY AND DELICATE SCENT
DEFINES THIS GERMAN NOBLE HOP.
USAGE: AROMA

STERLING

AN ALTERNATIVE TO EUROPEAN HOPS,
IT HAS A SPICY, SOPHISTICATED
SCENT AND ASSERTIVE FLAVOR.
USAGE: AROMA, BITTERING

STYRIAN GOLDINGS

THIS SLOVENIAN FUGGLES VARIANT HAS
A SWEET, RESINOUS, PLEASINGLY SPICY
AROMA WITH A LITTLE FLORAL EDGE.
USAGE: FLAVOR, AROMA, BITTERING

SUMMIT

PRESENTS AN UP-FRONT PERFUME
OF ORANGE AND TANGERINE.
USAGE: BITTERING

TARGET

HAS AN INTENSE GRASSY, HERBAL, MINERAL-LIKE CHARACTER AND A FLORAL SCENT MORE INDEBTED TO BRITAIN THAN TO THE WEST COAST.

USAGE: BITTERING

TEAMAKER

ORIGINALLY DEVELOPED FOR ITS ANTIMICROBIAL PROPERTIES, THIS HOP VARIETY PROVIDES GREEN TEA-LIKE AROMAS AND NO BITTERNESS.

USAGE: AROMA

TETTNANGER

THIS NOBLE HOP HAS A FULL, RICH FLAVOR MIXED WITH A SPICY, FLOWERY NOSE THAT VERGES ON HERBAL.

USAGE: FLAVOR, AROMA

WARRIOR

OFFERS A CLEAN, SMOOTH BITTERNESS THAT WORKS IN HOP-FORWARD ALES.

USAGE: AROMA, BITTERING

WILLAMETTE

THE AROMA IS DECIDEDLY HERBAL, EARTHY, AND WOODY, WITH A LITTLE FLORAL FRUITINESS TO BOOT.

USAGE: FLAVOR, AROMA

Engineering Better Bitterness

Blind Tiger Ale House is among New York City's best beer bars, dispensing more than 30 meticulously sourced drafts and cask ales daily, from peppercorn-spiked pumpkin ales to stouts flavored with oysters. But one August evening, the throngs ringing the bar ignored these esoteric offerings, awestruck by a visit from a rare beast. "It's all thanks to Randall the Enamel Animal," said Blind Tiger co-owner Alan Jestice.

Randall is no feral creature. Rather, it's a traveling educational tool devised by Delaware's Dogfish Head. The brewery took a sealed cylindrical water filter and retrofitted it to attach to a keg's draft line. The filter is then filled with loosely packed flavoring agents, such as whole-leaf hops or fresh mint. When poured, beer passes through Randall, snatching aromatics and flavors. It works well with a potent ale like Dogfish Head's 90 Minute IPA, which boasts 9 percent alcohol by volume (ABV). The alcohol strips flavorful oils from the leaves,

Dogfish Head's Randall the Enamel Animal, which infuses beers with the flavor of fresh hops.

essentially instant-infusing the beer. The *Enamel Animal* moniker references the fact that drinking highly hopped, resinous beer can taste gritty, providing the sensation that it's dissolving tooth enamel—in a good way! (In September 2010, Dogfish Head released the souped-up Randall 3.0. The reengineered Randall is now double-barreled, helping reduce foam.)

Randall aside, Dogfish Head isn't the only brewer turning to technology to extract hops' full flavors. For instance, Harrisburg, Pennsylvania's Troëgs Brewing Company creates its HopBack Amber Ale and Imperial Amber Nugget Nectar by circulating the beers through a hops-stuffed vessel called, appropriately, the hopback. This process infuses the beer with garden-fresh flavors and aromas, which are complemented by the brew's sweet, malty caramel base. (This technique is popular at breweries nationwide, from Tempe, Arizona's Four Peaks to Hood River, Oregon's Full Sail and North Carolina's Mother Earth.)

Not to be one-upped, Sierra Nevada invented a stainless steel cylinder dubbed the hop torpedo, which harvests hops' oily resins and leaves the bitterness behind. How? Envision an espresso machine: A basket is filled with plump, whole-cone hops, then loaded into the torpedo and pressure sealed. The device is placed in a fermentation cellar, and beer is sent rushing through the torpedo to extract maximum aroma and flavor.

But Dogfish Head's Randall creates the most dramatic results. During this night's experiments, pine and spruce tips imbued the 90 Minute IPA with a Christmas-tree nose and an evergreen-fresh flavor that accompanies the piney profile. Bourbon ball candy and fresh mint created an overly sweet, faux mint julep; in that case, the Randall washed too much sugar into the beer. Randall works best when stuffed with sticky, stinky hops, which impart heady, intense aromatics—beer as fresh as the day it was brewed.

"That's what's great about a Randall," Jestice says. "It's not meant to transform a beer. It amplifies beer's natural flavors."

FOUR TO TRY

NUGGET NECTAR
TROËGS BREWING COMPANY
ABV: 7.5%

NUGGET NECTAR IS THIS PENNSYLVANIA BREWERY'S CROWN JEWEL. THE IMPERIAL AMBER IS BASED ON ITS AROMATIC HOPBACK AMBER ALE (SO-CALLED BECAUSE THE ALE FLOWS THROUGH A HOPS-STUFFED CONTAINER CALLED THE HOPBACK), BUT CRANKED TO 11. THE RESULT IS AN ALE WITH IPA-LIKE CHARACTER (93 IBUS, PLENTY OF PINE AND CITRUS) BALANCED OUT BY A SWEET, CARAMEL BACKBONE. IT'S LIP-SMACKING, NOT LIP-PUCKERING.

SILVERBACK PALE ALE
WYNKOOP BREWING COMPANY
ABV: 5.5%

TO FASHION THE SNAPPY PALE ALE, DENVER'S OLDEST BREWPUB USES THE WEST AFRICAN SPICE GRAINS OF PARADISE (A MEMBER OF THE GINGER FAMILY) TO ADD A NOVEL LEMON-PEPPER NOTE, AS WELL AS BREWMASTER ANDY BROWN'S HOMEMADE "HOPINATOR" HOPBACK. STUFFED WITH CENTENNIAL HOPS, IT GIVES SILVERBACK A CITRUSY SNIFF.

HOP KNOT IPA
FOUR PEAKS BREWING COMPANY
ABV: 6%

SO-CALLED BECAUSE SEVEN HOPS ARE WOVEN IN AT SEVEN DIFFERENT TIMES (INCLUDING A HOPBACK CRAMMED WITH WHOLE-LEAF HOPS) DURING THE BREWING PROCESS, THE ARIZONA BREWERY'S IPA PRESENTS PLENTY OF PINE AND CITRUS AROMA. THE TASTE IS INITIALLY INTENSELY BITTER, THEN BACKS OFF INTO A LIGHT, ENJOYABLE RIDE.

HOP JUICE DOUBLE IPA
LEFT COAST BREWING COMPANY
ABV: 9.4%

THIS SOUPED-UP IPA EMPLOYS EVERY FORM OF HOPS (EXTRACT, PELLETS, FLOWERS) AT EVERY STAGE OF BREWING (MASH, HOPBACK, FERMENTER, BRIGHT TANKS) TO MAKE THIS BEAST. CARAMEL-TOUCHED MALT SWEETNESS KEEPS THE RESIN-STICKY ALE FROM DIVING INTO THE ORANGE-BITTER DEEP END.

Delta Force

One day in 2009, international agricultural company Hopsteiner rang the crew at Boston's Harpoon Brewery and made an offer as mysterious as it was alluring. The hop merchant had created an experimental hop variety dubbed Delta. Would Harpoon be interested in buying some of the crop? Always eager to do some R&D, the brewery accepted, then set out to decode the Delta hop's riddle. "There's absolutely nothing online about this hop," says Harpoon brewer Charlie Cummings. "Hopsteiner doesn't even list Delta on its website."

After digging, Cummings and his crew discovered that Delta is a cross of two well-known varieties: the earthy English Fuggles and floral Cascade—the quintessential flavor of West Coast beers—which is itself a blend of Fuggles and the Russian hop Serebrianker.

When the hops arrived at Harpoon, Cummings brewed a test batch of a British-style extra special bitter (ESB), liberally dosing it with the Delta for both aroma and bitterness. His first taste was a revelation. "Fuggles is usually a pretty subtle hop, but this had a stronger, more assertive character—an American punch," he says. The flavor of the beer was similarly complex, with citrusy, melon-like notes and an herbal, grassy quality. "We made a very quick decision to brew that ESB as one of our 100 Barrel Series beers," Cummings says of Harpoon's special line of experimental beers.

The result was the Single Hop ESB, America's first production beer to feature the Delta hop. It balances the beer's nimble, malt-forward body with a fruity kick. It's a familiar yet foreign flavor, one that's as agreeable as it is unusual. It's already caught the eye of Shipyard Brewing Company in Portland, Maine, which uses Delta in its summery Wheat Ale, and other brewers are waiting for the next crop to start their experiments. "People are always looking for the next new hop," Cummings says, "and this is a pretty great one."

WHEAT ALE
SHIPYARD BREWING COMPANY
ABV: 4.5%
AT FIRST BLUSH, THIS FILTERED WHEAT BEER MAY EVOKE A STATUS QUO
GOLDEN SUMMER BREW. BUT TAKE A WHIFF, AND YOU'LL NOTICE DELTA'S
BEGUILING AROMA: EARTHY AND GRASSY, LIKE ENGLAND BY WAY OF THE WEST
COAST. THE INTOXICATING SCENT IS PAIRED WITH A LEAN PROFILE AND A LOW
ABV, MEANING THAT WHEAT IS FIT FOR A LONG-HAUL DRINKING SESSION.

The Full Nelson

While some hops' applications are discovered in the lab, others
are found by serendipity. A couple of years back, Pat McIlhenney,
brewmaster and owner of Southern California's Alpine Beer
Company, traveled to New Zealand, where he was smitten by the

redwood forests, verdant ferns, and colorful flora and fauna. Upon returning to California, the retired firefighter began researching New Zealand hops and discovered that, because there are scant natural pests and no known hop diseases, New Zealand hops require few, if any, pesticides. Add the facts that the growing season is the opposite of America's and that, thanks to a favorable exchange rate, New Zealand hops are often cheaper than their American counterparts (even factoring in shipping), and McIlhenney was sold.

He settled on a breed curiously named Nelson Sauvin. ("Nelson" refers to a region in central New Zealand, while "Sauvin" is shorthand for the grape variety sauvignon blanc.) "It's got an intense, grape-like quality," McIlhenney says of the strain, which recalls the fruity, tropical sauvignon blanc. "It shaped up to be the perfect hop." He found a home for Nelson Sauvin in his rye-based IPA named, naturally, Nelson, which quickly became one of Alpine's top sellers, giving McIlhenney a particularly envious problem: "We sell it faster than we can make it," the brewer says.

Should you be unable to source Nelson, never fear: Other brewers are quickly cottoning to the quirky New Zealand hop. It's part of the hop mix in beers such as the Big Barrel Double IPA from San Diego's Karl Strauss Brewing Co., the IPA from Kelso of Brooklyn, and the Punk IPA from Scotland's BrewDog. "It's one of our favorite hops to use," says BrewDog head brewer James Watt, who rhapsodizes about Nelson Sauvin's flavors of lychee and mango.

And though McIlhenney is loath to sing his beer's accolades too loudly ("That's like naming your favorite child," he says), he can't help himself: "Nelson is my wife's and my favorite beer," he says. "When a beer is that good and stands out that much, it's hard not to be excited."

THREE TO TRY

PUNK IPA
BREWDOG
ABV: 6%

WHEN SCOTLAND'S BREWDOG SET OUT TO FASHION ITS FLAGSHIP IPA, BREWMASTER JAMES WATT CRAVED A MODERN INTERPRETATION. NO NEED FOR ENGLAND'S CLASSIC CARAMEL FLAVOR, THANKS. INSTEAD, HE OPTED FOR A DOUBLE-BARRELED BLAST OF NELSON SAUVIN AND AHTANUM HOPS, WHICH GIVES THE GOLDEN ALE AN EARTHY, TROPICAL PERFUME. ITHE LIGHT BODY PACKS THE FLAVORS OF ORANGE PEEL AND PINE RESIN, SOMEWHAT LEAVENED BY BISCUIT MALT. SOME SPRITZY EFFERVESCENCE SEALS THE DEAL.

BiG BARREL DOUBLE IPA
KARL STRAUSS BREWING COMPANY
ABV: 9%

OVER THE LAST SEVERAL DECADES, SAN DIEGO'S FIRST BREWERY SINCE PROHIBITION HAS BECOME A MAINSTAY DUE TO ITS MIGHTILY HOPPED TOWER IO IPA AND RED TROLLEY ALE, WHICH

SMACKS OF DARK FRUIT. HOWEVER, MY FAVORITE IS KARL'S BIG BARREL. THE MALTY, MEDIUM-BODIED DOUBLE IPA (90 IBUS) IS DOCTORED WITH NELSON SAUVIN HOPS, EVOKING TROPICAL FRUIT AND A WHITE WINE-LIKE CHARACTER.

NELSON
ALPINE BEER COMPANY
ABV: 7%

HOPS FANATICS WORSHIP CALIFORNIA'S ALPINE, WHICH IS HOME TO DELIRIOUSLY BITTER ELIXIRS SUCH AS AROMATIC PURE HOPPINESS AND ITS BIG BROTHER, EXPONENTIAL HOPPINESS (IT'S FINISHED WITH A "BODY BAG" FILLED WITH HOPS AND OAK CHIPS). FINER STILL IS NELSON, A GOLDEN IPA MADE WITH RYE AND LOADS OF NELSON SAUVIN HOPS. THE KIWI HOPS PROVIDE AROMAS OF PEACHES AND PINE, WELL SUITED TO NELSON'S FRUITY FLAVORS, WINE-LIKE ASTRINGENCY, AND DISTINCT RYE SPICE. DESPITE THE 7 PERCENT PUNCH, IT'S ACES ON A HOT AFTERNOON.

Coming Up Ace

Jeremy Goldberg was having a problem with his IPA. Namely, it wasn't selling well. So when the head brewer at Massachusetts's Cape Ann Brewing discovered that his supplier was discontinuing Brewer's Gold—a piney, pungent British bittering hop that flavored his IPA—he took it as a sign to rejigger the recipe.

Some of his employees who were avid homebrewers told Goldberg about the unusual Sorachi Ace hop. Japan's Sapporo Breweries originally developed the variety, but the brewery was unable to find a commercial use for the uniquely lemony hop. Goldberg would. To temper Sorachi's citric character, he paired it with the herbal Chinook hop, creating their earthy, creamy Fisherman's IPA. "People ask, 'Do you put butter in it?'" Goldberg laughs.

Whereas Cape Ann uses Sorachi Ace as a flavoring component, New York's Brooklyn Brewery created a summery beer expressly as a platform for the singular hop. "When I smelled Sorachi Ace, the first thing that came to mind was, 'That'd make a great saison,'" says head brewer Garrett Oliver. For summer 2009's Brewmaster's Reserve series, he created the dry, austere, single hopped Belgian saison called, fittingly, Sorachi Ace.

Though Oliver was confident that the beer would do well, the results outstripped his expectations. Sorachi Ace became the fastest-selling release in the series. "Even though we made twenty-five percent more than usual, we sold out early," he says. While the inventive Brewmaster's Reserve beers (like the Cookie Jar Porter) are mainly one-offs and rarely bottled, the overwhelming demand for Sorachi Ace led Oliver to revive it and make it a year-round release. The beer rolled off the factory line in large-format bottles, but the production run might have been a tad smaller than expected. "People working at the brewery said, 'It's a shame that some of these will *accidentally* fall off the bottling line,'" Oliver jokes.

THREE TO TRY

SORACHI ACE
BROOKLYN BREWERY
ABV: 6.5%

I DRINK SO MUCH BEER I SOMETIMES SUFFER FROM PALATE FATIGUE. BUT OCCASIONALLY, A NOVEL BEER SHOCKS ME FROM MY HOPPY STUPOR—LIKE SORACHI ACE. THE NAMESAKE JAPANESE HOP GIVES THIS CLOUDY, TARNISHED-GOLD SAISON THE BRIGHT AROMA OF LEMONS AND THE FLAVOR OF . . . BUTTER? YES, BUTTER MAKES IT BETTER, AS DOES VIGOROUS CARBONATION. PLENTY OF FLORAL, PEPPERY FLAVORS KEEP SORACHI GROUNDED, HELPING IT CLOSE OUT CRISP.

SUM'R ORGANIC SUMMER ALE
UINTA BREWING COMPANY
ABV: 4%

SALT LAKE CITY'S UINTA CRAFTS GREAT PILSNERS AND PALE ALES, BUT I LIKE ITS FOUR+ SERIES OF BEERS BEST. SO-CALLED BECAUSE THEY'RE MADE WITH FOUR PRIMARY INGREDIENTS (WATER, HOPS, YEAST, AND BARLEY PLUS A BREWER'S SKILL), FOUR+ BREWS ARE AS CREATIVE AS THEY ARE DELICIOUS, AND NONE MORE SO THAN SUM'R. THIS SEASONAL DRINKS LIGHT AND CLEAN, WITH A LOVELY LEMONY PROFILE, THANKS TO JAPAN'S SORACHI ACE HOP.

FISHERMAN'S IPA
CAPE ANN BREWING COMPANY
ABV: 6%

MADE IN GLOUCESTER, MASSACHUSETTS, THE COPPER IPA IS SMOOTHER AND MALTIER THAN ITS WEST COAST COMPATRIOTS. INSTEAD OF A BITTER PUNCH, THERE'S A TOFFEE-LIKE, NEARLY BUTTERY FLAVOR AND AN HERBAL BOUQUET. FISHERMAN IS FORTIFYING ON A COLD AFTERNOON.

SUM'R

ORGANIC SUMMER ALE
SIX 12 OUNCE BOTTLES

USDA ORGANIC

Tea Time

Some brewers are compelled to create increasingly bitter beers. Others are eager to explore the opposite end of the mouth-puckering spectrum. Several times, Widmer Brothers Brewing Company in Portland, Oregon, has brewed its TEAser XPA. If you were lucky enough to get a pint, you would've found a heady aroma of grassy, floral hops. But sipping the pale-golden TEAser revealed that the piney aromatics and gentle, iced tea–like flavors didn't correlate with the beer's bitterness—there was almost none. "You get a wonderful bouquet without the beer being a tongue-scraper," says Widmer co-owner Rob Widmer. He's one of America's first brewers to experiment with TEAser's signature ingredient: the Teamaker hop.

Teamaker was released in 2006 by the Agricultural Research Service Forage Seed and Cereal Research Unit at Corvallis, Oregon. The scientists' goal in developing the variety was to harness the natural antimicrobial properties of hops while subtracting the trademark bitterness caused by the flower's alpha acids. Teamaker was engineered with low alpha acids and high beta acids, which impart aroma but no bitterness—perfect for tea.

One of Teamaker's proposed applications is livestock production. In lieu of antibiotics, the hop could be incorporated into animal feed to lessen microbial and fungal illnesses. That's great news for farmers. Brewers were nonplussed. "It was a homeless hop," Widmer says. He first heard of Teamaker from longtime Oregon hop grower Goschie Farms and was intrigued: "You can have too much bitterness, but you can't have too much hop aroma."

For the first batch, in 2008, he bought enough Teamaker hops to craft about fifteen barrels of TEAser, though the brewers were unable to resist including a tiny amount of traditional hops. Allagash Brewing also experimented with Teamaker, using it in conjunction with Simcoe and Sorachi Ace hops in the Hugh Malone Belgian-style

IPA. "Brewers' nature is to add bittering hops," Widmer says. "Next time, I'd be tempted to skip the bittering agents completely."

Secret Citra

With brewers more or less having access to identical hops, creating a proprietary variety with uncommon aromatic and bittering qualities can pay delicious dividends. A few years ago, the brewers at Sierra Nevada were aflutter over hop variety 394. In conjunction with Deschutes and Widmer Brothers, Sierra Nevada had funded the research and development of this strain with a strange flavor profile—a hard-to-pin-down mix of citrus, mango, and papaya. "There's even something strangely Southeast Asian about the hop," says Sierra Nevada's Bill Manley. "This was one of the most promising hops we'd seen in some time."

Sierra's brewers played around with 394, polishing and tweaking recipes to serve as the novel hop's coming-out party. By late 2008, Sierra Nevada had its eureka moment. The tropical 394, christened Citra, would drive the flavor of the Torpedo Extra IPA. When it was released in early 2009, it was Sierra's first addition to its year-round lineup since 1980.

If that sounds like lots of time and research to develop beer for a single hop strain, it is. But unlike small brewpubs or microbreweries, Sierra Nevada and other larger brewers are uniquely positioned to do the time-consuming legwork. "We have labs and a researcher with a background in hop compounds," says Manley. "Smaller craft brewers would just have to buy a lot of hops and hope for the best."

Since Sierra Nevada cracked the seal on Citra, other brewers have quickly adopted the hop. In Madison, Wisconsin, Ale Asylum puts Citra in its Bedlam! Trappist IPA, while Flying Fish's Exit 16 Wild Rice Double IPA uses it in combination with Chinook hops, and Clown Shoes Beer in Ipswich, Massachusetts, uses Citra, Simcoe, and Centennial hops in its Eagle Claw Fist Imperial Amber Ale. With the word out, amateur brewers are clamoring to experiment with the trademarked hop. "We get requests ten times a week from homebrewers asking where to find Citra," Manley says. "It just takes somebody to break the ice."

THREE TO TRY

TORPEDO EXTRA IPA
SIERRA NEVADA BREWING CO.
ABV: 7.2%
WHEN TORPEDO WAS RELEASED IN 2009, IT WAS SIERRA NEVADA'S FIRST NEW YEAR-ROUND BEER SINCE 1980. THE BOLD, BRASH TORPEDO HAS ALL THE CITRUS AND PINE COMPONENTS YOU'D EXPECT FROM AN AMPED-UP IPA, BUT THEN THERE'S THAT SMELL: MANGO, PAPAYA, AND OTHER EXOTIC TROPICAL FRUIT, COURTESY OF THE CITRA HOP. A MORSEL OF MALT SWEETNESS KEEPS THE BITTERNESS IN CHECK.

EXIT 16 WILD RICE DOUBLE IPA
FLYING FISH BREWING CO.
ABV: 8.2%
WILD RICE, BROWN RICE, AND WHITE RICE GIVE THIS DOUBLE IPA A DRY, CRISP CHARACTER, WHICH LETS THE CHINOOK AND CITRA HOPS SING BRIGHT AND FRESH. ON THE NOSE: TANGERINE, CITRUS, MANGO, PAPAYA, AND PINE, OH MY!

CITRA BLONDE SUMMER ALE
WIDMER BROTHERS BREWING COMPANY
ABV: 4.3%
BEFITTING ITS BEACH-SEASON RELEASE, THE BLONDE SUNBURN IS A LIGHT AND LOVELY SUMMER SIPPER, WITH A DAB OF BARELY THERE BITTERNESS. WHAT'S THE DRAW? THE DISTINCT AROMA OF CITRUS AND TROPICAL FRUIT, DUE TO DRY-HOPPED CITRA.

Back in Black

In 2006, a few months before Mitch Steele became head brewer at San Diego's Stone Brewing Company, he had a revelation at Boston's Extreme Beer Fest. Among the many beer samples, one stood out above all others: a black IPA from Shaun Hill of the Shed Restaurant and Brewery in Vermont. (He now runs Vermont's Hill Farmstead Brewery.) Despite the beer's ebony tint, it was super-bitter and thirst quenching, not at all overwhelmed by roasted flavors or a heavy body. "I thought it was an amazing style, and I knew I wanted to brew it at Stone," says Steele.

He and his fellow brewers spent about a year dialing in the recipe, trying to solve the riddle of achieving a rich, obsidian hue without an overbearing roasty essence or heavy body. "We wanted it to drink like an IPA but look like a stout," says Steele. The solution

was dehusked black malt, the kind used in the German black lagers dubbed schwarzbiers. "That allowed the hops to come through" in Stone's 11th Anniversary Ale, released in 2007. It was such a hit that, by 2009, it became a full-time brew, since named Sublimely Self-Righteous Ale.

Consider the black IPA a seasonal chameleon: crisp and bracing enough to slake thirst on all but the hottest days, while malty enough for a breezy eve by a lake. This sleight-of-hand style has rapidly expanded with

21st Amendment Brewery's Back in Black, Dogzilla Black IPA from Idaho's Laughing Dog, and Deschutes's Hop in the Dark.

Since black IPA is an oxymoron ("How can a pale ale be dark?" says Deschutes's digital marketing manager, Jason Randles), the name Cascadian dark ale—referencing the Pacific Northwest's Cascades range, where many hop farmers and brewers are located—has been proposed. But this smacks of regionalism, especially considering the Northwest isn't the only region where this beer is brewed, and highly hopped dark beers were crafted in the United Kingdom more than a century ago. Besides, Steele says, "CDA doesn't imply that it's a really hoppy beer. If you order a CDA, what does that even mean? You need to have *India* in there. It's an IPA."

HOPS...

THREE TO TRY

HOP IN THE DARK C.D.A.
DESCHUTES BREWERY
ABV: 6.5%

PRACTICE MAKES PERFECT FOR THE BREWING PRIDE OF BEND, OREGON. MORE THAN A YEAR OF EXPERIMENTATION—AND 22 TEST BATCHES—CREATED THIS RAVEN-COLORED ALE THAT, DUE TO A QUARTET OF HOPS (CASCADE, AMARILLO, CENTENNIAL, AND CITRA) PACKS A HEADY IPA BOUQUET. THE MALT PROFILE IS SMOOTH, WITH A TOUCH OF COFFEE TO BALANCE OUT THE CITRIC BITTERNESS. P.S.: C.D.A. STANDS FOR CASCADIAN DARK ALE. IT'S A NOD TO THE NORTHWEST'S CASCADE MOUNTAIN REGION, WHERE MANY HOPS ARE GROWN.

ALPINE BLACK IPA
OTTER CREEK BREWING
ABV: 6%

A LIBERAL DOSE OF CITRA, CENTENNIAL, AND APOLLO HOPS GIVES THIS CARAMEL-KISSED, MIDNIGHT-COLOR IPA A CITRIC SCENT, WITH A DETOUR TO TROPICAL FRUIT. THE BITTERNESS IS PRESENT AND BOLD.

O'DARK:30
OAKSHIRE BREWING
ABV: 6.3%

BREWMASTER MATT VAN WYK FEELS THIS ONYX BREW IS DISTINCT FROM A BLACK IPA, EVEN THOUGH THE LABEL OF O'DARK:30 IDENTIFIES IT AS "CASCADIAN DARK ALE AKA BLACK IPA." "A CDA IS ESSENTIALLY A HOPPY, DARK BEER," HE SAYS, "BUT IT DOESN'T JUST TASTE LIKE AN IPA." SEMANTICS ASIDE, O'DARK:30 POURS THE COLOR OF A MOONLESS NIGHT. IT OFFERS THE SCENT OF THE PACIFIC NORTHWEST—CITRUS, PINE—MIXED WITH THE FLAVORS OF ROASTED COFFEE AND CHOCOLATE.

INTERNATIONAL SPOTLIGHT: NEW ZEALAND'S EPIC BREWING COMPANY

DO YOU LIKE TO TRAVEL? DO YOU FAVOR SWEET, FIZZY, BARELY BITTERED BEERS THAT ARE ABOUT AS POTENT AS POND WATER? THEN BOOK A FLIGHT TO LOVELY NEW ZEALAND, WHERE FLAVOR-DEPRIVED LAGERS RULE WITH A HEAVY, WATERY FIST.

THIS IS PARTLY DUE TO A NEW ZEALAND PHENOMENON KNOWN AS THE "SIX O'CLOCK SWILL." STARTING IN 1917, THE GOVERNMENT MANDATED THAT PUBS CLOSE AT 6 P.M. SO WHEN WORKERS CLOCKED OUT AT 5 P.M., THEY HAD ONE MAD HOUR TO SLAKE THEIR THIRSTS. THE PREFERRED TIPPLES WERE LIGHT AND EASY LAGERS—ALL THE BETTER TO POUND BY THE PINT. THOUGH THE 6 P.M. CLOSURES WERE LIFTED IN 1967, KIWIS' PREFERENCE FOR INNOCUOUS LAGERS LINGERED LIKE A BAD HANGOVER.

"MOST PEOPLE THOUGHT THAT BEER WAS BEER. THEY SHOPPED ON BRAND AND PRICE," SAYS NEW ZEALAND BREWER LUKE NICHOLAS. "I WANTED TO GET PEOPLE OUT OF THE MIND-SET THAT BEERS WERE YELLOW, COLD, AND FIZZY." TO SHAKE DRINKERS FROM THEIR DOLDRUMS, NICHOLAS TOOK A DRASTIC STEP. IN 2006, HE UNLEASHED EPIC BEER, A PORTFOLIO OF PALE ALES, IPAS, AND OTHER HOP-FORWARD BREWS MORE AT HOME ON AMERICA'S WEST COAST. "PEOPLE WERE LIKE, 'WHAT THE HELL ARE YOU DOING? THAT'S TOO MUCH FLAVOR.' I TOTALLY FREAKED OUT NEW ZEALAND," NICHOLAS SAYS.

Epic Brewing's brewmaster and owner Luke Nicholas.

THE BITTER BEGINNING

THAT FREAK-OUT WAS A LONG TIME IN THE MAKING. WHILE STUDYING IN CALIFORNIA IN THE 1990S, NICHOLAS DEVELOPED A TASTE FOR HOPPY ALES AND A TALENT FOR BREWING. WHEN HE RETURNED HOME IN 1996, NICHOLAS ANGLED FOR A JOB AT BRITISH-STYLE BREWPUB COCK & BULL, NEAR AUCKLAND. THEY WEREN'T HIRING. NICHOLAS DIDN'T CARE. "I WENT DOWN AND ASKED FOR A JOB EVERY WEEKEND FOR A YEAR UNTIL THEY HIRED ME," NICHOLAS RECALLS. HE BREWED FOR THEM FOR TWO AND A HALF YEARS, BEFORE LEAVING TO TOIL FOR THE WEBSITE REAL BEER. THEN CAME 2001'S DOT-COM CRASH. BYE-BYE, INTERNET. WELCOME BACK, BREWING.

HE CAUGHT ON WITH AUCKLAND'S STEAM BREWING, WHICH PRODUCED BEERS FOR COCK & BULL. STILL, NICHOLAS YEARNED TO RE-CREATE THOSE CALIFORNIA HOP MONSTERS. THE BOSSES GAVE NICHOLAS THE GO-AHEAD TO BUILD A SEPARATE BRAND, ONE FOCUSING ON HOP-FORWARD BREWS: EPIC, SO NAMED BECAUSE HE CRAVED FLAVORS AND AROMAS AS BIG AND BURLY AS A WEIGHTLIFTER. HE SPENT 2005 TINKERING WITH RECIPES BEFORE RELEASING THE AROMATIC EPIC PALE ALE IN 2006. THE RESPONSE? AT THE NEW ZEALAND INTERNATIONAL BEER AWARDS THE PALE ALE WAS ANOINTED "SUPREME CHAMPION BEER."

"THAT WAS A GOOD SIGN," NICHOLAS SAYS, LAUGHING. DESPITE THE ACCOLADES, HIS EMPLOYERS SAW NO FUTURE FOR EPIC. "THEY OWN A CHAIN OF PUBS, AND THEIR CORE BUSINESS WAS EXPANDING PUBS," HE EXPLAINS. "I WASN'T GOING TO LET MY VISION AND DREAM OF CRAFT BEER DIE." IN OCTOBER 2007, HE BOUGHT THE EPIC BRAND AND ENTERED AN ARRANGEMENT THAT ALLOWED HIM TO CONTINUE BREWING AT STEAM. THAT WAS FORTUITOUS, BECAUSE "I DIDN'T HAVE TO RAISE $2 MILLION TO OPEN," NICHOLAS SAYS.

TASTEFUL MARKETING

MONEY. IT'S ALWAYS AN ISSUE FOR NEW BREWERIES. "I DIDN'T HAVE POCKETFULS OF CASH TO PAY FOR ADVERTISING, SO I HAD TO SHOCK PEOPLE TO GET THEM TO REMEMBER MY BEER," HE SAYS. HE WAGED A HOP ASSAULT ON ALL LEVELS, FROM HIS ELEGANTLY DRY-HOPPED LAGER TO BITTER BEAST ARMAGEDDON IPA, WHICH RATES A DEVILISH 6.66 PERCENT ABV. "PEOPLE WENT, 'YUP, THAT IS WHAT I'M LOOKING FOR.'"

NICHOLAS ALSO TOOK HIS PROMOTIONS ONLINE. HE USED BLOGS TO ANSWER CUSTOMERS' QUESTIONS (Q: IS EPIC PALE ALE VEGAN? A: YES.), AND WAS THE FIRST BREWERY TO SIGN UP FOR TWITTER. THOUGH THE MESSAGING SERVICE IS NOW A UBIQUITOUS MARKETING TOOL, NICHOLAS WAS AHEAD OF

HIS TIME IN USING TWITTER TO KEEP FANS INFORMED ABOUT RELEASES, EVENTS, AND NEWS. "YOU CAN TALK TO YOUR DRINKER, WHICH IS SO POWERFUL," SAYS NICHOLAS.

NOW THAT HE HAS NEW ZEALAND'S EYES AND STOMACHS, NICHOLAS HAS CONTINUED TO INNOVATE. HE RELEASED MAYHEM, AN AMERICAN-STYLE STRONG PALE ALE GIVEN AN AROMATIC PUNCH BY LOCAL HOPS, AS WELL AS THE SMOOTH, RICH THORNBRIDGE STOUT. GIVEN HOW MUCH NICHOLAS LOOKS TO AMERICA FOR INSPIRATION, IT'S A NO-BRAINER THAT EPIC BEERS ARE NOW SOLD IN THE UNITED STATES. STILL, NICHOLAS TAKES HIS GREATEST PRIDE IN HOW HE'S AFFECTED THE KIWI CONSUMER.

"PEOPLE NOW DRINK EPIC PALE ALE AS THEIR EVERYDAY DRINK," NICHOLAS SAYS, MARVELING AT HIS SUCCESS. "I'VE CHANGED THE ENTIRE MARKET."

With the Grain

Like grapes to wine, grains are crucial to creating the hot soup that becomes beer. But each grain is not created equally. Some malts impart sweetness, others spiciness or espresso bitterness. An African grass called sorghum enables the creation of gluten-free beer suited for people with celiac disease. And rice and oats? Read on.

A stalk of sorghum.

A QUICK GUIDE TO THE FERMENTABLES THAT FUEL YOUR BEER

BARLEY

BARELY SERVES AS THE BUILDING BLOCK OF BEER. THE GRAIN IS TRANSFORMED INTO BREW-READY MALT BY TAKING A HOT-WATER BATH, WHICH BEGINS GERMINATION AND CAUSES THE GRAIN TO CREATE ENZYMES NECESSARY TO TRANSFORM PROTEINS AND STARCHES INTO FERMENTABLE SUGARS. WHILE THERE'S NO GLOBAL SYSTEM FOR CLASSIFYING THE HUNDREDS OF VARIETIES OF MALT, THE GRAIN CAN BE CONDENSED INTO TWO BROAD CATEGORIES:

1. BASE MALTS: THESE CONSTITUTE THE LION'S SHARE OF THE GRAIN BILL. THESE MALTS ARE TYPICALLY LIGHTER COLORED AND PROVIDE MOST OF THE PROTEINS, FERMENTABLE SUGARS, AND MINERALS REQUIRED TO CREATE BEER.

2. SPECIALTY MALTS: THESE CAN HELP HEAD RETENTION, INCREASE BODY, AND ADD COLOR, AROMA, AND FLAVOR, SUCH AS COFFEE, CHOCOLATE, BISCUIT, AND CARAMEL. ALL SPECIALTY GRAINS CAN BE USED IN CONJUNCTION TO FOSTER UNIQUE FLAVOR PROFILES. POPULAR VARIETIES INCLUDE:

   - CRYSTAL (OR CARAMEL) MALTS, WHICH ARE SPECIALLY STEWED, CREATING CRYSTALLINE SUGAR STRUCTURES WITHIN THE GRAIN'S HULL THAT ADD SWEETNESS TO BEER.

   - DARK MALTS, WHICH ARE HIGHLY ROASTED, RESULTING IN ROBUST FLAVORS FIT FOR STOUTS, SCHWARZBIERS, BOCKS, AND BLACK IPAS.

   - ROASTED MALTS, WHICH ARE KILNED OR ROASTED AT HIGH TEMPERATURES TO IMPART CERTAIN FLAVOR CHARACTERISTICS.

UNMALTED BARLEY IMPARTS A RICH, GRAINY CHARACTER TO BEER, WHICH IS IMPORTANT IN STYLES SUCH AS DRY STOUT. UNMALTED BARLEY HELPS HEAD RETENTION, BUT IT WILL MAKE A BEER HAZY.

RYE

MIXED WITH BARLEY, RYE CAN IMPART COMPLEXITY, CRISPNESS, A SHARPENED FLAVOR PROFILE, AND SUBTLE SPICINESS, AS WELL AS DRY OUT A BEER. IT CAN ALSO BE KILNED TO CREATE A CHOCOLATE OR CARAMEL FLAVOR. THE DOWNSIDE IS THAT SINCE RYE CONTAINS NO HULLS, THE GRAIN TENDS TO CLUMP UP AND TURN TO CONCRETE DURING BREWING.

WHEAT

THIS GRAIN'S PROTEINS HELP GIVE BEER A FULLER BODY AND MOUTHFEEL AND MAKE A FOAMY HEAD AS THICK, LUSTROUS, AND LASTING AS SHAVING CREAM. A LARGE WHEAT BILL OFTEN CREATES A LIGHT, SMOOTH, HAZY BREW, SUCH AS A HEFEWEIZEN OR A WITBIER.

CORN

WHEN USED IN BEER, AMERICA'S FAVORITE COB-BASED VEGETABLE PROVIDES A SMOOTH, SOMEWHAT NEUTRAL SWEETNESS. MORE CRUCIALLY, CORN LIGHTENS A BEER'S BODY, CURTAILS ITS HAZINESS, AND CAN STABILIZE FLAVOR.

OATS

USED IN CONJUNCTION WITH BARLEY, OATS CREATE A SILKY, CREAMY BREW WITH A FULL-BODIED FLAVOR. THEY'RE WELL SUITED TO STOUTS.

RICE

AS AN INGREDIENT IN BEER, RICE HAS LITTLE OR NO DISCERNIBLE TASTE. INSTEAD, IT HELPS CREATE SNAPPY, CRISP FLAVORS AND A DRY PROFILE, AS WELL AS LIGHTEN THE BEER'S BODY.

SORGHUM

MADE FROM THE AFRICAN GRASS, SORGHUM IS A GLUTEN-FREE ALTERNATIVE TO BARLEY AND OTHER GRAINS. IT IS USED TO CREATE GLUTEN-FREE BEER. MOST BREWERIES USE PREPARED SORGHUM SYRUP, WHICH IS HIGHLY CONCENTRATED WORT. SOME SORGHUM-BASED BREWS CAN HAVE A SOUR EDGE.

Rye Rising

In the late 1990s, Georgia was a barren land for hoppy beer. Brown ales, stouts, and lightly bittered pales dominated tap lines. Seeing a niche that needed to be filled, Brian "Spike" Buckowski and John Cochran started planning Terrapin Beer, an Athens brewery specializing in bold brews with a bitter edge.

They decided their first release would be a hopped-up, West Coast–style pale ale, something in the Sierra Nevada vein. The problem was, southern beer drinkers balked at the plan. "They said they didn't like the bitterness sitting on their tongue," recalls Buckowski, Terrapin's brewmaster. "Remember, this was 1997 in the South. Back then, anything hoppier than a Budweiser was too bitter."

While flipping through recipes, Buckowski fondly recalled college days spent sipping rye whiskey. "I liked that spicy character that dried out your palate," he says. Perhaps rye malt could curtail lingering bitterness in beer? Buckowski crafted a brew that incorporated about 10 percent rye (the remainder was a blend of barley malts) and citric, earthy hops. The result was fresh and clean, with a crisp, thirst-quenching character and a bitterness as fleeting as a sun shower. "Thirty seconds later, you're ready to take another sip," Buckowski says of what became Terrapin's Rye Pale Ale.

Though it was "created out of necessity of pleasing palates in the Southeast," Buckowski soon discovered that rye beer held national appeal. Six months after Rye Pale Ale's spring 2002 release (hey, opening a brewery takes time), it won gold at Denver's Great American Beer Festival. "As far as [American] rye beers go, we were definitely one of the pioneers," he says.

Nowadays, Terrapin isn't alone in its rye pursuits. Brewers nationwide have begun embracing the grain, which can add complexity, sharpness, subtle spiciness, and dryness to beer styles ranging from piney IPAs to chocolaty porters and even more

eclectic, experimental beers. New York's Ithaca Beer Co. makes
the brawny Old Habit strong ale (as part of their Excelsior! series)
with a quartet of rye malts and ages it in Rittenhouse Rye whiskey
barrels. Missouri's O'Fallon Brewery offers the buttery Hemp
Hop Rye, and Bear Republic and Real Ale are both resuscitating
Germany's hefeweizen-like roggenbier.

RYE RULES

With brewing, it's helpful to think of rye as a supporting actor. Top
billing on the grain bill is usually reserved for barley malts. This
may also be a matter of taste, but it's mainly due to an evolutionary
advantage: Barley contains husks, which keep the mash (the grains
steeped in boiling water) loose and permit drainage of the wort—
the broth that becomes beer. By contrast, rye is huskless and, like
a sponge, sops up water. Compounding matters, rye can create a
sticky, viscous mash, something "like concrete," says Matt Van Wyk,
brewmaster at Oakshire Brewing in Eugene, Oregon. To prevent
coagulation, which is common when using 20 percent or more rye,
brewers can add enzymes or, as Van Wyk does, rice hulls. They
make the mash fluffy without altering flavor, allowing rye to work
its magic without driving brewers bonkers.

For Van Wyk, rye was crucial in creating Line Dry Rye Pale
Ale, Oakshire's summer seasonal. "We wanted to make a drinkable,
sessionable beer, but we didn't want to make something that was
boring," he explains. "We wanted some complexity." To achieve
that, he dialed up Oregon blackberry and buckwheat honey, citric
Centennial hops, and rye. "The rye adds crispness, a spicy character,
and helps dry out the beer, which is great in a summer seasonal,"
says Van Wyk, who has seen Line Dry become a top seller.

Rye is ideal not only in summery beers, but also in robust ales
and cool-weather brews. Real Ale Brewing Company in Blanco,
Texas, employs rye to smooth out its Sisyphus barleywine and
cut its richness, while Nashville-based Yazoo Brewing Company's

chocolaty Sly Rye Porter gets a dry finish from the grain. A potent double IPA? It's the perfect platform for rye, which balances the sweet, caramel character of Shmaltz Brewing's He'Brew Bittersweet Lenny's R.I.P.A.

For Brian Owens, head brewer at O'Fallon, rye was the secret ingredient required to unlock a curious ingredient's potential. One day, brewery owner Tony Caradonna mentioned that he'd like O'Fallon to brew a hemp-based beer. "I was skeptical, because the first thing that came to my mind was marijuana," says Owens. Duty bound, he bought toasted hemp seeds and brewed several pilot batches, discovering that the seeds' flavor had nothing in common with the skunky, pungent herb; instead, they possess a delicate nuttiness—too delicate, in fact. To enhance the subtle taste without overpowering the seeds (they're imported from Canada and tested to ensure there's no THC content), Owens turned to rye. "It added a layer of flavoring and a spicy sharpness that makes it nice and drinkable," Owens says of his silky, ruby-hued Hemp Hop Rye.

Pleased with the results, Owens began exploring other brews that deserved a rye dose. One he settled upon is an amped-up IPA called Ryely Hoppy, a special Brewer's Stash release. It's a tribute to both the grain and his young son. "My son's name is Ryely," Owens says, laughing. "I love rye beers, so my wife and I thought, 'Perfect, let's name him Ryely.'"

A HEFEWEIZEN BY ANOTHER NAME

Creating a new breed of rye beers can be thrilling, but other brewers are instead finding success in reviving long-forgotten styles. For Real Ale, the opportunity to dig into history books arose after it bid good riddance to its old brewhouse in 2006. It was an indoor-outdoor setup (basically, a carport attached to a basement) that "was a glorified homebrewing system," recalls head brewer Erik Ogershok. Brewing on jerry-rigged equipment was a pain, especially when crafting the balanced, well-hopped Full Moon Pale

Rye Ale. However, in the new building, brewing with rye was a relative snap.

Like teens given keys to a sports car, Ogershok and Real Ale decided to take their shiny new equipment for a spin. While Full Moon possessed 17 percent rye, what would happen if they brewed a beer containing 35 percent rye or higher? To do "something different and prove a point, we decided to make a roggenbier," Ogershok says.

You may blank on the German beer that fell out of favor a century ago, but you're likely familiar with its summery sibling, hefeweizen. Whereas hazy hefeweizens are wheat driven, roggenbiers (*Roggen* is German for *rye*) contain up to 50 percent rye. When fermented with hefeweizen yeast, roggenbiers "end up with a smooth, velvety body. That clovey spiciness of the yeast goes well with the spicy rye. It almost tastes like pumpkin pie," Ogershok says of his beer, which has attracted a rabid local following, along with the darker, maltier Dunkelroggen.

Though it's too early to call this a revival, roggenbier is slowly catching on with brewers bewitched by rye. Toronto's Mill Street Brew Pub serves Schleimhammer Roggenbier, while Avery Brewing in Boulder, Colorado, turns out the creamy, chewy, limited-release Jerry's Roggenbier. Terrapin's Buckowski crossed a roggenbier with a smoky rauchbier to create the RoggenRauchBier. It was big, smoky, and challenging—just like roggenbier's uphill struggle in the marketplace, especially when compared with hefeweizen.

The issue, says Peter Kruger, master brewer at Bear Republic Brewing Company in Healdsburg, California, might be less about flavor than about semantics. "Hefeweizen has all these soft consonants," says Kruger, whose brewery makes a roggenbier. "With roggenbier there are lots of hard consonants. Just the name sounds hardcore." Adds Ogershok, "If we called it 'German rye ale,' it'd probably be easier to sell." However, he has faith in this once-forgotten style. After all, he says, "in America, it took time for people to become familiar with hefeweizen. With roggenbier people are like, 'What the hell is *that*?' As brewers, it's incumbent upon us to be rye educators."

ALL RYE, ALL THE TIME

Given that relatively small quantities of rye can create a gummy mash, it might seem like inviting disaster to craft an all-rye beer. But where others saw a fool's errand, Bear Republic saw a worthy challenge. One day in winter 2007, the brewers were unwinding with a couple of beers, discussing rye malt. Rye had long been popular at Bear Republic, driving the flavor of its burly, aggressively bittered Hop Rod Rye IPA. "One brewer said, 'What would a 100 percent rye beer taste like?'" Kruger recalls. "We thought, 'What do we have to lose? Let's go for it.'"

To transform the "brewing from impossible to very, very difficult," Kruger says, the team used enzymes and rice hulls to break up the grain bed. They carefully monitored the mash's temperature, since wild fluctuations could turn the wet grains to stone. This made the brewing somewhat easier—but it took much, much longer. An average Bear Republic brew day lasts about eight hours. This session lasted seventeen nerve-wracking, grueling hours. "That," Kruger recalls, "was not a fun day."

The hard work was forgotten when the brewers sampled the surprising result, cheekily called Easy Ryeder. Despite its grain bill, the hazy, coppery beer's spiciness was restrained, resulting in a smooth refreshment. Easy Ryeder was, well, easy drinking. "If you didn't tell people it had rye in it, they might not have known," Kruger says.

Though Kruger has sworn off brewing Easy Ryeder again, the experience has not dissuaded the brewery from continuing its rye research. At 2010's Great American Beer Festival, Bear Republic won gold with its Belgian-inspired Ryevalry. "Even though it was so weird, it was a beer that all of us loved," Kruger says of the double IPA that was brewed with 30 percent rye, then fermented with a Belgian ale yeast to create a bitter, spicy pleasure.

Terrapin's Buckowski, too, continues to be bitten by the rye bug. His Rye Squared is a supercharged riff on his flagship brew. He collaborated with Colorado's Left Hand Brewing in 2008, as part of their Midnight Brewing Project, to create the limited-release Terra-Rye'zd black rye lager (50 percent rye), and even snuck 10 percent rye malt into the tart, hoppy, oak-aged Monstre Rouge imperial Flanders red ale he made with Belgium's De Proef Brouwerij. As for the future, Buckowski dreams of perhaps blending chocolate rye and dark rye malts to create a rye stout. "There's always a side project where we can use more rye," Buckowski says. "Any way we can exploit rye, we certainly will."

FIVE TO TRY

BLACK HEMP BLACK ALE
O'FALLON BREWERY
ABV: 5.8%
THE MISSOURI BREWERY'S WINTER SEASONAL IS A WEIRDO MASH-UP OF TOASTED HEMP SEEDS, OATS, RYE, WHEAT, AND AMARILLO AND CITRA HOPS—TIED TOGETHER WITH BELGIAN YEAST. SURPRISINGLY, THE BEER REMAINS BALANCED, WITH A NICE CITRUSY, TROPICAL CURRENT COURSING THROUGH THE BLACK DEPTHS.

SLY RYE PORTER
YAZOO BREWING COMPANY
ABV: 5.7%

WITH SLY, THE TENNESSEANS TAKE RYE TO THE DARK SIDE, FORMULATING A MEDIUM-BODIED ENGLISH PORTER THAT SMELLS OF CHOCOLATE AND CARAMEL AND FEATURES FLAVORS OF DARK FRUIT AND SWEET ROASTED MALTS. THE RYE SHINES AT THE SPICY, DRYING END.

HOP ROD RYE
BEAR REPUBLIC BREWING CO.
ABV: 8%
AGGRESSIVE AND UNCOMPROMISING, HOP ROD ROARS FROM THE BOTTLE A DEEP AMBER WITH A BULKY TAN HEAD AND LACING LIKE A SPIDER WEB. THE UNABASHEDLY FLORAL BOUQUET—

CITRUS, PINE—CONTAINS TRACES OF CARAMEL AND SPICE. TASTE-WISE, BITTERNESS IS BALANCED BY A SWEET-SPICY PROFILE AND A PEPPERY FINISH ROOTED IN EARTH.

RYE PALE ALE
TERRAPIN BEER CO.
ABV: 5.5%

THE GEORGIA BREWERY'S FLAGSHIP BREW FROM DAY ONE, RPA DECANTS A WARM HONEY-ORANGE AND OFFERS A CITRUSY HELLO SMOOSHED AGAINST TOASTED MALTS. ON FIRST SIP, THE MEDIUM-BODIED ALE REVEALS A FLORAL, HERBAL BITTERNESS, WHICH IS TEMPERED BY SWEET MALT AND RYE AS PRICKLY AS A PORCUPINE.

HE'BREW R.I.P.A. ON RYE
SHMALTZ BREWING COMPANY
ABV: 10%

R.I.P.A. ON RYE IS A COPPERY CREATURE CAPPED BY A BEIGE HEAD. THE SCENT OF THIS LIMITED-RELEASE DOUBLE IPA CALLS TO MIND CARAMEL, VANILLA, PINE, AND RYE—BOTH THE GRAIN AND THE WHISKEY, THANKS TO A STAY IN SAZERAC BARRELS. WHEN SIPPED: HONEY, BISCUIT, BITTERNESS.

EDUCATION BY THE PINT

DESPITE GARNERING INTERNATIONAL ACCLAIM FOR DENMARK'S MIKKELLER, HEAD BREWER AND OWNER MIKKEL BORG BJERGSØ REMAINS A PART-TIME SCHOOLTEACHER, CLIMBING INTO A CLASSROOM ONCE A WEEK. HOWEVER, THOSE OTHER SIX DAYS A WEEK HE'S ALSO A TEACHER, INSTRUCTING STUDENTS SITTING NOT AT A DESK BUT AT THE BAR.

"IT'S INTERESTING TO TEACH PEOPLE ABOUT INGREDIENTS," BJERGSØ SAYS OF HIS LINE OF EDUCATIONAL BREWS, WHICH ARE AS INSTRUCTIONAL AS THEY ARE DELICIOUS. TO HELP DRINKERS UNDERSTAND DIFFERENT YEAST STRAINS AND HOPS, HE BREWS A UNIFORM BATCH OF BEER AND THEN TWEAKS ONE COMPONENT. IN MIKKELLER'S SINGLE HOP SERIES, BJERGSØ'S VARIABLE IS THE HOP, WITH EACH BEER EXCLUSIVELY DOSED WITH A SINGLE VARIETY. LINE UP A FEW SELECTIONS, AND YOU'LL BE ABLE TO DISCERN THE DIFFERENT AROMATIC AND BITTERING PROPERTIES AMONG VARIETIES SUCH AS CHINOOK, CENTENNIAL, AND NELSON SAUVIN.

AFTER EXHAUSTING MIKKELLER'S HOPS LESSON, ENROLL IN THE YEAST SERIES. "YEAST IS ONE OF BEER'S MOST IMPORTANT INGREDIENTS," BJERGSØ SAYS. THE MIX OF HOPS AND MALT CAN MAKE OR BREAK A BEER, BUT IT'S YEAST THAT DEVOURS THE SUGARS AND TRANSFORMS GRAIN SOUP INTO ALCOHOL. TO DEMONSTRATE, BJERGSØ INOCULATES EACH YEAST RELEASE WITH A DIFFERENT STRAIN, RANGING FROM HEFEWEIZEN TO LAGER TO UNTAMED BRETTANOMYCES. "NINETY PERCENT OF ALL STYLES ARE DEFINED BY THE YEAST," HE EXPLAINS.

BREWERIES ACROSS AMERICA ARE ALSO TURNING HAPPY HOUR INTO STUDY HALL. IN HOUSTON, SAINT ARNOLD BREWING CO.'S DRAFT-ONLY MOVABLE YEAST SERIES FEATURES BATCHES OF WORT (THE UNFERMENTED BROTH

CREATED BY BOILING GRAINS WITH WATER), SPLIT IN HALF, WITH A DIFFERENT YEAST STRAIN PITCHED IN EACH. (FOR EXAMPLE, THE AMBER ALE WAS DOSED WITH BELGIAN TRAPPIST YEAST TO CREATE THE ALTARED AMBER.) IN ENTERPRISE, OREGON, TERMINAL GRAVITY BREWING AND PUBLIC HOUSE HAS ITS SINGLE-HOP IMPERIAL IPA SERIES, WHILE BELLINGHAM, WASHINGTON'S BOUNDARY BAY BREWERY & BISTRO RUNS THE ONGOING TRADITION SINGLE HOP PALE ALE SERIES. NOT TO BE OUTDONE, PENNSYLVANIA'S SLY FOX SPENT MORE THAN FIVE YEARS BREWING NEARLY THREE DOZEN UNIQUELY HOPPED IPAS BEFORE REVISITING THE HOP PROJECT, AS IT'S KNOWN, WITH SUBTLER, MORE NUANCED PALE ALES.

WITH EDUCATIONAL BEERS, LEARNING'S SO MUCH FUN, YOU MIGHT JUST MAKE A PLAY FOR EXTRA CREDIT.

No Barley, No Problem: Gluten-Free Beer

One day, a Houston doctor rang Russ Klisch, the president of Milwaukee's Lakefront Brewery. The call concerned a serious medical condition: the doctor's. The doc bemoaned the fact that he couldn't drink beer because it contained gluten. "What's the deal with gluten?" Klisch asked.

Gluten, the doctor explained, is several different proteins found in certain cereal grains such as rye, barley, and spelt. Most people easily digest gluten. But for an estimated two and a half to three million Americans suffering from celiac disease, an autoimmune disorder, ingesting gluten causes crippling stomach pain and serious issues with digestion. This means no bread. No pasta. No beer. A single bottle could make a celiac sufferer sicker than the nastiest hangover.

The doctor wondered if Lakefront would brew a beer he could drink. Klisch was intrigued, especially because the doctor had rung him from Houston. "I asked why he called me," Klisch recalls. "He said he'd recently visited Wisconsin and noticed that Lakefront made an organic beer. He said, 'If you can make an organic beer, you can make a beer for me.'"

GLUTEN FREE – WHEAT IS MURDER

Up for the challenge, Klisch and his colleagues experimented with recipes, settling upon a blend of rice (which is gluten free) and sorghum extract, an ingredient used in wheat-free baking. Ta-da! Lakefront devised New Grist, a crisp, golden potion that looks, smells, and drinks much like its gluten-y counterpart. "Everyone who wants to should be able to drink a beer," Klisch says.

A decade ago, pickings for gluten-free beer were as slim as a gnat's eyelash. But as celiac sufferers have grown more visible and vocal, breweries have begun finding ways to kick barley and wheat to the curb. Connecticut's Bard's Tale Beer Company relies on the grass sorghum to craft its smooth Bard's beer, while Britain's Green's mixes millet, sorghum, buckwheat (which is wheat and gluten free, despite the name), and brown rice to make its English- and Belgian-style ales. Wisconsin's Sprecher Brewing offers the light, cider-like Shakparo Ale, brewed with sorghum and millet. Even Anheuser-Busch InBev sells the wheat-free, sorghum-based Redbridge, a beer

I like better than Bud. For celiac sufferers, ditching wheat no longer means ditching great beer.

PROCESS SERVED

Brewing gluten-free beer isn't as simple as just leaving out the barley or wheat. These grains are beer's essential components. They provide the sugars and proteins that yeast feasts on, spurring fermentation. As a substitute, brewers turn to gluten-free alternatives such as buckwheat, millet, flax, or, most commonly, sorghum grass, which has a high sugar content. Since making sorghum malt is a labor-intensive process, many brewers use formulated extracts, such as Briess Malt & Ingredients Co.'s white sorghum syrup. It's calibrated to mimic standard malt extracts, allowing brewers to easily manufacture gluten-free beer. Kind of.

"Brewing with sorghum creates a hazy beer," Klisch explains. New Grist, as well as other sorghum-heavy gluten-free beers, requires heavy-duty filtration to achieve that Caribbean-clear look. In addition, brewers must take painstaking precautions to prevent any cross-contamination.

"While brewing, you have to ensure that the beer isn't contaminated by wheat products," says Brian Kovalchuk, the CEO of Bard's Tale Beer Company. The firm was conceived when die-hard beer fans Kevin Seplowitz and Craig Belser were diagnosed with celiac disease. Instead of giving up their favorite beverage, they were inspired to create sorghum-driven Bard's (originally sold as Dragon's Gold). Since the first bottle rolled off the production line, Bard's has expanded to more than 40 states. That may seem like insane success, but when discussing gluten-free brews, market saturation doesn't translate to overwhelming demand.

"Our product is different than a craft beer," Kovalchuk explains. "While there are microbrews specific to cities and regions, there's not a gluten-free beer that's specific to a location." Instead of capturing consumers with novel flavors or regional pride, as is the

standard craft-beer playbook, gluten-free beers must appeal to
the middle ground. That explains why brands, such as Redbridge
and Bard's Gold, are somewhat interchangeable: easy drinking,
lager-esque beers.

Moreover, with a total American market of two to three million
celiac sufferers—and not all of them beer drinkers, or old enough
to consume alcohol—gluten-free beers are a national product out
of necessity. They're sold primarily at supermarkets, beer stores,
and restaurants specializing in gluten-free cuisine (like New York's
excellent Risotteria). You won't find Bard's Gold poured by the pint
at your local tavern, because "there's a question of running the beer
through draft lines that may be contaminated [with the residue of
beers containing gluten]," Kovalchuk says. "I don't want people to
drink my beer and say, 'I got sick.'"

SICK IN THE STOMACH

By now, you may be yawning. Where's that craft-beer daring? Will there ever be a gluten-free double IPA dosed with wild raspberries? Perhaps. For instance, in England, Green's fashions fine Belgian-inspired tripels and dubbels, and a crisp pilsner. Innovation is easy. The issue is, "Will the retailers carry that much variety of gluten-free beer?" Kovalchuk asks.

Doubtful. If drinkers had their druthers, I doubt they'd choose gluten-free beer. Though this style has mainstream appeal ("I have a friend who drinks New Grist all the time, simply because he likes the flavor," Lakefront's Klisch says), lager-like, gluten-free beers are pale wallflowers compared to barrel-aged stouts and IPAs. The thing is, for celiac sufferers, there's no choice. That can be heartbreaking, especially if the person you love can no longer enjoy the beers you love brewing.

That was the quandary for John Kimmich. Since 2003, the brewmaster at Waterbury, Vermont's Alchemist Pub and Brewery has devised wonderful weirdoes such as Uncle Daddy pumpkin hefeweizen and Wellness, a "probiotic" fruit beer concocted with Vitamin C–packed raspberries and antioxidant-stuffed pomegranates and ginseng. Despite Kimmich's mad-fermentationist streak, he had never tinkered with gluten-free beer. That changed when he feared his wife, Jennifer, had stomach cancer. For months, Jennifer suffered from stomach pain so intense that most mornings she was doubled over in agony.

But Jennifer tested negative for cancer. After a run through the medical ringer, the couple discovered that Jennifer suffered from celiac disease. "When we first found out, I thought, Oh my gosh, that's devastating," Kimmich says. "You're never going to drink another one of my IPAs." After a year on a gluten-free diet, "there was a 180-degree change," Kimmich says. "She never felt better." Jennifer began sampling gluten-free beers. To her dismay, she was unable to find one that tickled her taste buds. She was accustomed to her husband's innovative brews. How could she sip such *normal* beer?

"That really got me motivated to try something new," says Kimmich. He played around with white sorghum syrup, gauging its quirks—it creates a tangy finishing note. Kimmich realized sorghum would mate well with tart, dry saisons and ales inoculated with wild yeasts such as *Brettanomyces*, which provide funky, pungent flavors.

"It's very complementary to those kinds of beers," says Kimmich, who devised a range of super-tasty gluten-free brews. The Celia Saison is flavored with coriander and orange peel, while Celia IPA has a grapefruit punch.

More important, Jennifer can now drink her husband's brews, like Celia Framboise, spiked with *Brettanomyces*. "It produces this beautiful, horsey character," Kimmich says. "It just shines." And wins prizes. It took home the gold at 2009's Great American Beer Festival, which began recognizing gluten-free beer as a category in 2007. (Celia IPA took the bronze.)

Now Kimmich keeps a couple of Celia beers on

tap, and he's constantly concocting new gluten-free brews, such as a Belgian-style pale ale. His beers have been largely well received, but then he'll read a review that'll bristle his feathers. Of the Celia IPA, one Rate Beer reviewer wrote that it had "some 'hollowness' in the body with lack of grain. [It's] great for a gluten-free [beer], so-so for an IPA, and I rated to the latter."

"Of course my Celia IPA won't taste like my Holy Cow IPA—it's a different category," Kimmich says. "Those reviews can be kind of misleading. Many reviewers aren't judging gluten-free beers against gluten-free beers. If it has zero barley, it's pushing the definition of beer."

And that's the rallying cry for craft brewing.

TEN TO TRY

BARD'S
BARD'S TALE BEER COMPANY
ABV: 4.6%
CREATED BY TWO SERIOUS BEER GEEKS WHO, IN THEIR THIRTIES, WERE DIAGNOSED WITH CELIAC DISEASE, BARD'S IS A GLUTEN-FREE, SORGHUM-BASED BREW THAT RECALLS THE CLASSIC AMERICAN LAGER. THE BEER POURS A TRANSPARENT GOLD, WITH A SUBTLE AROMA OF PEARS AND A LIGHT, WISPY HEAD. IT DRINKS CIDER-LIKE, FINISHING DRY AND SHARP.

ENDEAVOR
GREEN'S GLUTEN FREE BEERS
ABV: 7%
BASED IN BRITAIN, GREEN'S QUENCHES THE THIRST OF THOSE WHO CANNOT HAVE GLUTEN WITH TERRIFIC WHEATLESS AND BARLEYLESS BEERS SUCH AS BOTTLE-FERMENTED QUEST TRIPEL BLONDE ALE, AMBER-STYLE MISSION, AND, MY FAVORITE, ENDEAVOR. THIS BELGIAN DUBBEL DECANTS AS DARK AS RUBIES, GIVING OFF A COMPLEX SCENT OF LICORICE AND DARK CHOCOLATE. THE FLAVOR FOLLOWS THE AROMA, WITH THE ADDED BONUS OF BEING CREAMY AND AS RICH AS DADDY WARBUCKS.

NEW GRIST
LAKEFRONT BREWERY
ABV: 5.7%
MILWAUKEE'S LAKEFRONT PRODUCED AMERICA'S FIRST GLUTEN-FREE BEVERAGE THAT THE U.S. GOVERNMENT PERMITTED TO CARRY THE NAME BEER. THIS STRAW-PALE LIBATION—CONCOCTED FROM SORGHUM AND RICE—HAS AN AROMA

OF HAY AND CLOVES, WHILE THE TASTE IS A LITTLE LEMONY AND SWEET. IT'D BE PERFECT FOR CRACKING OPEN ON A THERMOMETER-SPIKING SUMMER AFTERNOON, BUT IT'S SUITABLE YEAR-ROUND.

Celia Framboise
THE ALCHEMIST PUB AND BREWERY
ABV: 7.1%
WHEN HIS WIFE WAS DIAGNOSED WITH CELIAC DISEASE, VERMONT'S JOHN KIMMICH DEVISED HIS CELIA LINE OF GLUTEN-FREE BREWS SO SHE COULD ONCE MORE DRINK HIS BEER. THE CELIA SAISON IS SERIOUSLY TART AND REFRESHING, AND THE FRAMBOISE IS FIRST-RATE. IT'S REDOLENT OF POMEGRANATE AND RASPBERRY AND POSSESSES THE BRETTANOMYCES YEAST'S TRADEMARK BARNYARD PROFILE. NEGATIVES? SADLY, THE BEERS ARE POURED ONLY AT THE PUB.

Shakparo Ale
SPRECHER BREWING CO.
ABV: 5.7%
SPRECHER FIRST CREATED THIS WEST AFRICAN-STYLE ALE FOR MILWAUKEE'S AFRICAN WORLD FESTIVAL. HOWEVER, THE SORGHUM-AND-MILLET CONCOCTION (THEY'RE THE FAVORED FERMENTABLES IN SUB-SAHARAN AFRICA, SINCE WHEAT AND BARLEY ARE RARE) WAS SUCH A HIT THAT THE BREWERY HAS MADE SHAKPARO A YEAR-ROUND STAPLE.

GOOD CALL. SHAKPARO IS GENTLE AND THIRST SLAKING, PACKING AN APPLE CIDER-LIKE PROFILE. IT'S SUMMERTIME BY THE BOTTLE.

REDBRIDGE
ANHEUSER-BUSCH INBEV
ABV: 4%
ANHEUSER-BUSCH BREWS REDBRIDGE, BUT THAT'S NOT NECESSARILY BAD. MADE WITH SORGHUM, REDBRIDGE IS NO SLOUCH. THE GLUTEN-FREE OFFERING POURS A PRETTY AMBER AND EXHIBITS A TEA-LIKE AROMA. TASTEWISE, EXPECT A MILD EARTHINESS CUT WITH SOME SWEET MOLASSES, BERRIES, AND A SMIDGEN OF CITRIC BITTERNESS.

G-FREE
ST. PETER'S BREWERY
ABV: 4.2%
G-FREE IS A FINE ADDITION TO THE GLUTEN-FREE FIELD. THE LOW-ALCOHOL BEER TAKES ITS CUES FROM CZECH PILSNERS, RESULTING IN A BRISK, EFFERVESCENT ALE THAT OFFERS UP A CITRIC BOUQUET—THANK YOU, AMARILLO HOPS.

Daura
ESTRELLA DAMM
ABV: 5.4%
WHEREAS MOST GLUTEN-FREE BEERS ELIMINATE ALL WHEAT, RELYING INSTEAD ON SORGHUM OR MILLET, SPAIN'S DAURA IS MADE WITH MALT. THAT'S POSSIBLE DUE TO A PROPRIETARY TECHNIQUE THAT

REMOVES THE GLUTEN FROM BARLEY MALT, MAKING IT PALATABLE FOR THOSE WITH CELIAC DISEASE. HENCE, DAURA TASTES PRETTY DARN CLOSE TO STANDARD BEER. IT'S BUBBLY AND PALE YELLOW, WITH A FULL BODY AND A BIT OF A BITTER KICK. AT THE WORLD BEER AWARDS, DAURA HAS WON BEST GLUTEN-FREE BEER FOR TWO YEARS RUNNING.

3R RASPBERRY ALE
NEW PLANET GLUTEN FREE BEER
ABV: 5%
THANKS TO RASPBERRY PUREE AND ORANGE PEEL, 3R DECANTS AS PINK AS A KITTEN'S NOSE, WITH FAINT NOTES OF BERRIES AND BISCUITS. IT GLIDES DOWN LIGHT, CRISP, AND SEMISWEET, AND RASPBERRIES LINGER ON THE FINISH.

MESSAGÈRE ROUSSE
MICROBRASSERIE NOUVELLE FRANCE
ABV: 5%
THIS QUEBEC-BASED MICROBREWERY'S WELL-CARBONATED ROUSSE—FANCY TALK FOR A RED ALE—IS DEVISED WITH RICE SYRUP AND BUCKWHEAT, GLUCOSE EXTRACT, BUCKWHEAT, AND MILLET. IT POURS A RICH MAHOGANY AND TASTES OF SUGAR-DIPPED DRIED FRUITS AND OAK.

Yeasts and Other Microscopic Critters

Thanks to yeasts' appetites, watery wort becomes boozy beer. Yet all yeasts are not equal: Fungi strains are as unique as fingerprints, and each one devours wort differently. Some leave plenty of sugary sweetness behind, while others create beer as lean and dry as champagne. Other fungi, as well as certain bacteria, can make beer that's as puckering and perplexing as it is pleasing. Welcome to the wild, wild yeasts.

Pucker Up, Buttercup

Our noses have been conditioned to equate *sour* with *rotten*. One whiff of expired milk will make you send it down a sink. Beers can also easily go bad. I've cracked countless past-their-prime ales that recall road-kill skunk. But the truth is, in a brewer's practiced hands, sour can be sublime.

Category-wise, *sour ale* is a catchall, encompassing a laundry basket of beer styles. Many are indigenous to Belgium, home to lip-scrunching gueuzes, lambics, krieks, and Flemish sour ales. But just as they've done with German pilsners and Russian imperial stouts, American brewers have given foreign styles a Stars and Stripes spin. Their tools are wild yeasts, bacteria, wooden barrels, and a desire to break down walls no one wants broken down.

Take Dann Paquette. Back in the mid-1990s, Paquette (now co-owner of Pretty Things Beer and Ale Project; see page 207) was toiling at Massachusetts's now-defunct North East Brewing Company, where brewers conducted barrel experiments. (Long before others leapt on the wooden bandwagon, North East served bourbon-barrel stouts directly from a cask.) Paquette sought out used wine barrels and sourced *Brettanomyces* yeast.

Brettanomyces, often shortened to Brett, makes grape juice reek of Band-Aids, horse stables, or even rancid cheese. Yet in a balanced, well-made beer, these challenging flavors can add uncommon complexity. In Paquette's underground "infection factory," he administered *Brettanomyces* yeast to his beers, as well as souring bacteria such as *Lactobacillus* and *Pediococcus*, then sent them to sleep in oak.

Inside the dark, wet wood, the bacteria went to work. They reproduced as rapidly as rabbits, rearranging the beer's molecular makeup, ushering in lemon-sourness and an earthy, barnyard funkiness by turns sweet and tart. Paquette was so proud of his funky, sour suds he took them to the Great American Beer Festival in 1998. His eyes were on a medal. "I thought it'd be insanely popular," Paquette says.

However, Paquette forgot an important lesson. For the initiate, that first sip of Brett-infected beer can be as foreign—and off-putting—as a spoonful of rank, custardy durian fruit. Soon after he started pouring, volunteers moved a trashcan in front of North East's booth. "People are spitting out your beer," a volunteer explained. Paquette was crestfallen. "I made the judgment that sour beers would never catch on in America," he says. "Of course, I was wrong."

Rather, he was ahead of the curve. In 1999, Belgian native Peter Bouckaert, the brewmaster at Fort Collins, Colorado's fittingly named New Belgium Brewing Company, released the burgundy-barreled La Folie Sour Brown Ale. It was just weird enough to work, and now it's one of three wood-aged beers from New Belgium. Then there's the case of Vinnie Cilurzo, a mad scientist masquerading as a brewer.

Cilurzo has a well-earned reputation as a trailblazer. At San Diego's Blind Pig Brewery, he was among the first brewers to drop an absurdly hopped double IPA. Now at Russian River Brewing Company in Santa Rosa, he's continued his hopped-up streak with the cultish Pliny the Elder. But it's within the barrels that he's found his true muse.

"I like making beers with bugs and critters," says Cilurzo of his sour, Belgian-style ales fermented with unpredictable *Brettanomyces*. "We're charting unknown territory and transforming beer." Cilurzo has experimented with Brett since 1999. His innovations include woodsy blonde ale Temptation and sour-cherry-spiked brown ale Supplication, respectively aged in French oak chardonnay and pinot noir barrels, and the tart Beatification.

Unlike normal beers, which ferment predictably and can be drinkable in as few as two or three weeks, Brett beers "aren't even tasted until they're six months old," Cilurzo says. His beers often age for a year, sometimes two, before they're blended together to meet Cilurzo's exacting, idiosyncratic standard. "We make funky, challenging beers we like to drink," Cilurzo explains, "and thank God, there are people out there who like to drink them."

PUCKER YOUR PALATE AT THESE SOUR-BEER FESTS ACROSS THE COUNTRY

STONE SOUR FEST
STONE BREWING WORLD BISTRO AND GARDENS, ESCONDIDO, CALIFORNIA
STONEWORLDBISTRO.COM/SOURFEST
CELLARING EXPERT CICERONE (CERTIFIED BEER SOMMELIER) AND "DR." BILL SYSAK HUNTS DOWN DOZENS OF THE WORLD'S RAREST SOURS TO SERVE AT THIS ANNUAL ONE-DAY FESTIVAL.

SOUR BEER FEST
THE JUG SHOP, SAN FRANCISCO
THEJUGSHOP.COM
THE LONG-RUNNING WINE, BEER, AND SPIRITS STORE OFFERS TWO SESSIONS: FRUITY SOURS, THEN BRETTANOMYCES-INFECTED AND BARREL-AGED ALES.

BROUWER'S SOUR BEER FEST
BROUWER'S CAFÉ, SEATTLE
BROUWERSCAFE.BLOGSPOT.COM
HELD DURING SEATTLE BEER WEEK, THIS EVENT FEATURES MORE THAN 40 SOURS SERVED ON DRAFT, COUNTING CASCADE AND CANTILLON.

WHERE THE WILD BEERS ARE
MINNEAPOLIS, MINNESOTA; BROOKLYN, NEW YORK
WHERETHEWILDBEERSARE.COM
THE FESTIVAL IS A COLLABORATIVE AFFAIR: ATTENDEES BRING BOTTLES OF
SOUR BEER, AND IN TURN RECEIVE DRINK TICKETS TO SAMPLE OTHER BREWS.

BOULDER SOUR ALE FEST
THE AVERY TAP ROOM, BOULDER, COLORADO
AVERYBREWING.COM
AVERY BREWING HOSTS THIS STAR-STUDDED LINEUP FEATURING MORE THAN
35 SOURS, INCLUDING OFFERINGS FROM NEW HOLLAND, GREEN FLASH, ODELL,
AND BOULEVARD.

LAMBIC BEER FESTIVAL
DELILAH'S, CHICAGO, ILLINOIS
DELILAHSCHICAGO.COM
EACH MAY, PUNK BAR DELILAH'S IS HOST TO THIS FAR-REACHING TASTING THAT
TYPICALLY INCLUDES MORE THAN A DOZEN GUEUZES, RARE FAROS (A SPICED,
BLENDED LAMBIC WITH CANDI SUGAR, A BELGIAN SUGAR USED IN BREWING), AND
MORE THAN 60 ASSORTED LAMBICS.

Sorry, Brett—You're Not Always Wanted

When it comes to making sour beers, Brett is not the end-all, be-all.
Sometimes, an unbridled Brett infestation can make beers as palatable
as sewer scum. "Over time, *Brettanomyces* will continue to crunch and
break down any carbohydrates left in the beer, causing it to become
mustier, more sour and thin out," says Ron Gansberg, the brewmaster
at Portland, Oregon's Cascade Brewing. Over the last decade, Gansberg
has earned a reputation as one of the Pacific Northwest's finest barrel
magicians, using *Lactobacillus* bacteria (which ceases reproducing
when the beer reaches a certain pH level) to create sour ales of
uncommon grace, balance, and nuance. "Drinking a sour beer shouldn't
be an event unto itself," Gansberg says.

To achieve that standard, Gansberg maintains an intimate relationship with his stock of more than 300 oak casks. He samples each of the developing beers, taking careful notes and deciding which barrels should constitute each blended batch. He follows no algorithm or recipe, instead relying on sensory monitoring to tell him when his food-

Cascade Brewing brewmaster Ron Gansberg.

friendly, wine-like ales are ready. There's nary a miss among them.

His blended Sang Rouge spends upward of two years fermenting and aging in French oak wine barrels, resulting in an oaky profile of sour, dark fruit. Kriek Ale gets its kick from six months sitting in oak in the company of bing and sour pie cherries. Apricot Ale is constructed by fermenting a sweet Belgian tripel for up to sixteen months in French-oak wine barrels with ripe apricots that Gansberg occasionally harvests himself. Each year's batch is a bit different, but that's just fine by Gansberg.

"We're shepherding a living organism, and each year it tends to change different aspects of the beer," Gansberg says. "We're not interested in making the same beer. We just want it to be as good as the previous year's batch—or better."

MEET THE FERMENTATION-MAD MICROBES THAT ARE MAKING BEERS SOUR

LACTOBACILLUS

THIS BACTERIA (WHICH SOURS MILK, THUS CREATING YOGURT) IS OFTEN USED TO MAKE SOUR GERMAN ALES SUCH AS SALT-KISSED GOSE AND BERLINER WEISSE, ALONGSIDE BELGIAN-STYLE FLANDERS RED AND BROWN ALES. ITS FERMENTATION RESULTS IN THE PRODUCTION OF LACTIC ACID, WHICH CREATES A DRY, TANGY PROFILE IN THE BREW.

PEDIOCOCCUS

THIS ANAEROBIC BACTERIA (IT SURVIVES WITHOUT OXYGEN) CREATES A BY-PRODUCT DUBBED DIACETYL, WHICH CREATES FLAVORS SUCH AS BUTTERSCOTCH AND BUTTER (IT'S USED IN THE MANUFACTURE OF BUTTER SUBSTITUTES). BUT GIVEN TIME, THE DIACETYL IS REABSORBED, RESULTING IN A REFRESHING ACIDITY.

BRETTANOMYCES

THIS SLOW-GROWING, HARD-TO-KILL WILD YEAST HAS AN INSATIABLE HUNGER, DEVOURING COMPLEX SUGARS AND CARBOHYDRATES THAT OTHER YEASTS FIND UNPALATABLE. IT'S BEHIND THAT EARTHY, HORSEY, LEATHER-LIKE SCENT. BREWERS BOTH FEAR AND REVERE THE YEAST, THE PRESENCE OF WHICH IS CONSIDERED A DEFECT IN WINE.

Spontaneous Creation: Wild Ales

Creating great sour beers takes passion and patience, two qualities you'll find in Ron Jeffries. Based in Dexter, Michigan, Jeffries runs Jolly Pumpkin Artisan Ales, the country's first 100 percent oak-aged sour brewery. "I think we're fairly, well, *unique* may be too strong of a word," says Jeffries of his rustic-farmhouse creations that are unfiltered and unpasteurized, "but we make fairly *different* beer."

Using an arsenal of microbes, Jeffries creates sour beers as unique as they are transcendent. Take La Roja. The amber ale is blended from beer aged in used oak barrels for two to ten months, creating a spicy, sour-caramel flavor rivaling fine wines for nuance. Or the Weizen Bam, made by mixing German hefeweizen yeast with wild and sour yeasts and bacteria. "We're not trying to create straight-ahead flavors—I want subtlety and hints," Jeffries says. But it's Lambicus Dexterius that is among his most impressive accomplishments.

Belgian lambics are created via spontaneous, or open, fermentation, which means that they grab yeasts lurking in the environment, instead of being inoculated with brewer's yeast. At century-old breweries, such as Belgium's famed lambic house Cantillon, contamination is a snap. Yeasts and bacteria lurk in nearly every nook and cranny. They've settled into the surroundings, calmly awaiting their next wort feast. In newer breweries, which may lack a critical mass of microscopic critters, creating a lambic requires a little luck—and a lot of waiting. Jeffries set out to create an American-born Belgian lambic in October 2005. "I wanted to be the first lambic production brewery in the U.S.," Jeffries says. He brewed a batch of beer heavy on raw wheat, then let the wort cool down overnight in an open fermentation tank. (Traditionally, Belgian brewers use coolships, which are large, shallow, open trays.) Once the wort cooled, airborne yeasts and bacteria infested the liquid, which was then racked into Jeffries's "sourest" oak barrels.

Numerous batches of lambic were brewed, with the beer spending years maturing. The first bottle, a blend of the batches, wasn't released until New Year's Eve 2009. The result of four years of labor and waiting, Lambicus Dexterius was low in carbonation, with hints of citrus and a deeply fruity, acidic sourness. It's a little bit of Belgium, from a little city in Michigan.

Jolly Pumpkin is not the only American brewery tinkering with spontaneous fermentation. Block 15 Restaurant & Brewery, in Corvallis, Oregon, which has a comprehensive "extended cellaring program," installed a coolship in fall 2010. Also, Allagash Brewing Company, in Portland, Maine, has built an authentic Belgian coolship. The inoculated wort, which is transferred to oak barrels where it snoozes until ready, has so far resulted in extremely limited-run beers in their Coolship series, such as the pink-tinted Cerise, aged with tart cherries, and Allagash Red, made with raspberries. If you're lucky, the brewers may bring a bottle to a festival or a special dinner.

The wort-filled coolship at Portland, Maine's Allagash Brewing is a buffet for yeasts and bacteria.

A Sour Challenge

For American brewing's barrel-aging vanguard, lack of creativity is not the problem. Instead, other issues conspire to keep barrel aging a speck within the craft-beer constellation.

For starters, there's space. Storing barrels require tons of square footage, multiplied by the months and years it takes to age the beer—with no guarantee that the liquid inside will be suitable for consumption. Second, most breweries are not climate controlled. This wreaks havoc with wood aging, which kowtows to Mother Nature. In the summer, beers ferment quickly. When the mercury drops, fermentation slows to a sludgy crawl. In the winter, Jolly Pumpkin's Jeffries receives calls from distributors wondering when his beers will be ready. "I tell them, 'Well, hope for a heat wave,'" Jeffries says. "That doesn't always make them too happy, but I can't speed up the process."

Most critically, there's the cleanliness concern. *Brettanomyces* is a hardy bugger that's not easily assassinated, especially after it's hunkered down in the dark, moist crevices of a cask. Or on a brewing gasket or a tube. An errant spore could spell doom for a batch of beer. "If Brett got into our regular production beer while it's fermenting, it could be devastating," says Gary Fish, owner of Deschutes Brewery in Bend, Oregon. So "we were absolutely fastidious with our cleaning process" when creating Dissident, a sour brown ale aged in barrels filled with mashed cherries.

"Using Brett is a little like playing with fire," says Joe Mohrfeld, a brewer at Odell Brewing, in Fort Collins, Colorado, which released the big, malty Brett-infected brown ale Saboteur. "The joke is, it's really hard to grow the particular strain of Brett you desire when you want it to grow, but it grows like crazy when you don't want it to grow." Odell ensures that the Brett doesn't contaminate other brews by isolating equipment and using a separate bottling line. Plus, the brewery's in-house lab technicians rigorously test beers to ensure there's no cross-contamination, a lesson that Russian River's Cilurzo learned firsthand.

"I'm not ashamed to admit that once, very early on when I wasn't nearly as experienced, we forgot to change a tube when we bottled Damnation," Cilurzo says. "The Damnation with Brett tasted awesome, but it wasn't what it was supposed to be." Nowadays, Cilurzo ensures no more delicious snafus by embracing kosher-style cleanliness methods: duplicates of every brewing gasket and tube— one for beers with Brett, one for normal beer.

For brewers, these are high, irritating hurdles to surmount for sour beers that may never have mass appeal. But today's labors of love could be drinkers' favorite beers tomorrow. Just look at India pale ales: Twenty years ago, few brewers could've crystal-balled the future and predicted that the tongue-twisting, face-scrunching bitter ales would be all the rage.

"Sour," proclaims Greg Hall, the former brewmaster at Chicago's Goose Island, "is the new hoppy."

NINE TO TRY

JULIET
GOOSE ISLAND BEER CO.
ABV: 6.7%
FORMER BREWMASTER GREG HALL MAY BE LAUDED FOR HIS BARREL-AGED BOURBON COUNTY STOUT (SEE PAGE 110), BUT HE ALSO HAS A STEADY HAND WITH SOURS. MOUTH-PUCKERING MADAME ROSE IS CONCOCTED WITH SOUR CHERRIES AND AGED IN OAK WINE BARRELS FOR SEVERAL YEARS. BETTER YET IS JULIET, A BELGIAN ALE DOCTORED WITH WILD

YEASTS, THEN RESTED IN CABERNET BARRELS ALONG WITH A BUSHEL OF BLACKBERRIES. FRUITY, TART, AND SHOT THROUGH WITH TANNINS, JULIET IS A FINE FIT FOR A DINNER TABLE.

ROSSO E MARRONE
CAPTAIN LAWRENCE BREWING COMPANY
ABV: N/A

WOOD VIRTUOSO SCOTT VACCCARO TURNS OUT OAK ODDITIES SUCH AS GOLDEN DELICIOUS, A TRIPEL AGED IN APPLE-BRANDY BARRELS, AND FLAMING FURY, A SOUR ALE AGED IN WINE BARRELS WITH FRESH PEACHES. EVEN FINER IS ROSSO, WHICH IS ADULTERATED WITH BRETTANOMYCES, MIXED WITH RED GRAPES, AND SENT TO SLEEP IN OAK WINE CASKS. ROSSO IS INSANELY EFFERVESCENT, WITH AN IN-YOUR-FACE ACIDITY AND A BALANCE BROUGHT ON BY SWEET, RIPE FRUIT AND A DRY FINISH.

BRUTE
ITHACA BEER CO.
ABV: 7%

PART OF ITHACA'S EXCELSIOR! SERIES, THIS CLOUDY, STRAW-COLORED ALE MADE WITH BARLEY, WHEAT, CORN, AND AGED HOPS SPENDS MONTHS NAPPING IN OAK CASKS INFESTED WITH BRETTANOMYCES BEFORE BEING FINISHED WITH A COCKTAIL OF CHAMPAGNE YEASTS. THE OUTCOME IS TRANSCENDENT: A LAYERED BOUQUET (FUNK, WOOD, LEMON, SOUR) LEADS TO A TART, SOMEWHAT CITRUSY CHARACTER CUT WITH GREEN APPLES, LEATHER, AND LIVELY, SPARKLING CARBONATION.

THE VINE
CASCADE BREWING
ABV: 8.33%

TO CREATE THIS "NORTHWEST SOUR," AS HE CALLS IT, BREWER RON GANSBERG BLENDS GOLDEN ALES, TRIPLES, AND BLONDE QUADS REFERMENTED WITH THE JUICE OF FRESH-PRESSED WHITE WINE GRAPES. IT PACKS A PUCKERING SOURNESS, WITH A SWEET FRUIT FOUNDATION. ZIPPY BUBBLES. A DRY, OAKY CLOSE. INCREDIBLY DRINKABLE.

TEMPTATION
RUSSIAN RIVER BREWING CO.
ABV: 7.25%

A YEAR SPENT DOZING ALONGSIDE BRETTANOMYCES IN FRENCH OAK CHARDONNAY BARRELS IMBUES THE BLONDE ALE WITH NOTES OF FRUIT AND OAK, AND A BIT OF BARNYARD THAT MATES WELL WITH THE AROMAS OF LEMON AND GRASS. TEMPTATION TASTES OF WHITE GRAPES, PEARS, AND SOUR APPLES, CONCLUDING OAKY AND DRY. NOT AS SOUR AS YOU'D EXPECT.

DUCHESSE DE BOURGOGNE
BROUWERIJ VERHAEGHE
ABV: 6%

TO CREATE THIS FLEMISH RED ALE FROM BELGIUM, BREWERS BLEND WILD YEAST-INFECTED ALE THAT'S

SPENT EIGHTEEN MONTHS IN OAK BARRELS WITH EIGHT-MONTH-OLD BEER. THE REDDISH-BROWN OUTCOME IS TRANSCENDENT: THE TART SCENT OF CURRANTS AND BLACK CHERRIES SEGUES TO A SMOOTH, SOUR-SWEET FRUIT TASTE AND A LONG, SHARP FINISH.

OUDE KRIEK VIEILLE
BROUWERIJ OUD BEERSEL
ABV: 6.5%

THE BELGIAN BREWERY'S KRIEK IS CONSTRUCTED BY ADDING CHERRIES TO SPONTANEOUSLY FERMENTED, BARREL-MATURED GUEUZE (A BLEND OF YOUNG AND OLD LAMBICS). THE FRUIT'S FLAVOR AND RUBY HUE SLOWLY SEEP INTO THE LAMBIC, CREATING AN IMMENSELY DRY, MODERATELY SOUR SIPPER BURSTING WITH TART CHERRIES, OAK, AND LEATHER.

IRIS
BRASSERIE CANTILLON BROUWERIJ
ABV: 5%

BREWED ONCE A YEAR, THE SPONTANEOUSLY FERMENTED, UNBLENDED BELGIAN LAMBIC TAKES A DIFFERENT PATH TO YOUR GLASS. TYPICALLY, LAMBIC IS MADE WITH AGED HOPS (THE FLAVOR AND AROMA SHOULD COME FROM THE FERMENTATION, NOT THE BITTER FLOWERS), BUT CANTILLON USES A 50-50 BLEND OF DRIED AND FRESH HOPS FOR IRIS, AGES IT FOR TWO YEARS, THEN COLD-HOPS THE BEER TWO WEEKS BEFORE IT'S BOTTLED. THE PAYOFF IS A FRESH BOUQUET OF LEMONS, APRICOTS, AND GRANNY SMITH APPLES. THERE'S A WOODY BITTERNESS AND, BECAUSE THERE'S NO WHEAT, SWEET CARAMEL TO MATCH THE DRY ACIDITY.

GOUDENBAND
BROUWERIJ LIEFMANS
ABV: 8%

LIEFMANS'S TAKE ON THE FLANDERS OUD BRUIN ("OLD BROWN") IS AS COMPLEX AS SHERRY OR PORT—AN AROMA OF RAISINS, EARTH, CHOCOLATE, AND RICH MALT. GOUDENBAND TASTES LESS TART THAN SWEET AND HAS HINTS OF BROWN SUGAR, PLUMS, AND NUTS. THE ALCOHOL HERE IS WARMING.

TWO

GOING TO EXTREMES:

Exploring the Great Heights and Not-so-Dizzying Lows of Booze in Craft Beer

GETTING A BEER BUZZ USED TO BE SO CUT-AND-DRIED. During the reign of weak lager, I could drink a couple cans of fizz water and barely feel my cheeks flush. More beer made me more drunk. Less beer left me sober. Today, a single complex, roasty imperial stout may leave me marble mouthed and staggering.

It's a by-product of craft brewers' almighty taste quest, in which they're using heroic amounts of hops and malt to devise ever-more flavorful—and, due to the time required to craft them, rarer—beer. But booze need not equal flavor. At the opposite end of the spectrum, brewers are devising highly delicious, low-alcohol session beers fit for sipping by the six-pack. Go big? Go small? Choosing between these extremes isn't always so simple.

Searching for Release(s)

In Portsmouth, New Hampshire, bars close at 1 a.m. After finishing last-call drinks, many bargoers will stumble to hole-in-the-wall Gilly's for hamburgers, hot dogs, and other greasy belly fillers. However, once a year in this historic New England town, drinkers won't head home after last call. Instead, they'll line up in front of downtown's Portsmouth Brewery.

While the brewpub's Dirty Blonde Ale and Black Cat Stout are bang-up, they're not the sorts of beers for which you'll sacrifice sleep. That honor is reserved for Kate the Great. Kate is a Russian imperial stout made with massive amounts of malt and brown sugar, then aged for months with port-soaked wood. This gives the milkshake-creamy, coal dark beer beguiling notes of oak and fig, chocolate cake, and caramel. Kate is special. Kate is rare. Only 900 bottles of Kate are available every year, all sold in one day in a first-come, first-served fashion.

Hence, if you want to take Kate home, you best not go home. Before sunrise, brewery employees will pass out sheets from a page-a-day calendar, 450 in all. Each page lets people purchase two bottles of Kate when the brewery opens at 9 a.m. In 2010, every page was spoken for in less than one hour. (In 2011, the brewery switched to scratch-off lottery tickets sold for $2 apiece, with proceeds going to charity. The 900 winning tickets—peppered among 10,000—allowed winners to purchase one bottle apiece for $15.) "It was never our intention to have a high production of bottles," says Portsmouth brewmaster Tod Mott. "When it's gone, it's gone."

In the modern craft-brew constellation, the stars are extreme beers. Since Jim Koch used the phrase to describe the heady Samuel Adams Triple Bock, which was released in 1994 with a then-outlandish 17.5 percent ABV, extremes have become a uniquely

Thirsty revelers lined up for a rare taste of Portsmouth Brewery's Kate the Great imperial stout.

American construct, microbrewers' liquid rebuttals to mainstream beer. These power-lifting brews, which range from resinous double IPAs to imperial pilsners and barrel-aged stouts (*see pages 105–118 for more on barrel aging*)—and everything in between and beyond—attract outsize attention and adoration. Just like in a high school locker room, strength often equals popularity.

Once a novelty, extreme beers have become commonplace. The mild-mannered 5 percent lager has lost its luster in lieu of muscular brews such as Dogfish Head's 18 percent 120 Minute IPA and Lagunitas Brewing Company's nearly 10 percent Brown Shugga'. More flavor, more hops, more booze. Does bigger equal better? Not always. I mean, how many 10 percent imperial IPAs can you sip and still stand upright? But in today's topsy-turvy craft-beer world, extreme is the new norm.

More Than Just a Beer

Many extreme beers are as common as a Coors Light. Pretty much year-round, you can knock your socks off with a 22-ounce bomber of Green Flash Brewing Co.'s intense, weed-like Imperial IPA, measuring a mild-mannered 9.4 percent ABV and 101 IBUs. However, some extremes are as scarce as sunny days in Seattle. The strapping beers' relative rarity, whether due to skimpy production or Internet-stoked fervor, requires breweries to orchestrate special-release events. They attract strong-beer devotees like picnic ants to spilled soda pop.

At Three Floyds Brewing in Munster, Indiana, each April thousands flock to Dark Lord Day for a bottle of the fierce, 15 percent Russian imperial stout. Up in Brooklyn Center, Minnesota, Surly Brewing makes a day out of selling its release of Darkness, another RIS, with serious bitterness and hints of cherries and chocolate. Sexual Chocolate is the lure at Foothills Brewing in North Carolina. Part celebration, part gathering of a like-minded malty tribe, these release events take beer devotion to an extreme.

I know it's ludicrous. Who would drive hours, or fly across the country, to wait in line though the night just to buy a strong beer? After all, dozens of double-digit beers are ready and willing to wallop you with hops and malt. "Your average drinker of Fat Tire and Sierra Nevada will not show up for a beer-release day," explains Ben Weiss, the sales and marketing manager at Placentia, California's the Bruery, which releases its Black Tuesday Russian imperial stout every October.

Instead, these gold-letter days appeal to craft diehards. Maybe you're one of them. I know I am. There's a charm to gathering with hundreds of folks who love the same potent, bubbly liquid. In certain respects, these beer-release days are like bygone Grateful Dead gigs (minus the acid, of course). The main event is a sideshow to the extracurricular activities.

At Three Floyds' annual Dark Lord Day, the release of the Dark Lord Russian imperial stout (sense a theme in beer styles?) is wrapped in an all-day event featuring bands and thousands of beer fans sharing favorite brews. Surly also brings out bands for Darkness Day, as does Foothills Brewing. "We try hard to cultivate the whole weekend as a beer event," says Jamie Bartholomaus, Foothills' president and brewmaster. Come February, the brewpub is consumed by lust for Sexual Chocolate, a strapping imperial stout infused with cocoa. Sexual Chocolate (oh, how I love typing those letters) was first brewed for Valentine's Day in 2007. Like Foothills' beers at the time, it was draft only, sold on tap and by the growler.

The beer was so rapturously received that customers hand-bottled Sexual Chocolate. "I was getting questions like, 'How do I sanitize a bottle?'" Bartholomaus says. No more growlers. (The same thing happened at Surly, where drinkers dumped glasses of Darkness into bottles to trade and share.) The next year, he slid his imperial stout into bottles, and so began Winston-Salem's most anticipated beer event: Sexual Chocolate Weekend, Afros and seventies shirts recommended.

The weekend begins with pre-Sex Friday, wherein revelers gather at Foothills toting treasured beers. Foothills provides finger foods, bands strum, and everyone shares their rare elixirs. "We're a bar, so we don't usually allow people to bring in beer, but this weekend is special," Bartholomaus says. The tasting lasts till the wee hours, when beers lovers are allowed to line up outside at 4 a.m. "They're literally

drinking all night and hanging out with their buddies and having fun," he says.

There's a fuzzy line between fun and *too much* fun. In 2010, when beer lovers, some of whom flocked from California and Washington, started purchasing the 1,000 Sexual bottles at 11 a.m., Bartholomaus was nowhere to be found. "I was unable to stand up," he says, laughing. "I had so much fun Friday night that I was lying in my car most of the day."

INTERNATIONAL SPOTLIGHT: SCOTLAND'S BREWDOG

HALFWAY THROUGH THE MILLENNIUM'S FIRST DECADE, AMERICAN BEER DRINKERS WERE FINALLY SAVORING CRAFT BREWS AS DELICIOUS AS THEY WERE INVENTIVE. HALFWAY AROUND THE WORLD, SCOTTISH BUDDIES JAMES WATT AND MARTIN DICKIE WISHED THEY COULD SAY THE SAME THING ABOUT BRITISH BREWING.

MOST BREWERIES MAKE "BLAND, LIGHTLY HOPPED, MILDLY MALTY BEER," DICKIE LAMENTS. "IT'S BORING, THOUGHTLESS, LACKLUSTER, AND INSIPID BEER." INSTEAD OF COMPLAINING, THEN SWILLING ANOTHER PINT OF DRAB LAGER, DICKIE AND WATT MADE A PACT TO PRODUCE BEERS THEY CRAVED. IN 2007, THE DUO FOUNDED BREWDOG, LAUNCHING THE KIND OF LIQUID REVOLUTION UNDER WAY ACROSS THE ATLANTIC.

WITH DICKIE SERVING AS DIRECTOR AND WATT AS BREWMASTER, THE TWOSOME BEGAN RELEASING BEERS LIKE THE UNCOMPROMISINGLY BITTER PUNK IPA, HOPPED-UP 5 A.M. SAINT AMBER ALE, AND TROPICAL-TINGED TRASHY BLONDE. THEY'RE BEERS THAT ARE WORLDS APART FROM BRITAIN'S LOW-ALCOHOL MILDS AND BITTERS.

"WE WANTED TO SHAKE THINGS UP AND GET AWAY FROM A 'REAL BEER' MENTALITY TO A 'GREAT BEER' MENTALITY," DICKIE SAYS. "WE ARE RAISING THE BAR OF BEER PRODUCED IN THE U.K. AND INFORMING THE DRINKER THAT THEY SHOULD NOT HAVE TO ACCEPT WHAT THE MULTINATIONALS OR LAZY

BREWERS TERM BEER. BEER SHOULD BE A PLEASURE, NOT A CHEAP, TASTELESS COMMODITY."

SUCH BRASH VERBAL SHOTS QUICKLY GARNERED BREWDOG MEDIA ATTENTION, WHICH HAS BEEN CENTRAL TO THE COMPANY'S GROWTH. AFTER ALL, THE BREWERY'S REMOTE LOCATION IN NORTHEAST SCOTLAND'S FRASERBURGH IS HARDLY A CRAFT-BEER HOTBED. TO SPUR INTERNATIONAL INTEREST, THE TWOSOME TURNED TO TWITTER, YOUTUBE, BLOGS, AND FACEBOOK. "AS A YOUNG COMPANY, SOCIAL MEDIA AND BEER BLOGGERS HAVE BEEN INSTRUMENTAL IN GETTING THE WORD OUT IN THE UNITED STATES," DICKIE SAYS.

THE BACKLASH BEGINS

SOMETIMES, TOO MUCH ATTENTION CAN BE A TERRIBLE THING. NO STRANGERS TO CONTROVERSY, OR CONTROVERSIAL STATEMENTS, THE BURGEONING BREWERY BECAME A PARIAH IN SUMMER 2008 FOLLOWING THE RELEASE OF TOKYO. IT WAS AN IMPERIAL STOUT BREWED WITH CRANBERRIES AND JASMINE, DRY-HOPPED, AND THEN AGED ON FRENCH OAK CHIPS. OH, AND IT CLOCKED IN AT 18.2 PERCENT ABV. THIS TYPE OF BOUNDARY-PUSHING, HIGH-PROOF EXPERIMENT IS OLD HAT IN AMERICA. BUT IN THE U.K., THIS STRONG BEER—THE MOST POTENT TO DATE IN BRITAIN—BROUGHT THE MEDIA CIRCUS TO BREWDOG.

"WHAT JUSTIFICATION CAN THERE POSSIBLY BE TO BRING AN EXTRA STRONG BEER ON TO THE MARKET?" JACK LAW, CHIEF EXECUTIVE OF ALCOHOL FOCUS SCOTLAND, ASKED THE FINANCIAL TIMES. "SUPER-STRENGTH DRINKS ARE OFTEN FAVORED BY YOUNG PEOPLE AND PROBLEM DRINKERS. IS THIS REALLY WHO THE BREWERY WANTS TO TARGET?"

MIND YOU, THE AVERAGE BOTTLE OF TOKYO COST AROUND 10 QUID (ABOUT $15), MAKING IT ONE OF THE PRICIEST BEERS IN THE UNITED KINGDOM. WHY WOULD A LAGER LOUT SPEND THAT MUCH ON BOOZE WHEN HE COULD BUY CHEAPIE VODKA OR LOW-COST, HIGHLY BOOZY CIDER? "THE ONLY PEOPLE SEEKING OUT TOKYO ARE BEER ENTHUSIASTS," SAYS DICKIE, EXASPERATED. "IN THE U.K., THERE'S A LOT OF POLITICAL TENSION AROUND ALCOHOL MISUSE, BUT IF YOU LOOK AT THE DATA, IT'S NOT ANY WORSE THAN IT WAS TWENTY YEARS AGO."

TABLOID HYSTERIA CAN ALSO BE ADVANTAGEOUS. WITH THE SCOTTISH PARLIAMENT AGITATING TO BAN TOKYO, BREWDOG RESPONDED BY RELEASING NANNY STATE. THE OVERLY HOPPED, "MILD IMPERIAL ALE" REGISTERS A ROBUST 1.1 PERCENT ABV. POINT MADE.

A TEST OF STRENGTH

SINCE THEN, BREWDOG HAS MADE AN ART FORM OF ATTRACTING MEDIA INTEREST. ITS ATLANTIC IPA WAS AGED ABOARD A MACKEREL TRAWLER NAVIGATING THE TEMPESTUOUS NORTH ATLANTIC. THEN CAME TACTICAL NUCLEAR PENGUIN, WHICH, AT 32 PERCENT ABV, WRESTED AWAY THE TITLE OF THE WORLD'S STRONGEST BEER FROM GERMANY'S SCHORSCHBRÄU. THE GERMANS RESPONDED BY RELEASING THE SCHORSCHBOCK 40 PERCENT. BREWDOG CAME BACK WITH THE 41 PERCENT IPA CALLED SINK THE BISMARCK! (WHILE FERMENTATION ALONE CAN'T CREATE SUCH ELEVATED ABVS, A FREEZE-DISTILLING PROCESS PROVIDES A HANDY RUNAROUND. SINCE ALCOHOL FREEZES AT A FROSTIER TEMPERATURE THAN WATER, REMOVING ICE RESULTS IN A CONCENTRATED LIQUID WITH A SUPERCHARGED ALCOHOL LEVEL.)

SCHORSCHBRÄU THEN RELEASED SCHORSCHBOCK 43 PERCENT. BREWDOG'S REBUTTAL WAS A DOZEN BOTTLES OF END OF HISTORY, A 55 PERCENT MONSTROSITY STUFFED INSIDE A DOZEN TAXIDERMIED STOATS AND SQUIRRELS. NATURALLY, THE "COMPETITION" WAS ACCOMPANIED BY CHEEKY YOUTUBE VIDEOS AND TONS OF TWEETS. (AS OF PRESSTIME, THE BOOZY RECORD HOLDER IS NOW DUTCH BREWERY 'T KOELSCHIP, WITH ITS 60 PERCENT START THE FUTURE.)

FUN AND GAMES ASIDE, BREWDOG FACES SEVERAL SERIOUS CHALLENGES THAT CAN'T BE LAUGHED AWAY. AFTER FACTORING IN IMPORT

BrewDog's burly, 55 percent End of History beer, was sold inside taxidermied critters.

TAXES AND SHIPPING, THE COST IN AMERICA OF BREWDOG'S CORE BRANDS—LIKE PUNK IPA—CAN BE TWO AND A HALF TO THREE TIMES THE COST OF A COMPARABLE BEER, SUCH AS A STONE IPA. "IT'S HARD FOR OUR CUSTOMERS TO PAY THAT MUCH FOR A SIMILAR PRODUCT," DICKIE LAMENTS.

BUT MANY BREWDOG BEERS ARE UNIQUE. IN 2010, IT LAUNCHED THE ABSTRAKT LINE, WHICH FOCUSES ON ONE-OFF OFFBEAT OFFERINGS LIKE A VANILLA BEAN—INFUSED BELGIAN QUAD AND A TRIPLE DRY-HOPPED IMPERIAL RED ALE. "WE WANT TO STAY AT THE FOREFRONT OF THE INDUSTRY," DICKIE SAYS. "IF WE'RE NOT CONSTANTLY THINKING ABOUT HOW BEER CAN PROGRESS, THEN WE'RE NOT DOING OUR JOB."

Give Me More!

A cynic might say that breweries are artificially manipulating demand of extreme beers, much like how gem firms restrict the inventory of sparkly diamonds. Fewer products equal higher prices, and everyone laughs all the way to the bank.

That's far from the truth. Creating an extreme beer is often a time-intensive labor of love, whose genesis comes at the expense of a brewery's other beers. When Tod Mott makes Kate, he ties up several of the brewing tanks for up to five months. That's an eternity when some beers take only two or three weeks to go from grain to glass. "We only have so much supply and there's too much demand," Mott says of Kate.

Adds Bartholomaus of Sexual Chocolate, "It's a tank drain. It's four months before it's even ready. To us, the real cost is the lack of opportunity to make more batches of beer." That's why Sexual Chocolate averages around $15 a bottle, which is about how much you'll spend for Three Floyds' Dark Lord. Surly's Darkness is about $18. But the Bruery's Black Tuesday imperial stout costs nearly $30 a bottle, which is a small price to pay when you consider the hell brewers endured to produce it.

Back in summer 2008, the Bruery embraced a challenge: to make a strong stout, and to make it taste good. On Tuesday, July 1, brewers gathered at 4:30 a.m. and began their experiment. They used 2,500 pounds of grain, more than twice as much as a typical batch. Things went well until a pump started leaking. Attempting a fix worsened the leak. Catastrophe ensued when brewmaster Patrick Rue tried to clear a valve blockage, sending spent grain and 170-degree water coursing out in "a tidal wave of hot shit, all over my arms, legs, in my boots," Rue wrote on his blog.

Before the valve was sealed, the brewery had taken on several inches of water. Grain coated walls, equipment, limbs. "Everything went wrong," says marketing manager Weiss, who was assisting that day. "It was a total disaster." After cleanup, the hard work continued. To reach nearly 20 percent ABV, the beer was fed extra nutrients for

A glass of the Bruery's rare, potent Black Tuesday imperial stout.

weeks, occupying fermenters and preventing other beers from being brewed. *Then* the stout was consigned to bourbon barrels for more than a year. Time. Space. Resources. Money. This big stout was a big resource drain.

"It's a really expensive beer to make," Weiss explains. When the stout was deemed ready, there was enough to fill about 1,200 champagne-size bottles. In honor of the beer's disastrous Tuesday brew day, the beer was named Black Tuesday. Before the official release day, Black was put on draft in the Bruery's tasting room. "It was ranked number four in the world before it was released," says Weiss. "People went crazy online. We obviously knew there would be some sort of hype around the beer, but we never imagined the amount of hype."

So let's take a step back for a second. The Bruery has only 1,200 bottles of its labor-intensive creation, for which rabid beer fans are frothing at the mouth. The Bruery set limits of three bottles a person, no small chunk of change at $30 apiece. Still, on October 27, 2009—the last Tuesday of the month—the Bruery sold out of Black Tuesday. "We had some pretty angry people, who got nothing out of it except for a few samples after waiting in line for five hours," Weiss says.

Know Your Limits

Scarcity is just one reason why brewers restrict the purchase of their special-release extremes. Theoretically, in a free-market system, a coordinated gang could purchase the entire supply of an extreme run. Purchasers could create an inflated secondary market for the stout, much like scalping tickets. This may sound like a conspiracy theory, but it's already occurring on a lesser scale.

Every couple of weeks, Weiss fields a phone call from a specific kind of inquisitive customer. "They ask, 'Do you have this? Do you have that?' They just run down a list of what we make. They seem to know nothing about beer. They just want to buy it, so they can sell it on eBay and make $150."

Or more. While an average bottle of Black Tuesday sells for about $175 on eBay, Weiss has seen it go for as much as $230. Thus, the Bruery's three-bottles-per-customer restriction. "If we didn't put limits, we would've sold out after the first forty people," he says. Surly allows Darkness Day attendees to buy eight bottles each, allocating a thousand more for off-premise purchases. At Three Floyds Brewing, Dark Lord fans purchase a ticket—proceeds go to charity—which ensures they can nab a bottle. Not that this stops people from hawking scores: Beernews.org reported that within 24 hours of the end of the event in 2010, more than 25 Dark Lord listings appeared on eBay.

What's a brewery to do? Devote its fermentation tanks to burly, over-the-top brews? That's fun for neither brewers nor consumers. No one wants to be pigeonholed into making a single beer until their end days. Creativity is brewing's lingua franca, and it'd be a dark world if we drank only dark, potent beer. And really, do you need to drink a 12 percent Russian imperial stout every night?

"We can't make enough, which is a great scenario," Mott says of Kate the Great. "It goes away in two weeks; then I get to make another beer."

EXTREME BEER RELEASES WORTHY OF YOUR VACATION TIME

*CHECK WITH BREWERIES FOR CURRENT RELEASE SCHEDULES.

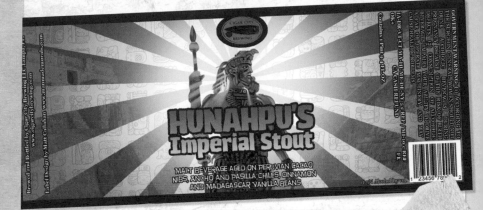

HUNAHPU'S IMPERIAL STOUT

CIGAR CITY BREWING,
TAMPA, FLORIDA
CIGARCITYBREWING.COM
ABV: 11.5%

HEAPS OF RAW PERUVIAN CACAO
NIBS, ANCHO AND PASILLA CHILES,
MADAGASCAR VANILLA BEANS, AND
CINNAMON IMBUE THE IMPERIAL
STOUT WITH A COMPLEX EXOTICISM
WORTH ANY WAIT.

SEXUAL CHOCOLATE IMPERIAL STOUT

FOOTHILLS BREWING, WINSTON-
SALEM, NORTH CAROLINA
FOOTHILLSBREWING.COM
ABV: 9.75%

SCORING THE SILKY, COCOA-INFUSED
IMPERIAL STOUT IS HALF
THE FUN: THE NIGHT
BEFORE THE RELEASE,
ATTENDEES SHARE
RARE BREWS—AND
OCCASIONALLY HIT AN
AREA, UM, GENTLEMAN'S
CLUB.

THE ANGEL'S SHARE

THE LOST ABBEY, SAN
MARCOS, CALIFORNIA
LOSTABBEY.COM
ABV: 12.5%

NAMED AFTER
THE SPIRITS THAT
EVAPORATE FROM
WOOD BARRELS
DURING AGING,

THE ANGEL'S SHARE IS AN INTENSE STRONG ALE SPORTING FLAVORS OF CARAMEL, VANILLA, AND OAK, OAK, OAK—HELLO, YEARLONG NAP IN BRANDY OR BOURBON CASKS.

PLINY THE YOUNGER

RUSSIAN RIVER BREWING COMPANY, SANTA ROSA, CALIFORNIA
RUSSIANRIVERBREWING.COM
ABV: 11%

PLINY THE ELDER IS ONE OF AMERICA'S BEST DOUBLE IPAS. SO WHAT HAPPENS WHEN RUSSIAN RIVER RELEASES ITS BURLIER, MORE BITTER RELATIVE? IT SELLS OUT IN LESS THAN TEN HOURS, LIKE IT DID IN 2010. GET IN LINE NOW.

PERSEGUIDOR

JOLLY PUMPKIN ARTISAN ALES. RELEASE TAKES PLACE AT JOLLY PUMPKIN CAFÉ AND BREWERY IN ANN ARBOR, MICHIGAN
JOLLYPUMPKIN.COM
ABV: VARIES

PERSEGUIDOR IS SNOWFLAKE UNIQUE: EACH YEAR'S RELEASE IS MADE FROM A SELECTION OF JOLLY'S SOUR AND FARMHOUSE-STYLE ALES (SOMETIMES AGED FOR MORE THAN EIGHTEEN MONTHS), WHICH ARE BLENDED, CONSIGNED TO OAK FOR SIX MONTHS, AND THEN BOTTLE CONDITIONED FOR ANOTHER SIX MONTHS.

BLACK TUESDAY

THE BRUERY, PLACENTIA, CALIFORNIA
THEBRUERY.COM
ABV: VARIES

AS IF THE OPPORTUNITY TO PURCHASE THIS POTENT IMPERIAL STOUT ISN'T LURE ENOUGH, THE BRUERY SWEETENS THE DEAL BY SERVING SAMPLES OF CHOCOLATE RAIN, WHICH IS BLACK TUESDAY WITH COCOA NIBS AND VANILLA BEANS ADDED.

DARK LORD RUSSIAN-STYLE IMPERIAL STOUT

THREE FLOYDS BREWING COMPANY, MUNSTER, INDIANA
3FLOYDS.COM
ABV: 15%

THIS IMPERIAL STOUT IS SO CULTISHLY REVERED, YOU NEED A WILLY WONKA–LIKE GOLDEN TICKET TO PURCHASE A BOTTLE DURING DARK LORD DAY—DLD, TO THE THOUSANDS WHO FLOCK. BRING A COOLER OF YOUR FAVORITE BREWS SO YOU CAN TRADE BEERS.

DARKNESS

SURLY BREWING CO., BROOKLYN CENTER, MINNESOTA
SURLYBREWING.COM
ABV: 9.8%

TO CELEBRATE THE RELEASE OF THIS HALLOWEEN-THEMED RUSSIAN IMPERIAL STOUT, SURLY BUSTS OUT WITH AN ALL-DAY BASH FEATURING BANDS, GRUB, AND GOBS OF KILLER BREWS.

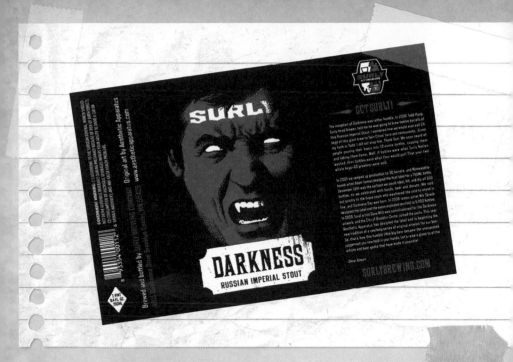

Class Is in Session

Back in the 1990s, Chris Lohring helped spearhead the Northeast's nascent craft-brewing movement. He cut his teeth at Maine's Kennebunkport Brewing Company before cofounding Boston's Tremont Brewery. There, he turned out terrific British-style ales and porters until he sold Tremont to Portland's Shipyard Brewing Company in 2001. Lohring stayed aboard to facilitate Tremont's move, then backpedaled from the beer world.

A one-year sabbatical stretched to six. Though he was consulting on product designs for gadgets such as semiconductors and sports equipment, Lohring kept abreast of craft brewing's evolution. "I was frustrated by the focus on higher-alcohol beers," Lohring says of the swell of super-charged double IPAs and Russian imperial stouts.

At Notch Brewing, founder Chris Lohring focuses on flavorful low-alcohol beer.

"I'm not anti–extreme beer, but I drink those kinds of beers maybe a hundredth of the time."

Lohring liked low-alcohol beers, the kind he could kick back two or three of and still cruise home without worrying about a DUI. But in the low end, "I didn't see lots of flavorful options. So I decided to go and make a session beer myself."

In spring 2010, Lohring, in conjunction with old friend Shipyard, launched Notch Brewing. It is America's first company committed to crafting balanced, flavorful beers that clock less than 4.5 percent—session beers, so called because you can have several of them in a drinking session. Notch's slogan: "full flavor, long drinking, no headache."

Session Lesson

That motto's not totally true. Drink enough of any beer, and you'll be searching for aspirin the next bleary-eyed morning. But with session beers, you've got to try a whole lot harder to get schnookered, because getting drunk isn't the point of sessions.

In the United Kingdom, session beers are typically less than 4 percent ABV, encompassing most of the country's milds and bitters. (This is due to a mix of chit chatty pub culture and tariffs, wherein beers are taxed according to alcohol level.) In America, the Brewers

Association guidelines state that a session beer sits between 4 percent and 5.1 percent. I find that too high. Instead, I look to Lew Bryson, a Philadelphia-based beer writer who runs the online Session Beer Project. The site, which espouses the pleasures of gently boozy brews, sets straightforward guidelines. Session beers should be "4.5 percent alcohol by volume or less, flavorful enough to be interesting, balanced enough for multiple pints, conducive to conversation and reasonably priced." Or, in simpler terms, "low alcohol but not low taste."

While flavor bombs boasting double-digit ABVs dominate top-50 lists at Beeradvocate.com and Ratebeer.com, there's been a small, slow groundswell of swell small beer. In Bryson's hometown, the Philadelphia Brewing Company's Kenzinger is a zippy, golden 4.5 percent refreshment. Down In Virginia, Starr Hill Brewing Company's Dark Starr Stout is a coffee-hinted 4.2 percent treat. And rich, creamy Guinness Draught? That Irish standout measures a relatively meager 4.2 percent.

Big taste can come in small packages.

Turn Back Time

Just as the cost of eggs and milk has incrementally crept north over the years, so too has craft beer's alcohol content. During the microbrewery boom of the 1990s, many of the British- and European-influenced microbrews hovered around 5 percent.

Though different, those suds weren't *radically* different from big brewers' watery pilsners and pale lagers clogging the marketplace. To set themselves apart, liquid artisans began tinkering with more potent and assertively flavored ales. This had penny-pinching pluses too, since "lagers cost more to produce," Bryson explains. "They must be chilled, and you have to age them longer." But what began as a rebellion against the carbonated mainstream grew into "this knee-jerk reaction that lagers were bland," Bryson says.

Nowadays, a beer with a sub–5 percent ABV is as antiquated as dial-up Internet. With shelves sagging with barley wines and strong ales, "our minds have been skewed to think six or seven percent is typical," Notch's Lohring says. This is not to bad-mouth craft brewers. The world's a far tastier place with Bear Republic's Racer 5 IPA (7 percent) and Stone Brewing Co.'s Arrogant Bastard strong ale (7.2 percent) on tap. The drawback is that after three of these stellar brews, you're three sheets to the wind—or more, if you're getting intimate with a 22-ounce Russian imperial stout.

Beer writer Lew Bryson's online Session Beer Project champions low-alcohol brews.

"Who thought of putting a twelve percent beer in a twenty-two-ounce bottle?" Bryson says. "There's a slam on light beer: 'People who drink them don't like drinking beer; they like to pee.' But if you're only drinking eight percent beers, you don't like to drink. You just like to get drunk."

Full Flavor, Low Booze

For brewers, restricting ABV is not a handicap when it comes to making memorable, flavorful beer. In fact, swimming in alcohol's shallow end can be artistically rewarding. "Most innovation happens when there's a limitation," Lohring explains.

He relates the story of Mark Sandman, the former frontman for 1990s alternative band Morphine. While most bassists opt for four, five, or six strings, Sandman used a two-string bass to create his signature deep, haunting sound. "He said that the limitation forced him to be creative," Lohring says. "That's what it's like for me: I'm forced to be creative in ways that I wouldn't be otherwise."

Lohring's low-alcohol experiments have included the wheaty, unfiltered Summer Session (4.5 percent) doctored with German hops; malt-forward, subtly sweet Session Red (4 percent); and dry, floral Hop Session amber ale (4.5 percent). "That's the one request I kept getting: Make a hoppy beer that I can enjoy and not have it be seven percent alcohol," Lohring says of his brew, which is dense with layers of flavors, not mouth-scrunching bitterness. "Session beers are all about balance."

For Scott Smith, the brewmaster at Pittsburgh's East End Brewing Company, creating inspired session beers was born out of a somewhat selfish need. As a self-professed "lightweight, I was looking for something I could have a small glass of at lunch and still remain productive," he says. "For an afternoon of drinking, nothing beats a growler of low-alcohol beer," Smith says.

His low-ABV quest blossomed into the innovative Session Ales series (under 4.5 percent ABV). Operating under "*Iron Chef*–like constraints," Smith plays with sourness and hoppiness, which don't contribute to alcohol content. Since each Session Ale is limited to about seven barrels apiece and is available only at the brewery via growler fill, the beers don't linger. With small batches, Smith can take chances and get his "beer-geek juices flowing." To date, he's devised more than 40 unique low-alcohol releases, ranging from a hoppy wheat to a blueberry-rye ale to a Russian bread beer called kvass.

Most Session Ales are one-offs, but some have staying power. His English-style Fat Gary Nut Brown Ale, which began as a 3.7

percent experiment, is now available year-round and selling like hotcakes. "It blows my mind that in a world of 'hoppiest' and 'strongest,' this tiny, quiet beer is lighting up the sky," Smith says.

You Can't Put Session in a Corner

In the beer world, flavors define categories for beer. If I tell you that a beer is an IPA, you'll expect hops and bitterness. If I pass you a pilsner, you'll anticipate a snappy, effervescent ale. However, if I blindfolded you and handed over a session, you might be clueless.

"The term suffers from having to be explained," Bryson says. "Any term you have should be immediately understood. I feel the same away about *session* as I do about gastropubs—I love the place, but I hate the name. *Low-alcohol beer* is kind of boring."

Instead, brewers fall back on stock phrases, such as *summer beer*. Sure, it evokes the season, but the term expires as soon as leaves start dropping. Then there's the issue of supply. At Brooklyn's the Diamond, a "beer-centric establishment" (as they like to call themselves), in Greenpoint, owner Dave Pollack splits his brew selection between "strong" and "session" beers—5.5 percent and under.

"For me, our list is bullshit," Pollack says. "Brewers say, 'This is our session beer,' but it's 5.2 percent." To Pollack, the ideal session brew is about 4 percent, but it's a number nearly as rare as a unicorn in America's craft-beer universe. Moreover, not just any ol' low-ABV brewski will do. "I'm looking for session beers of distinction," says Pollack, whose taps often include aromatic Southern Tier Brewing Company's Hop Sun Summer Wheat Beer (5.2 percent), a sparkling pilsner, and a kölsch.

By now, many of Pollack's customers are familiar with the phrase "session beer," but consumer education is never ending. That's also an issue for Lohring. "People are so used to tasting beer instead of drinking it," he says. Since session beers are subtler, a single taste is not enough to gauge mouthfeel, aromas, and nuances. "I tell people, 'Don't taste them, drink them. Have two pints and tell me if you like them.'"

In its own way, this is rekindling a forgotten concept: sitting back and savoring a beer. At its core, beer should be about the camaraderie it creates, an accompaniment to playing cards or conversation. Pinpointing a barrel-aged ale's aromas can be a barrel of fun, but there's something to be said to drinking for drinking's sake—without getting lit up like fireworks on the Fourth of July. Imperial stouts and double IPAs will always have their day, just not as everyday beers.

As Lohring says, "Craft beer enhances our time together; session beer extends it. Who doesn't want to extend the good times?"

TEN TO TRY

LEVITATION ALE
STONE BREWING CO.
ABV: 4.4%
SURE, SOUTHERN CALIFORNIA'S STONE HAS MADE ITS BONES ON BOLD, UNCOMPROMISING BREWS SUCH AS PALATE-PUNISHING ARROGANT BASTARD ALE AND HEARTY, HOPPY OLD GUARDIAN BARLEY WINE ALE. HOWEVER, STONE'S SCALED BACK ITS ABV ATTACK—WITHOUT FORFEITING FLAVOR—ON THE COPPER-TONED LEVITATION. THE EASY SIPPER IS PROPPED UP BY A CARAMEL BACKBONE, WITH A NOSE OF FLORAL HOPS AND A MILD MOUTHFEEL THAT CLOSES CLEAN AND AS BALANCED AS A GYMNAST.

BRAWLER
YARDS BREWING COMPANY
ABV: 4.2%
THIS BRAWLER WON'T BEAT YOU INTO AN ALCOHOLIC STUPOR. INSTEAD, THE LIP-SMACKING SESSION OFFERING FROM PHILADELPHIA'S YARDS IS AN EXCELLENT ENGLISH-INFLUENCED ALE. THE GARNET-TINGED TREAT PACKS A PRONOUNCED MALT PROFILE—ON YOUR SNIFFER, YOU'LL

NOTICE BISCUITS AND CARAMEL. BRAWLER SLIDES DOWN QUICK AND SMOOTH, WITH A LIGHT, DRYING FINISH. IT'S ALL PLEASURE, NO PUNCH.

AVRIL
BRASSERIE DUPONT
ABV: 3.5%

AVRIL IS A BELGIAN BIERE DE TABLE—AKA TABLE BEER. BRING A BOTTLE TO YOUR NEXT DINNER PARTY, WHERE GUESTS WILL BE TAKEN ABACK BY THE PALATE-PRICKLING BEER'S FUNKY AND EARTHY PROFILE, CUT WITH GENTLE FLAVORS OF GRASS AND WHEAT. WAIT TILL EVERYONE'S HAD A SECOND GLASS AND IS ACTING LOOPY BEFORE SPILLING THE BIG SECRET: AVRIL'S DAINTY ABV.

DONNYBROOK STOUT
VICTORY BREWING COMPANY
ABV: 3.7%

THIS PENNSYLVANIA OUTFIT'S IRISH DRY STOUT IS DISPENSED ONLY ON DRAFT VIA NITROGEN POUR, WHICH GIVES THE BLACK BEER A FIRM AND CREAMY KHAKI HEAD—ONE SIP, AND YOU'LL SPORT A FOAM MUSTACHE. WEAR IT WITH PRIDE. DONNYBROOK IS DARK AND DEEPLY REFRESHING, OFFERING UP A LIGHT BODY AND LOTS OF ROASTY AROMAS AND FLAVORS. YOU'LL HAVE NO PROBLEM SIPPING THIS SILKY DELIGHT TILL LAST CALL.

PILSNER URQUELL
PILSNER URQUELL BREWERY
ABV: 4.4%

I KNOW WHAT YOU'RE THINKING. "WHY IS HE INCLUDING THIS MASS-MARKET PIECE OF CRUD ON THIS LIST?" THAT'S BECAUSE PILSNER URQUELL IS SESSION BEER PERSONIFIED. THE CLASSIC CZECH BEER HAS BEEN IN PRODUCTION SINCE 1842, AND WHILE THE RECIPE HAS SHIFTED OVER THE ENSUING 170 YEARS, URQUELL REMAINS ROCK SOLID. THE SNAPPY, GOLDEN PILSNER—BACKED BY A HINT OF GRAPES—IS AS FIZZY AND QUENCHING AS SELTZER.

BITTER & TWISTED BLOND BEER
HARVIESTOUN BREWERY
ABV: 4.2%

IF YOU LIKE HOPS BUT CAN'T HANDLE AN IPA'S HEAD-SPINNING STRENGTH, TRY SCOTLAND'S BEAUTY OF A BLONDE BREW. CRACK THE CAP, AND OUT COMES A CLEAN, FLORAL PERFUME THAT'S AS FRESH AND DELICATE AS A COURT MAIDEN. YOU MIGHT EXPECT AN OVERLY BITTER BREW, BUT NO—IT'S BRISK AND

FRUITY, VEERING TOWARD LEMONS. HOW CAN A 4.2 PERCENT BREW BE SO TANGY? HOW CAN YOU NOT HAVE ANOTHER?

BITTER BREWER
SURLY BREWING CO.
ABV: 4.1%

COME SPRING AND SUMMER, MINNESOTA'S SURLY RELEASES THIS LIQUID ODE TO BEER MAKERS' CEASELESS TOIL. TANGERINE-TINGED BITTER BREWER IS OVERLOADED WITH THE AROMAS OF TOAST AND JAM, A ONE-TWO PUNCH THAT MAKES ME THINK OF MOTHER ENGLAND. HOWEVER, BB BOASTS AN AMERICAN PROFILE OWING TO COLUMBUS AND GLACIER HOPS, WHICH IMPART AN EARTHY BITTERNESS THAT'LL FLIP FROWNS UPSIDE DOWN.

HOP SESSION
NOTCH BREWING COMPANY
ABV: 4.5%

THE MAINE BREWERY'S COPPER TONED AMBER ALE HAS A STURDY MALT SPINE AND A HOP-FORWARD FRAGRANCE OF CITRUS AND PINE. PUTTING A BOW ON THE BEER: A SURPRISING COMPLEXITY AND PALATE-DRYING CLOSE.

BURTON BITTER
MARSTON'S BEER COMPANY
ABV: 3.8%

DESPITE ITS LOW ABV, BURTON BITTER HAS A GREAT BIG CARAMEL CHARACTER, NICE CREAMINESS, AND

GENTLE HOP BITTERNESS THAT KEEP YOU RETURNING FOR SECONDS. AND THIRDS.

DARK STARR STOUT
STARR HILL BREWERY
ABV: 4.2%

VIRGINIA'S STARR HILL MAKES ONE OF AMERICA'S FINEST IRISH DRY STOUTS. THE SECRET IS HEAPS OF ROASTED BARLEY, WHICH GIVE DARK STARR A CHOCOLATY, COFFEE-LIKE CHARACTER WHILE RETAINING A NIMBLE BODY. IN THE WORDS OF THE BREWERY: "THIS SIGNATURE BREW POURS LIKE VELVET AND DRINKS LIKE A SLICE OF GRANDMA'S PUMPERNICKEL BREAD."

AMERICAN SESSION ALE

NOTCH

HOP SESSION

4.5% ALCOHOL BY VOLUME

Brewed and bottled in Portland, Maine
12 FLUID OUNCES, 355 ML   NOTCHSESSION.COM

LOW GRAVITY
HIGH FLAVOR
LONG DRINKING

IN A BETTER TIME, LABORERS DRANK BEER AT LUNCH. THESE SESSION-STYLE BEERS WERE CRAFTED TO YIELD A HIGH FLAVOR AND LOWER ABV. EVERY BEER-BREWING COUNTRY HAS A TRADITION OF SESSION BEERS. NOTCH SESSION IS THE AMERICAN TRANSLATION OF THIS HISTORIC BEER STYLE. ✶

Falling in Flavor

At its most basic level, beer is composed of four ingredients: malt, water, hops, and yeast. From that quartet have emerged dozens of distinct beer styles, such as creamy, banana-scented hefeweizens, stouts as dark and roasty as a double espresso, and sour brews that recall carbonated lemonade.

But for many beer makers, using four ingredients is just too limiting. Thus, many brewers have begun acting like Middle Ages monks, who flavored their beers with gruit. This was a proprietary blend of bitter and astringent yarrow (a flowering plant), wild rosemary, and resinous, eucalyptus-like wild gale, along with various spices including cinnamon or caraway seeds. In large quantities, gruit was considered a euphoric stimulant and an aphrodisiac, and brewers often incorporated psychotropics such as henbane to enhance the effects. Whether due to public-health or religious reasons (those inebriated heathens!), gruit was largely phased out by the 1700s in favor of hops.

The Spice Is Right

This is not to diss hops. I love those pungent, floral cones something fierce. I've simply come to admire how brewers today are relying less on hops to drive flavor and are dipping their fingers into the fridge, spice rack, and apothecary's cabinet and conceiving beers as kooky as they are quaffable. In Italy, Birrificio Le Baladin's brewer, Teo Musso, makes his Egyptian-style ale Nora with ginger, myrrh, orange peel, and the ancient grain kamut, which has a nutty character. (A tiny amount of hops is used as a preservative.) Wisconsin's Furthermore Beer uses hardly any hops to create the tart, fall-friendly Fallen Apple, which is a blend of fresh-pressed cider and cream ale, and pairs hops with an unlikely flavor by cold-infusing its Knot Stock pale ale with cracked black pepper, resulting in a zingy curiosity.

Instead of an orchard, Michigan's New Holland Brewing Company takes its cues from Mexican cuisine in creating its malty El Mole Ocho, which is redolent of cocoa, chiles, and coffee. Statemates Short's Brewing Company are inspired by dessert, turning out sweet post-dinner treats such as Strawberry Short's Cake (made with milk sugar fermented with fresh strawberries) and S'Mores Stout, which receives its campfire-ready kick from graham cracker crumbs, marshmallows, and milk chocolate.

Are these beers with mass-market appeal? Maybe not. Maybe it doesn't matter. "When you're brewing beers out on the ledge, they're not going to go on tap at your local Hooters and sell three kegs a week," explains Sam Calagione, the president of Delaware's Dogfish Head Craft Brewed Ales, whose offbeat beers include Raison D'Etre, made with green raisins, and Chicory Stout, incorporating roasted chicory, Saint-John's-wort, and licorice root.

"We brew for our own palates first and what excites us, in the hopes of exciting some consumers out there," Calagione says. "We're going to keep flying our freak flag front and center and continue trying out fun stuff." Consider it a rallying cry for craft brewing.

FIVE UNUSUAL BEERS WORTH SAMPLING

BLOODY BEER
SHORT'S BREWING COMPANY
ABV: 8.5%

IN ORDER TO RE-CREATE A BLOODY MARY IN A BOTTLE, SHORT'S BREWING FERMENTS THE BEER WITH ROMA TOMATOES AND SPICES IT WITH CELERY SEEDS, PEPPERCORNS, FRESH HORSERADISH, AND DILL. CLAY-RED BLOODY SMELLS GARDEN-FRESH, WITH DILL THE STANDOUT SCENT. AS IT WARMS, IT RELEASES ITS SPICY, PEPPERY BOUQUET. THIS BEER WON A SILVER MEDAL IN THE EXPERIMENTAL CATEGORY AT THE 2009 GABF.

WELLS BANANA BREAD BEER
WELLS & YOUNG'S BREWING COMPANY
ABV: 5.2%

A BUNCH OF BANANAS GIVES THE COPPER BRITISH BREW A NOSE OF CHIQUITA AND NUTS AND A FLAVOR THAT, MOST CERTAINLY, BRINGS TO MIND BANANA BREAD. THOUGH I NORMALLY HATE A THIN, FIZZY BODY, IT WORKS WELL HERE. SWEETNESS WOULD'VE RUINED THIS SIPPER.

NORA
BIRRIFICIO LE BALADIN
ABV: 6.8%

NAMED AFTER ITALIAN BREWER TEO MUSSO'S WIFE, THE EGYPTIAN ALE SPICED WITH MYRRH, GINGER, AND ORANGE PEEL IS A COMPLEX STUNNER. ITS PERFUME IS FLORAL AND HERBAL, MILDLY REMINISCENT OF INCENSE, WHILE ORANGE STEERS THE TINT AND DELICATE, SEMIDRY FLAVOR.

La DRAGONNE
BFM BRASSERIE DES FRANCHES-MONTAGNES
ABV: 7.5%

DON'T BOTHER CHILLING THIS SWISS WINTER WARMER THAT IS, WELL, BEST SERVED WARM—LIKE TEA, NOT CASK ALE. THE CARBONATION-LESS ALE IS SPICED WITH EVERYTHING FROM CLOVES TO ANISE TO CARDAMOM, FORGING A SWEET, THICK TONIC THAT TASTES LIKE CHRISTMAS WITH A BITTER FINISH.

LEMON TEA ALE
MILL ST. BREW PUB
ABV: 5%

THE TORONTO BREWERY TURNS OUT THIS UNFILTERED AMBER-HUED ALE BY ADDING LEMON AND BLACK TEA LEAVES TO THE AGING TANK. THIS IMPARTS A DRY, SLIGHTLY TANNIC FINISH TO THE SMOOTH AND MALTY TIPPLE. IT'S GOOD AND QUENCHING.

INTERNATIONAL SPOTLIGHT: CANADA'S DIEU DU CIEL!

WIPE AWAY THAT MOLSON MIND-SET. LOSE THE LABATT OUTLOOK. WHILE CANADA'S MOST WELL-KNOWN BEERS MAY BE NORTH-OF-THE-BORDER BUDWEISER, THAT DOESN'T MEAN THE COUNTRY CAN'T BREW. SOME OF NORTH AMERICA'S MOST FLAVORFUL, INVENTIVE BEERS ARE BEING CRAFTED IN QUEBEC.

THE PROVINCE BOASTS MORE THAN 50 BREWERIES, FROM À L'ABRI DE LA TEMPÊTE'S VAUNTED SCOTTISH ALES TO CORSAIRE MICROBRASSERIE'S BITTER PALE ALES. THAT'S IMPRESSIVE FOR A REGION CONTAINING ABOUT SEVEN MILLION PEOPLE, FEWER THAN RESIDE IN NEW YORK CITY. "LOOK AT MONTREAL'S FLAG: IT FEATURES OUR CITY'S FOUR FOUNDING NATIONS— FRANCE, IRELAND, SCOTLAND, AND ENGLAND," EXPLAINS ALAIN THIBAULT, THE MAESTRO AT MONTREAL'S CONVENIENCE STORE-TURNED-BEER PARADISE DÉPANNEUR PELUSO. "BREWING IS OUR HERITAGE."

Dieu du Ciel's! Montreal brewpub.

Meet the Dieu du Ciel! crew: cofounder Stéphane Ostiguy, co-owner Isabelle Charbonneau, brewer and cofounder Jean-François Gravel, and co-owner Luc Boivin.

THIS HERITAGE IS PROUDLY ON DISPLAY AT MONTREAL'S DIEU DU CIEL!, A BREWERY WHOSE NAME LOOSELY TRANSLATES TO "OH MY GOD." IT'S AN APT DESCRIPTION FOR BEER MAKERS WHO TURN CLASSIC STYLES ON THEIR EARS. FOR STARTERS, THE STRONG SCOTCH ALE ÉQUINOXE DU PRINTEMPS IS MADE WITH MAPLE SYRUP. CLEF DES CHAMPS RYE ALE CONTAINS FLORAL MUGWORT AND HEATHER.

AND ROASTY, DECADENT PÉCHÉ MORTEL ("MORTAL SIN") IMPERIAL COFFEE STOUT IS CRAFTED WITH ENOUGH COFFEE BEANS TO KEEP DRINKERS BUZZING ALL NIGHT.

"I START WITH A TRADITIONAL STYLE AND THINK OF THINGS THAT MIGHT COMPLEMENT IT," HEAD BREWER JEAN-FRANÇOIS GRAVEL TOLD THE TORONTO STAR. "IF THEY WORK OUT, I'LL USE THEM. WHY NOT?"

PLAYING HOOKY PAYS DIVIDENDS

HERE'S A BETTER QUESTION: WHY DOES DIEU DU CIEL! EXIST? BACK IN THE MID-1990S, GRAVEL AND STÉPHANE OSTIGUY WERE TOILING AS GRADUATE STUDENTS IN A CHEMISTRY LAB. CONVERSATIONS OCCASIONALLY TURNED TO BEER, NAMELY GRAVEL'S EXPLOITS IN HOMEBREWING. "AT THE TIME, I DIDN'T HAVE MUCH KNOWLEDGE ABOUT CRAFT BEER," OSTIGUY SAYS. HE TOOK QUICKLY TO THE TOPIC, FINDING HIS FRIEND'S CREATIONS TO BE THE BEST, BAR. NONE. ABOUT A YEAR AND A HALF INTO THEIR FRIENDSHIP, OSTIGUY REMARKED TO GRAVEL, "YOUR BEERS ARE SO GOOD, AND SO MANY PEOPLE WANT TO BUY THEM. DO YOU EVER THINK ABOUT DOING SOMETHING WITH BEER?" "I HAD THIS CRAZY DREAM OF OPENING A BREWPUB IN MONTRÉAL," GRAVEL REMARKED.

"THAT'S A GOOD IDEA," OSTIGUY SAID.

WITH THOSE FOUR WORDS, THE DUO DOVE INTO THE BREWPUB PROJECT. AFTER A YEAR OF RESEARCH, THEY LEASED A LOCATION IN MONTREAL'S HIP PLATEAU MONT-ROYAL NEIGHBORHOOD AND SPENT NEARLY A YEAR RENOVATING THE SUNNY, WINDOWED SPOT. THE PROJECT WAS ALL CONSUMING—AT THE EXPENSE OF THEIR EDUCATION. OSTIGUY LOST INTEREST IN HIS BIOLOGY DOCTORATE, WHILE GRAVEL CARED LESS AND LESS ABOUT HIS MASTER'S IN APPLIED MICROBIOLOGY. "WE THOUGHT WE'D HAVE TIME TO FINISH OUR DEGREES, BUT WE SPENT SO MUCH TIME WORKING ON THE BREWPUB INSTEAD OF OUR STUDIES," OSTIGUY SAYS.

BY SEPTEMBER 1998, THE TWOSOME INDEFINITELY PAUSED THEIR COLLEGE CAREERS TO FOCUS ON DIEU DU CIEL! IT PROVED TO BE THE RIGHT CHOICE. OVER THE YEARS, THEY CONVERTED CUSTOMERS WITH THEIR CURIOUS CREATIONS, SUCH AS BLANCHE DE SEPTEMBRE WITBIER BREWED WITH GINGER AND CORIANDER, AND CARAMEL-FLAVORED FUMISTERIE, WHICH INCORPORATES HEMP SEEDS. THEN THERE'S THE ROSÉE D'HIBISCUS, A BEER AS PINK AS A LIGHTLY SEARED STEAK.

IT WAS BORN ONE DAY WHEN HEAD BREWER GRAVEL WAS WATCHING A DOCUMENTARY ON WESTERN AFRICA, WHICH INCLUDED A SEGMENT ON BISSAP—A TEA MADE FROM AN INFUSION OF HIBISCUS FLOWERS AND SUGAR. GRAVEL JOTTED DOWN THE RECIPE AND RE-CREATED THE DRINK AT HOME, REALIZING THE FLOWER'S FLORAL PROFILE AND ACIDITY WOULD COMPLEMENT A TWANGY BLANCHE (THE FRENCH NAME FOR WITBIER).

"WE FIRST BREWED IT AS A SPECIAL RELEASE FOR THE MONTREAL BEER FESTIVAL [MONDIAL DE LA BIÈRE] IN 2006, AND IT WAS SUPPOSED TO BE A ONE-SHOT DEAL," OSTIGUY SAYS, "BUT PEOPLE KEPT ASKING FOR THIS BEER." SO DIEU BREWED IT FOR THE FOLLOWING FESTIVAL. THE RESPONSE WAS EVEN MORE ENTHUSIASTIC. NOW, ROSÉE "IS THE BEER THAT PEOPLE TALK ABOUT THE MOST, AND TELL US HOW MUCH THEY LOVE IT," OSTIGUY SAYS.

DIEU FOR EXPANSION

THE PROBLEM WAS, THE BREWERY COULDN'T MAKE ENOUGH OF THE BEER THAT PEOPLE LOVED. DIEU DU CIEL! HAD MAXED OUT PRODUCTION. "WE DIDN'T HAVE ENOUGH TIME TO BREW A LAGER OR EXPLORE MORE UNUSUAL STYLES," OSTIGUY BEMOANS. SO IN 2008, THE ECLECTIC BREWPUB EXPANDED INTO A FULL-FLEDGED MICROBREWERY, OPENING A SECOND LOCATION 45 MINUTES OUTSIDE TOWN TO FOCUS ON ITS CORE BEERS, INCLUDING THE ELEGANTLY HOPPED DERNIÈRE VOLONTÉ BLONDE ALE. THAT LEFT THE MONTREAL BREWPUB FREE TO CONDUCT DELICIOUS EXPERIMENTS SUCH AS THE PÉNOMBRE BLACK IPA.

AS FOR THE FUTURE, THE BREWERY HAS CONTINUED TO EXPLORE THE FRINGES OF FERMENTATION, WORKING WITH WILD YEASTS, BARREL AGING, AND EVEN SPIKING BEER WITH ABSINTHE. "WE'RE TRYING TO SHOW PEOPLE EVERYTHING THAT BEER CAN BE," OSTIGUY SAYS.

Brasserie
Dieu du Ciel !
DERNIÈRE VOLONTÉ
Bière blonde
de style Abbaye
Abbey-style
blond ale

Bière forte
7 % alc./vol.
Bière sur lie
Refermentée en bouteille

Strong Beer
341 mL
Beer on lees
Bottle conditioned

Embouteillée le / Bottled on : | 01 | 02 | 03 | 04 | 05 | 06 | 07 | 08 | 09 | 10 | 11 | 12 | • | 10 | 11 | 12 | 13 |
La Dernière volonté est née d'une rencontre entre les traditions brassicoles belges et britanniques. Elle présente un nez complexe de fleurs et d'alcool, soutenu par des arômes fruités et légèrement maltés, le tout couronné par un fort bouquet de houblon. En bouche, elle est épicée et fruitée, et laisse deviner une discrète touche d'alcool. En finale, le houblon ferme la marche avec force
Ingrédients : Eau, orge maltée, blé, houblons, levure
Ingredients : Water, malted barley, wheat, hops, yeast

Pour déguster toute la gamme de nos bières en fût, visitez nos deux pubs :
• 29 Laurier Ouest, Montréal, 514-490-9555 • 259 rue de Villemure, St-Jérôme, 450-436-3438
Brassée et embouteillée par / Brewed and bottled by : Microbrasserie Dieu du Ciel inc.,
St-Jérôme, Québec, Canada, J7Z 5J4. www.dieuduciel.com – Infomicro@sympatico.ca
Illustration : yannick.brosseau@sympatico.ca

8 90761 12648 9

THREE

A TASTE OF THE PAST:

Saved From Extinction, These Beer Styles Have a Flavorful Future

JUST LIKE GIANT PANDAS AND SIBERIAN TIGERS, some species of beer are in danger of going extinct. But instead of habitat destruction or sport, these beer styles' endangered status is due to drinkers' fickle tastes. Brewing history is peppered with thousands of different beer recipes that, much like clothes or music, are constantly sliding in and out of fashion. In the nineteenth century, gold-rushing California miners drank lightly fruity, copper-colored steam beer. By the 1960s, that beer was nearly snuffed out—until Fritz Maytag took over a San Francisco brewery and began crafting what came be known as Anchor Steam. It takes only a single intrepid brewer to bring a style back to delicious life.

From full-bodied, corn-driven lagers popular in pre-Prohibition America to sour German beers spiced with coriander and salt and 9,000-year-old Chinese elixirs concocted with chrysanthemum flowers and hawthorn fruit, what's old is new again. Don't call it a comeback. These beers have been here for years.

Pre-Prohibition Lagers

If you were an American at the turn of the twentieth century, you likely drank a very different kind of lager. Unlike modern-day American lagers, which are synonymous with watery, innocuous brews such as Coors and Budweiser, pre-Prohibition beers were bracing and nuanced. They were crafted by European immigrants who arrived bearing yeast cultures and brewing know-how.

They began devising lagers such as a strong, all-malt bock, which was favored in the spring, sometimes marketed as a medicinal tonic, and popular in New York City. As an alternative to fruity ales, which once dominated the country, lagers were spiced with juniper berries and orange peel. Lightly sweet, gently hopped, amber-tinted Vienna lagers, which rose to fame in that city in the mid-1800s, also flourished in Texas and Mexico. (Negra Modelo is an enduring example of Vienna lager.) On the West Coast, mild, less hoppy Western lagers made with rice were popular, most notably from Portland, Oregon's Henry Weinhard's.

In the Midwest and on the East Coast, the dominant version was a pale lager. Its secret? Corn. While corn is today derided as a cheap adjunct, the indigenous ingredient was important to brewers. Since they found American barley harsh, a measure of corn added a calming sweetness that, when blended with imported German hops, created the quintessential robust, flavorful American lager.

Lager's decline was hastened by Prohibition, the Depression, the Dust Bowl, and, finally, World War II: ingredients were scarce. Breweries closed or consolidated, creating national brands. Increasingly, greater portions of rice were used, resulting in crisper, lighter beers sold from coast to coast.

Timeless Flavor

These unique German American lagers languished until a few intrepid breweries decided to restore the luster of the maligned style. For instance, Brooklyn Brewery staked its fate on an old-world lager. "When we came out with Brooklyn Lager, few people had even heard the word *lager*," says current brewmaster Garrett Oliver of the lightly hoppy, amber-colored Vienna lager, which was based on an old family recipe of Brooklyn brewer William Moeller. "It took a lot of convincing to get anyone to sell a beer that had an amber color," says Oliver.

To break Big Beer's distribution stranglehold, Brooklyn's founders bought a van and beverage truck and trekked cases of their lager—with labels stamped PRE-PROHIBITION—to retail stores and saloons. Bottle by bottle, the lager won over taste buds and became the company's flagship beer.

In Hood River, Oregon, Full Sail Brewing Co.'s Jamie Emmerson fell in love with old-school lagers thanks to a peculiar bottle. "It's a grenade. I wondered, what could I fill a grenade with?" the executive brewmaster recalls.

The grenade in question is the classic stubby beer bottle. In the post-atomic era, stubbies from now-bygone Pacific Northwest breweries such as Lucky, Pearl, and Rainier were synonymous with lager beer. But America's stubby era ended with Rainier Brewing Company's 1999 closing.

Full Sail brewmaster Jamie Emmerson is unafraid to show his affections for beer.

When the brewery was shuttering, Emmerson noticed that "people were buying pallets upon pallets of the stubbies. Drinkers loved the bottle—and the beer that was in it."

The problem was, Full Sail brewed few lagers. Its name was staked on premium, flavorful ales. For three or four years, Emmerson and his colleagues kicked around concepts for a stubby beer. A strapping porter? Brazen barley wine? Highly hopped ale?

"Let's look at something that's been done before," Emmerson remembers thinking, "but something that no one's doing." Like pre-Prohibition lagers. Emmerson spent nearly a year tweaking formulas. The just-right recipe resulted in a light, rich lager called Session and, later, Session Black, its roasty flavored sibling. "I took a sip and said, 'This is going to do just fine,'" Emmerson recalls of Session, which launched in 2006.

An Old-Fashioned Phenomenon

The trend toward pre-Prohibition lager is catching on countrywide. Nebraska's Lucky Bucket Brewing Co. cooks up the biscuity Pre-Prohibition Lager, while Craftsman Brewing Company in

Pasadena, California, cranks out the corn-influenced 1903 Lager. Each spring, Pennsylvania's Victory Brewing Company makes the limited-release, draft-only Throwback Lager using corn and yeast from Philadelphia's bygone Christian Schmidt Brewing Co. Even brewing colossus MillerCoors has entered the throwback game, releasing the hoppier, more full-bodied Batch 19 Pre-Prohibition Style Lager.

Despite evoking a nostalgic age of beer consumption, Emmerson admits that it's tough "to get today's drinkers over the hump of expectations that American lagers are bland. We're going to fight that for a while," he says. He has some unlikely allies in the battle: "My dad and his buddies are all old-school, light-beer drinkers, and they love Session. You don't get much more macro-drinking approval than that."

FOUR TO TRY

SESSION
FULL SAIL BREWING CO.
ABV: 5.1%

IN THIS AGE OF AMERICAN LAGERS MADE FROM CORN, RICE, AND EVERYTHING NOT NICE, IT'S REFRESHING TO SEE FULL SAIL FASHION ITS THROWBACK LAGER WITH 100 PERCENT MALT. SOLD IN ELEVEN-OUNCE "STUBBIES," SESSION WON'T STUN YOU WITH A FULL-THROTTLE HOP ASSAULT. INSTEAD, THIS CLASSIC AMERICAN LAGER DRINKS CRISP AND CREAMY, A PERFECT THIRST QUENCHER. ALSO SUPERB IS THE LIGHTLY ROASTY, SUBTLY CHOCOLATY SESSION BLACK (5.4 PERCENT), WHICH IS AS DRINKABLE AS IT IS DARK.

PRE-PROHIBITION STYLE LAGER
LUCKY BUCKET BREWING COMPANY
ABV: 4.5%

LUCKY BUCKET'S ROSTER OF BEERS SHOULD BE CAUSE FOR SOME SERIOUS NEBRASKAN STATE PRIDE. THERE'S THE ORIGINAL AMERICAN INDIA PALE ALE, WHICH IS AN AROMATIC LOVE LETTER TO CENTENNIAL, CASCADE, AND AMARILLO HOPS. CERTIFIED EVIL IS A BLENDED, PARTLY CABERNET BARREL-AGED DARK BELGIAN STRONG ALE. AND THEN THERE'S THE PRE-PROHIBITION LAGER, WHICH POURS THE COLOR OF GOLD DOUBLOONS. THE LIGHT MALTINESS WORKS WELL WITH THE SLIGHTLY BITTER AND FLORAL HOPS.

POINT SPECIAL LAGER
STEVENS POINT BREWERY
ABV: 4.66%

SINCE 1857, THE LAGER HAS SERVED AS THE WISCONSIN BREWERY'S FLAGSHIP. A MEASURE OF BREWERS GRITS (THAT'S CORN TO YOU) GIVES SPECIAL SOME SWEETNESS THAT'S AGREEABLE WITH THE GRASSY FLAVOR. SMOOTH, LIGHT, AND CRISP, IT'S AN IDEAL LAWNMOWER BEER.

YUENGLING TRADITIONAL LAGER
D.G. YUENGLING & SON
ABV: 4.4%

AS YOU'D EXPECT FROM AMERICA'S OLDEST BREWERY (CIRCA 1829), YUENGLING TURNS OUT A FINE PRE-PROHIBITION LAGER. COUNTING INGREDIENTS SUCH AS CORN AND CASCADE HOPS, THE MEDIUM-BODIED AMBER BREW HAS A BISCUITY, CARAMEL FLAVOR AND AN EASYGOING DRINKABILITY.

California Common

Thank California's gold rush for inspiring one of America's singular styles of beer. To capitalize on miners' prodigious thirst, brewers in the mid-1800s decamped to California, armed with lager yeast. Upon arriving, they discovered there was neither a ready supply of ice nor mechanical refrigeration. Without ice, it was impossible to chill bottom-fermenting lagers, which require cool-temperature fermentation.

Improvising, brewers used a special lager yeast that functions at a warmer temperature. And to chill the hot wort (the unfermented broth created by boiling grains with water), the scalding liquid was pumped up to large, shallow rooftop bins cooled by Pacific Ocean breezes. The result was an effervescent, malty, prominently hopped amber beer that miners gulped down by the gallon. Because of the highly carbonated beer's tendency to spray when a keg was tapped, or maybe due to the steam rising from the cooling wort, it came to be known as steam beer. That name has been trademarked by San Francisco's Anchor Brewing Company (one of the original brewers of steam beer), forcing other brewers to market their offerings of the beer as California Common.

"We used to call our beer Steam Engine Steam, but Fritz Maytag [of Anchor Brewery] made it his mission to make sure we didn't call it that," laughs Ken Martin, brewmaster at Durango, Colorado's Steamworks Brewing Co., whose California Common is called Steam Engine Lager. Since it won gold in 1997 at the Great American Beer Festival, the balanced, hop-spiced Steam Engine Lager has become their flagship beer, accounting for around half of brewery production.

Predictably Delicious

"It's such a great summer beer because you can sit down with three or four of these without breaking a sweat," says Martin, who also loves the style's brewing predictability. "You can set your watch to it," Martin says. "It ferments right on time. It filters great. I don't know if it found us or if we found it, but we're lucky to have it in our lineup."

Other breweries, too, have dusted off the California Common: In St. Paul, Minnesota, Flat Earth Brewing Co. has made waves with its generously hopped Element 115 Lager, while Maryland's Flying Dog Brewery churns out the full-bodied Old Scratch Amber Lager. Up in Wisconsin, Furthermore Beer kicks up its caramel-hinted Oscura with plenty of Fair Trade coffee beans.

"The brewing techniques may have originated in Europe, but we added our own American twist. This is a unique style, one of the few that are indigenous to America," Martin says. "I love that miners were making a go of it in the hardest conditions, yet they still wanted the luxury of beer."

FOUR TO TRY

STEAM ENGINE LAGER
STEAMWORKS BREWING COMPANY
ABV: 5.65%
IN STEAM ENGINE, THE DURANGO, COLORADO, BREWERY HAS CREATED ONE OF AMERICA'S MOST BALANCED AND LAUDED LAGERS. IT POURS THE COLOR OF A COPPER MINE, WITH AN AROMA OF CANDIED MALT AND SUBTLE CITRUS. THE STRONG CARAMEL BODY IS FAINTLY REMINISCENT OF WERTHER'S ORIGINAL CANDY, THOUGH WOODY HOPS AND A PINCUSHION-PRICKLY FINISH ASSUAGE THE SWEETNESS.

ELEMENT 115 LAGER
FLAT EARTH BREWING CO.
ABV: 5.5%
I'VE HEARD THE COMPLAINT COUNTLESS TIMES: "I HATE LAGERS BECAUSE THEY DON'T TASTE LIKE ANYTHING." "WELL, HAVE YOU HAD ELEMENT 115?" I'LL ASK, STEERING THEM TOWARD MY FAVORITE FLAT EARTH RELEASE. WITH ELEMENT, THE ST. PAUL, MINNESOTA, BREWERY HAS DEVISED A DEVILISHLY HOPPED CALIFORNIA COMMON OOZING GRAPEFRUIT. BUT MALT LASSOS THE ASTRINGENCY, RESULTING IN A LIP-SMACKER WITH A SWEET-BITTER CONCLUSION.

BOOTLEGGER
BAD ATTITUDE CRAFT BEER
ABV: 6.94%
PRODUCED IN THE ITALIAN-SPEAKING CANTON OF TICINO IN SWITZERLAND, NOT FAR FROM ITS BORDER WITH ITALY, BAD ATTITUDE BEERS TAKE THEIR INSPIRATION FROM U.S. CRAFT BREWING. HOBO IS AN AROMATIC IPA MADE WITH AMARILLO, CASCADE, AND NELSON SAUVIN HOPS, WHILE BOOTLEGGER IS A DRY, LIGHTLY FILTERED CALIFORNIA COMMON WITH A FRAGRANT HOP PERFUME. EVEN MORE AMERICAN: IT'S SOLD IN CANS.

OLD SCRATCH AMBER LAGER
FLYING DOG BREWERY
ABV: 5.5%
THE MARYLAND BREWERY DOES RIGHT WITH ITS COMMON. THE LIGHTLY CITRIC, SWEET-GRAIN SCENT SETS THE STAGE FOR A RICH, BREADY BREW CUT THROUGH WITH CARAMEL AND A SHORT, DRY FINISH.

Berliner Weisse

While ransacking Europe, Napoleon's soldiers discovered Berliner weisse, a tart German beer so effervescent that the combatants dubbed it the "Champagne of the north." Like sipping unsweetened lemonade, Berliner weisse—born in Berlin, naturally—is as immensely sour as it is refreshing. The bottle-conditioned, pale-golden wheat beer is concocted with warm fermenting yeasts and *Lactobacillus* bacteria, which imparts the refreshingly acidic flavor that makes it a great mate with raw oysters and light summer salads and citrus fruit.

Because tartness does not hold universal appeal, the Berliner weisse is often served *mit Schuss*: with a shot of flavored, colored syrup such as herbaceous woodruff (*Waldmeistersirup*), sweet raspberry *Himbeersirup*, or lemony *Zitronensirup*. Germans

traditionally take their Berliner served in a large, bowl-shaped glass with a straw, sucking it up like soda pop.

"It's great on a hot day," enthuses Patrick Rue, the owner of Placentia, California's the Bruery. "The Berliner weisse is such a low-alcohol beer"—around 3 percent on average—"that it can appeal to the most hard-core beer geek and to those who don't like beer." Rue brews Hottenroth Berliner Weisse (named after his grandparents), a mouth puckerer packed with both *Lactobacillus* and *Brettanomyces* yeast. "We have to really scrub down the equipment afterward," Rue says. "The Berliner is just as funky as a lambic."

That could be a clue to Berliner weisse's history. Beer writer Roger Protz has hypothesized that the style began when Huguenots, Protestants from France and Belgium's Flanders region, fled religious persecution and migrated to Germany; Berliner weisse might have developed from their favored sour red and brown ales. Alternately, Berliner weisse may be the evolution of the darker-hued, barley-and-wheat ale Halberstädter Broihan, which was originally brewed in the city of Halberstadt, about 130 miles southwest of Berlin.

While the beer's beginnings may be cloudy, its popularity was not: in the nineteenth century, there were an estimated 250-plus brewers producing Berliner weisse. However, a growing taste for lagers meant that, by the tail end of the twentieth century, only a handful of breweries producing Berliner weisse remained.

German Inspiration, American Made

While this sour style is not ready to be taken off life support, its pulse is stronger today than it has been in years. Berliner weisse is steadily produced at German breweries such as Weihenstephan and Berliner Kindl, and American outfits are increasingly turning to this Teutonic treat. The version offered at Philadelphia's Nodding Head Brewery & Restaurant is crisp and tangy, while Bell's Brewery in Kalamazoo,

Michigan, brews its Oarsman Ale in the style of the Berliner weisse—wheaty, refreshing, and low in alcohol. New Hampshire's White Birch Brewing has an invigorating Berliner weisse that drinks far lighter than its style-stretching 6.4 percent ABV. And Dogfish Head has made its tart and peachy Festina Pêche a seasonal mainstay.

"Berliner weisse has a wide range of appeal," says Rue, "as long as people get used to the idea of it being sour."

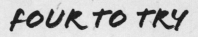

FOUR TO TRY

HOTTENROTH BERLINER WEISSE
THE BRUERY
ABV: 3.1%

THOUGH THE HAZY YELLOW HOTTENROTH—NAMED AFTER BREWMASTER PATRICK RUE'S GRANDPARENTS—LACKS BOOZY BOMBAST, IT BOASTS BOATLOADS OF OFFBEAT FLAVOR. IT'S CHOCKABLOCK WITH SOURNESS (HELLO, LACTOBACILLUS BACTERIA) PLUS A CITRIC TARTNESS THAT SIMULTANEOUSLY SHOCKS AND PLEASES THE TASTE BUDS. IT'S LIKE THE HAPPY OFFSPRING OF LEMONADE AND CHAMPAGNE.

1809
DR. FRITZ BRIEM
ABV: 5%

SOMEWHAT STRONGER THAN OTHER BERLINER WEISSES, THIS BEER, BREWED BY WEIHENSTEPHAN AND DOEMENS INSTITUTE, IS NONETHELESS FIRST-RATE: ITS PLEASINGLY SOUR, WHEATY SMELL MELDS WITH A BRIGHT AND ELEGANT CHAMPAGNE-LIKE TANG THAT'S BUOYED BY TRACES OF RASPBERRIES, PEARS, AND LEMONS.

BERLINER KINDL WEISSE
BERLINER KINDL BRAUEREI
ABV: 2.5%

DESPITE THE SCANT ALCOHOL CONTENT, THIS GERMAN-BREWED BERLINER WEISSE STILL HAS A SHARP APPLE ESSENCE MIXED WITH EARTHY MUSTINESS. IT TASTES OF GENTLY SPICED WHEAT AND IS AS LIP-SMACKING AND TART AS FALL'S FINEST CIDER.

BERLINER-STYLE WEISSE
BAYERISCHER BAHNHOF BRAU & GASTSTÄTTENBETRIEB
ABV: 3%

LOCATED IN LEIPZIG, GERMANY, THIS BREWERY'S BERLINER WEISSE OFFERS THE FRAGRANCE OF FRESH-CUT MELON, NEW LEATHER, AND WHITE WINE. TASTE-WISE, THE LIGHTLY ACIDIC LEMON CHARACTER IS GROUNDED BY PRONOUNCED WHEAT. IT'S AN EASYGOING EXAMPLE OF THE STYLE.

Gose

Putting salt in beer may seem sacrilegious, but for centuries the seasoning has been key to this strange, singular German beverage. Like the Berliner weisse, gose is one of northern Germany's traditional top-fermenting wheat beers. While both are sour, gose diverges by incorporating salt and coriander, a spice typically found in the Belgian witbier. Though some historians speculate that gose is related to Belgium's gueuze—a blend of aged lambics—gose originated in Goslar, a mining town in northwestern Germany and takes its name from the river Gose, which courses through the city.

Sharp, twangy gose proved popular and by the 1700s had caught on in Leipzig, located about 100 miles east, where it became a local favorite. Leipzig brewers also began manufacturing gose, and as recently as 1900 there were reportedly more than 80 licensed *gosenschenke*—that is, gose tavern—where one could get a glass of the salty stuff, which was sometimes served with a cumin-flavored liqueur. "You see that with many of the old north-Germany beer styles," explains beer historian Ron Pattinson, the author of *Porter!* and *Brown Beer*. "They drank them with spirits because the beers weren't very alcoholic."

Despite currying local favor, "gose was never the majority of beer drank in Leipzig," Pattinson continues. "The amount of gose produced was quite limited," likely because few people had mastered its tricky production. From its late-nineteenth-century peak gose gradually declined, as a lager craze swept Germany, wiping out small-scale breweries specializing in top-fermenting beer. Gose survived till World War II dealt it a deadly blow. Across Germany during that era, beer production temporarily ceased. When smoke and rubble were cleared, Leipzig found itself in Communist German Democratic Republic. In 1945, the last remaining gose brewery was confiscated and closed. Leipzig's Friedrich Wurzler Brauerei revived gose in 1949, but when the owner died in 1966, so did gose.

A One-Man Revival

The style lay dormant till the 1980s, when bar owner Lothar Goldhahn decided to restore Leipzig's Ohne Bedenken, once one of the city's most famous *gosenschenke*. To fill taps, he contracted breweries to craft gose. "It had been 20 years since people had gose, so he had people who drank gose try it," Pattinson says. It passed muster. After a rocky period where production ceased again, "there are more breweries making gose in Germany than any time since World War II," Pattinson says. "It's a remarkable comeback." He counts at least four gose-producing German breweries, including Brauhaus Hartmannsdorf, makers of the laser-tart Goedecke Döllnitzer Ritterguts Gose, and Gasthaus & Gosebrauerei Bayerischer Bahnhof, located in Leipzig's historic train station. Lately, it's been brewed in America, too.

"The salt changes the finish and makes it more appetizing," says Alex Ganum, the owner and head brewer of Upright Brewing Company in Portland, Oregon. "It makes you want to drink more of it." Ganum first fell in love with the style when attending a homebrew competition. "My friend was like, 'Oh, man you got to try this. It's so cool,'" Ganum recalls of the gose, which was soured with lemon juice.

FOUR TO TRY

GOSE
UPRIGHT BREWING
ABV: 5.2%

RELEASED IN LATE WINTER, THIS COLD-WEATHER SEASONAL HAS A BRIGHT, LEMONY SCENT CROSSED WITH A TRACE OF CLOVE, LEADING TO A WHEATY TANG THAT'S SHARPENED BY THE SALT. THE SOURNESS IS MUTED, THE DRY FINISH REFRESHING.

LEIPZIGER GOSE
GASTHAUS & GOSEBRAUEREI BAYERISCHER BAHNHOF
ABV: 4.6%

THIS UNPASTEURIZED, BOTTLE-CONDITIONED GOSE POURS A CLOUDY YELLOW HUE, SMELLING OF HERBS AND APPLES. IT'S LEMONY TART ON THE TONGUE, TASTING SOMEWHAT SWEET, BREADY, AND PIQUANT, THEN CLOSING CRISP AND ZINGY. COUNT YOURSELF LUCKY IF YOU FIND IT SOLD IN THE TRADITIONAL FLAT, CIRCULAR BOTTLE TOPPED BY A NARROW, ELONGATED NECK.

SPRING GOSE
CASCADE BREWING
ABV: 4.5%

SERVED ON DRAFT AT THE PORTLAND, OREGON, PUB, THIS GOSE HAS ARMLOADS OF AROMATICS (CHAMOMILE, LEMON PEEL, LAVENDER FLOWERS) BOUND TOGETHER BY SALT AND WHEAT. IT'S A LITTLE LIKE DRINKING A MEADOW. (CASCADE ALSO BREWS A SPECIAL GOSE FOR EACH OF THE OTHER THREE SEASONS.)

TINY BUBBLES
HOLLISTER BREWING COMPANY
ABV: 4.5%

THE CALIFORNIA BREWERY GARNERED SILVER AT THE 2010 GABF WITH ITS TART, TINGLY, DRAFT-ONLY GOSE BUILT WITH WHEAT, PILSNER MALTS, CORIANDER, LACTOBACILLUS BACTERIA, AND SALT—NOT TOO MUCH, SINCE SANTA BARBARA'S WATER IS HARD AND SALINIC. IF THE FLAVOR'S TOO SOUR, ADD A SHOT OF RASPBERRY OR CHERRY SYRUP.

Smitten with the style's flavor and low ABV—gose is traditionally less than 5 percent ABV—Ganum decided to brew his own version at Upright in fall 2009. He used a French saison yeast, then fermented it at cooler temperatures to give it a hefeweizen-like character. Cautious about overdoing it with the lactic acid and salt, he used too little of each at first. So he added more salt and lactic acid, then more still. The result was bright and acidic, offering notes of lemon and earth paired with a drying, quenching finish.

"That's probably the seasonal beer that's had the most requests. I always get, Oh, man, when are you going to brew the gose again?" Ganum says of the beer, which has become a winter-spring specialty.

Elsewhere, fellow Portland brewery Cascade Brewing creates a *Lactobacillus*-soured, draft-only gose for each season, while the Draught House Pub & Brewery in Austin, Texas, serves Sunshade Gose as a summer seasonal (sunshade—*Sonnenschirm*—is the German nickname for this hot-weather beverage). Indianapolis's Brugge Brasserie occasionally offers Bad Kitty Leipziger Gose. Ganum can understand the appeal. "It's different, exciting, and can still be aggressive," Ganum says. "Gose has an edge to it that appeals to people."

Ancient Ales

While pilsners and India pale ales have besotted drinkers for centuries, these styles are spring chickens in the annals of brewing. In one form or another, beer has existed for millennia. That much is understood. But did these ancient styles taste good?

To answer that, Sam Calagione, the president of Delaware's daring Dogfish Head, set out to re-create bygone beverages. "We're on this quixotic journey that no one tells us what beers should be," Calagione says. His Ancient Ales series includes Midas Touch, a delicate, floral beverage based on saffron, honey, white Muscat grapes, and barley found in 2,700-year-old drinking vessels in King Midas's tomb. The chocolaty, light-hued Theobrama ("food of the gods"), made with Aztec cocoa powder, cocoa nibs, honey, chiles, and annatto seeds, was concocted after scientists analyzed shards of Honduran pottery and discovered a chocolate-based alcoholic elixir used for ceremonies as far back as 1200 BC.

Not content to stop there, Dogfish ventured backward an additional eight millennia to a tipple inspired by traces of a fermented beverage found on 9,000-year-old preserved pottery excavated in northern China's Jiahu village. Called Chateau Jiahu, it is mildly carbonated with a sweet, fruity base. "We're showing the breadth of what can be made in a brewery," Calagione says.

The Old-Time Club

Though 9,000-year-old inebriants inspire Dogfish, other brewers are going back even further in time—like 45 million years. In California, microbiologist Raul Cano harvested a strain of *Saccharomyces cerevisiae* (brewer's yeast) from a chunk of amber that was up to 45 million years old. Like a scene from *Jurassic Park*, he brought the yeast back to life. Instead of creating a *T. Rex*, Cano used his yeast to brew. The result is Fossil Fuels Brewing Company, which makes wheat beer served around northern California.

Scotland's Williams Bros. Brewing Co. began in 1988, but the origins of many of its brews stretch back centuries. The brewery's catalog of historic Scottish ales include Ebulum, a fruity delight crafted with elderberries whose recipe dates back to the sixteenth century, and

Fraoch, based on heather ale, which has been brewed in Scotland since 2000 BC. Then there's Kelpie, which is fashioned from fresh seaweed. It's a nod to nineteenth-century coastal Scottish breweries that made beer with malted barley that was fertilized with seaweed.

Is Kelpie fit for a backyard BBQ or buying by the six-pack? Not really. But that's not the point. It's about dusting off the history books and demonstrating that, while today's brewers are mighty inventive, so were brewers a hundred—or a thousand—years ago.

"People like to think they're coming up with all these new ideas," says Amsterdam-based beer historian Ron Pattinson, who researches forgotten recipes and posts them on his blog *Shut Up About Barclay Perkins*. "I like coming up with all these examples that show it's already been done."

FIVE TO TRY

GROZET
WILLIAMS BROS. BREWING CO.
ABV: 5%

BASED ON A TRADITION OF DRINKS MADE FROM CEREALS, HERBS, AND FRUIT THAT STRETCHES BACK TO SIXTEENTH-CENTURY SCOTTISH MONKS, GROZET IS BREWED WITH MALT, WHEAT, HOPS, BOG MYRTLE, AND MEADOWSWEET, THEN GETS A SECOND FERMENTATION WITH GOOSEBERRIES. DON'T BE AFRAID. GROZET IS AN EASYGOING BREW, COLORED LIKE BARBIE'S HAIR AND PACKED WITH BRIGHT FRUIT FLAVORS. IT'S AS BRISK AS A DECEMBER DIP IN THE ATLANTIC.

CHATEAU JIAHU
DOGFISH HEAD CRAFT BREWERY
ABV: 10%

THE BREW IS BASED ON A 9,000-YEAR-OLD NEOLITHIC CHINA TIPPLE THAT WAS COMPOSED OF RICE, HONEY, AND FRUIT. IN ITS RE-CREATION, DOGFISH USED WILDFLOWER HONEY, BARLEY MALT, RICE FLAKES, MUSCAT GRAPES, HAWTHORN FRUIT, CHRYSANTHEMUM FLOWER, AND SAKE YEAST—NO BARLEY HERE. THE RESULT IS A WINE-LIKE ELIXIR WITH NOTES OF SWEET HONEY. THANKFULLY, THE DOGFISH TEAM WASN'T ENTIRELY HISTORICALLY ACCURATE. THE ORIGINAL LIKELY CONTAINED LUMPS OF FLOATING YEAST.

POOR RICHARD'S TAVERN SPRUCE ALE
YARDS BREWING COMPANY
ABV: 5%

FOR ITS ALES OF THE REVOLUTION SERIES, THE PHILADELPHIA BREWERY MAKES HISTORIC ALES INSPIRED OR CREATED BY FOUNDING FATHERS GEORGE WASHINGTON (PORTER), THOMAS JEFFERSON (GOLDEN ALE), AND BEN FRANKLIN. POOR RICHARD'S IS BASED ON THE LATTER'S ORIGINAL RECIPE, RELYING ON MOLASSES AND SPRUCE ESSENCE. THE EFFECT IS NOT UNLIKE A DISTILLED EVERGREEN TREE SPRINKLED WITH SUGAR. VERY CURIOUS.

ORIGINAL HOCHZEITSBIER VON 1810
BRAUEREI HOFSTETTEN
ABV: 6.3%

BASED ON THE MORE POTENT MÄRZENS SERVED AT MUNICH'S ORIGINAL OKTOBERFEST CELEBRATION, THE AUSTRIAN BREWER'S HOCHZEITSBIER VON 1810 IS A FULL-BODIED STUNNER. THE UNFILTERED DARK-AMBER LAGER HAS A FIRM, MALTY CHARM AND AN HERBAL, SOMEWHAT FRUITY HOPPINESS. IT'S A LAGER FOR HOP LOVERS.

SSS
BROUWERIJ DE MOLEN
ABV: 10.3%

HISTORIAN RON PATTINSON COLLABORATED WITH THIS SPLENDID DUTCH BREWERY TO TURN OUT A TRIPLE STOUT HAILING FROM LONDON, CIRCA 1914. THE TIME-TRAVELING DARK BEER BEGINS WITH A ROCKY TAN HEAD, PERFUMED WITH COCOA, MILKY COFFEE, AND ROASTED MALT. ZIPPY CARBONATION PROPELS SSS, AS FLAVORS DART FROM SEMISWEET CHOCOLATE TO EARTH, SMOKE, AND DARK FRUIT.

Barrel-Aged Brews

Matt Brynildson never dreamed of brewing beer. Post-college, Brynildson was a hops-flavor extractor for a spice firm. After his company "made the mistake of sending me to brewing school," he started a stint at Goose Island Beer Co. in Chicago, before finding a home at SLO Brewing in Paso Robles, California. When Firestone Walker Brewing Company bought the firm, Brynildson retained his brewmaster title—and found himself befuddled.

"I never learned to operate *that* in brewing school," says Brynildson of Firestone's revamped Burton Union: Every drop of rich, pleasantly hoppy DBA (Double Barrel Ale), floral Pale 31, and Walker's Reserve, a robust porter, spend six days in an oak-barrel fermenting system favored in nineteenth-century Britain. "Now I can't imagine making beer any other way."

Firestone Walker's Burton Union barrel-fermenting system in action with brewmaster Matt Brynildson sampling the fruits of his labor.

When railroads ruled the land, every beer in both America and Europe was seasoned and transported in wooden casks, which imparted flavors of lush vanilla and oak. It was—and remains—a time- and labor-intensive endeavor. When brewers began modernizing, using stainless steel vats, it ushered in an era of mass-produced beer.

Now brewers are coming full circle. In their quest for novel flavors, they've begun to use wooden barrels like chefs do spices: to transform the ordinary into the extraordinary. Barrels mellow and modify beer, providing woodsy notes and the essence of the cask's previous contents, which range from port to chardonnay to bourbon. But why stop there? With beer, it seems, things get better with age.

Liquor's Quicker

Of the many barrels available, whiskey and bourbon casks are most popular—and prevalent. By law, distillers can use charred barrels once, leaving the market flooded with casks that once contained Maker's Mark or Jim Beam. In a month or two, a freshly drained bourbon barrel can pass on 90-proof characteristics, without ratcheting up the alcohol content.

It took only a couple of days to make Rob Tod a barrel-aging convert. Back in 2004, the owner of Allagash Brewing Company in Portland, Maine, was bottling his Tripel ale when he faced a dilemma: A shipment of bottles was delayed, and he lacked enough glass for the full run. Since Tod needed space in his storage tanks, he pondered dumping the beer down a drain. Instead, he poured his strong, sweet-tasting Belgian ale into several empty Jim Beam casks, which he'd bought for future experiments. When he tasted the beer a couple of days later, "it was totally transformed," Tod says. "We originally wanted to call it an oak-aged tripel, but it was a different beer after oak aging. We made it a new beer," called Curieux.

While bourbon barrels worked their magic for Allagash's tripel, lighter pilsners and lagers would be overwhelmed by the boozy flavors. One of the best candidates for bourbon-barrel aging is a muscular barley wine or, better yet, a rich, inky, decadent stout.

Saint Louis Brewery consigns its Schlafly Barrel-Aged Imperial Stout to just-emptied Jim Beam barrels, while Maryland's Flying Dog Brewery ages its Wild Dog Barrel-Aged Gonzo Imperial Porter in Stranahan's Colorado Whiskey barrels. In Scotland, Harviestoun Brewery's rich, stout-like Ola Dubh Special Reserve offerings (aka black oil) are aged in retired Highland Park single-malt Scotch whisky oak casks 12, 16, or 30 years old.

The genesis of these bourbon- and whisky-barrel experiments can be traced to Chicago's Goose Island. In 1992, in order to commemorate the brewery's thousandth batch, former brewmaster Greg Hall decided to brew an imperial stout to knock everyone's socks off. The stout was poured into Jim Beam barrels and, 100 days later, Bourbon County Stout was born.

Goose Island's former brewmaster Greg Hall and his barrel-aged innovation.

"No one knew what to make of it," says Hall. He took his creation to the 1992 Great American Beer Festival, where it was disqualified for defying every category. But at the brewers-only tasting the night before the GABF opened, Hall's creation was validated. "We ran out before the festival even started," he says.

Since then, wood- and barrel-aged brews have become their own GABF categories (three, including beer, strong beer, and sour beer; *see more on that weirdo on page 45*), and Bourbon County Stout has grown into a phenomenon. Goose Island first bottled the brew in 2005, and began aging BCS in a blend of 12- to 16-year-old Heaven Hill and 21-year-old Pappy Van Winkle barrels. Now Goose Island has infused BCS with espresso, aged it with vanilla beans, and even given BCS a two-year nap in rare, 23-year-old Pappy Van Winkle bourbon barrels.

"There's no limit to what we can do with barrel aging," Hall says.

Beyond Bourbon

Though bourbon and whiskey may cast an aromatic spell, they're not brewers' sole wooden option. There's also a limited life span for barrels used to age pinot noir, chardonnay, brandy, and port (or even tequila; *see International Spotlight, page 113*). Each time a barrel is filled, less of the oaky, woodsy flavors leach out. An old barrel may no longer be useful

The barrel-aging program of Chicago's Goose Island.

to a winery, but a wine-soaked oak cask can add just the jolt that brewers are seeking.

Nebraska Brewing Co. uses a six-month sojourn in French oak chardonnay barrels to fashion two of its most winning reserve brews: the Belgian-inspired Mélange à Trois strong blonde and a special release of its Hop God IPA. The chardonnay maturation imparts a delicate fruitiness as well as luscious oak notes, softening the ales and providing wine-like characteristics. "I don't want the flavors to be separate," says head brewer Paul

Kavulak. "We're looking for flavors that intertwine and create a marriage."

Those flavors need not come from alcohol-soaked barrels. While Odell Brewing often ages stouts in old Buffalo Trace or Maker's Mark barrels (brewers travel to distilleries to hand-pick casks), the brewery took a different tack with the Woodcut Series. In 2007, the Fort Collins, Colorado, outfit purchased freshly constructed, lightly charred oak casks from Canton Cooperage in Kentucky.

The goal was to create delectable vanilla and subtle tannin characteristics without overwhelming the beer's natural flavors, explains brewer Joe Mohrfeld. So far, Odell has released only four Woodcuts (including a golden ale, a crimson ale, and a super-strong märzen lager), an average of about two a year—sometimes less. "We can never predict when the beer will be ready," Mohrfeld says. "Our marketing department doesn't like us, because they're like, 'We need to know when it'll be done!' But even we don't know. It's up to the wood and our brewers to determine when it is ready."

INTERNATIONAL SPOTLIGHT: MEXICO'S CUCAPÁ BREWING COMPANY

TEQUILA MAY HAVE MOVED BEYOND ITS LICK-SUCK-SWALLOW PAST, WITH WOODSY, LONG-AGED AÑEJOS AND BRIGHT, LIVELY BLANCOS ASSUMING TOP-SHELF PERCHES AT BETTER BARS, BUT MEXICAN BEER REMAINS A LIME-JUICED JOKE: AN ICY THIRST QUENCHER TO SLURP WHILE BROWNING ON A BEACH.

"IN MEXICO, 99.9 PERCENT OF THE BEER OFFERINGS ARE PALE LAGERS," EXPLAINS MARIO GARCÍA, CEO OF CUCAPÁ BREWING, WHICH IS LOCATED IN MEXICALI, MEXICO,

Meet Mario García, the CEO of Mexico's Cucapá Brewing.

NEAR THE U.S. BORDER. "CLEAR-BOTTLE BEER IS NOT CRAFT BEER. THAT'S
WHY THEY MAKE YOU SHOVE A LIME IN IT."

THIS WAS NOT ALWAYS THE CASE. MORE THAN A CENTURY EARLIER,
MEXICO WAS DOTTED WITH SMALL BREWERIES POURING ROBUST, FULL-
FLAVORED BEER. HOWEVER, A HUNDRED YEARS OF CONSOLIDATION LED TO TWO
CONGLOMERATES—GRUPO MODELO AND FEMSA—CONTROLLING MOST OF THE
COUNTRY'S BEER MARKET. COMPOUNDING MATTERS, THE COMPANIES OWN MOST
OF MEXICO'S ALCOHOL LICENSES. TO OBTAIN ONE, BAR OWNERS MUST AGREE
TO ONLY SELL MODELO OR FEMSA BEER. HENCE, TECATE, SOL, AND CORONA
REIGN SUPREME.

DaViD VS. GoliaTH

DESPITE CLEAR-BOTTLE BEER'S DOMINANCE, GARCÍA DECIDED
TO BATTLE THE BIG BOYS. IN 2002, CUCAPÁ (NAMED AFTER
A NEARBY MOUNTAIN RANGE AND AN INDIGENOUS INDIAN TRIBE)
OPENED AS A HUMBLE BREWPUB, THE FIRST OF ITS KIND IN A
QUARTER CENTURY. BY 2007, THE COMPANY DITCHED FOOD
AND MORPHED INTO A FULL-THROTTLE PRODUCTION BREWERY,
TURNING OUT THE KIND OF FLAVORFUL, FULL-BODIED BREWS
CURRYING FAVOR ACROSS THE BORDER.

CUCAPÁ'S LIQUID ROSTER COUNTS AMONG ITS OFFERINGS
OBSCURA, A DARK, NUTTY ALE WITH CHOCOLATY UNDERTONES;
REFRESHING CUCAPÁ HONEY, AN AMERICAN BLONDE ALE;
AND EVEN A BEEFY BARLEY WINE. IN OTHER WORDS, THESE
ARE NOT BEERS TO CHUG DURING SPRING BREAK IN CANCÚN.
BUT IN MEXICO, SWIMMING AGAINST THE MAINSTREAM
BEER CAN POSE SOME UNIQUE PROBLEMS. FOR EXAMPLE,
THE CHUPACABRAS PALE ALE PACKS A PLEASING SCENT OF
CITRUS, CUT WITH FLAVORS OF CARAMEL, FRESHLY TOASTED
BREAD, AND A BITTER JOLT—AROUND 45 IBUS, OR HALF AS
BITTER AS DOGFISH HEAD'S 90-MINUTE IPA. HOWEVER, FOR
MANY MEXICAN BEER DRINKERS, EVEN A TEENSY BIT OF
MOUTH-PUCKERING BITTERNESS IS AS WELCOME AS A CUPFUL
OF CURDLED MILK.

"WE HAD A COUPLE FESTIVALS THAT WE BROUGHT THIS
BEER TO, AND PEOPLE SAID, 'THIS BEER IS ROTTEN. IT'S
BITTER.' THEY ASSOCIATED BITTERNESS WITH THE BEER
BEING BAD," GARCÍA SAYS. "TRY EXPLAINING THAT TO A

COUPLE THOUSAND CONSUMERS AND YOU WON'T BE ABLE TO SPEAK THE NEXT DAY. THE CONSUMER FOR THAT CLEAR-BOTTLE BEER IS NOT EXACTLY A CRAFT-BEER CONSUMER. WE HAVE TO WORK HARD TO GET PEOPLE TO TRY OUR BEERS."

SINCE ITS BREWS HAVE LIMITED APPEAL TO MEXICAN DRINKERS (CUCAPÁ IS SOLD IN ONLY A DOZEN OR SO MEXICALI BARS, DUE TO BOTH LICENSING ISSUES AND DRINKERS' PALATES), CUCAPÁ TRIED CRACKING THE U.S. CRAFT-BEER MARKET. HERE, GARCÍA AND CO. RAN INTO THE SORT OF SKEPTICISM THEY WERE FIGHTING TO OVERCOME. "I'VE HAD SOME WEIRD LOOKS WHEN WE COME TO A DISTRIBUTOR AND OFFER THEM A CRAFT BEER," GARCÍA SAYS. "IT'S NOT UNTIL THEY TRY THEY BEER THAT THEY REALIZE THAT THERE'S GOOD BEER BEING MADE IN MEXICO. WE HAVE TO EDUCATE PEOPLE THAT WE'RE A TRULY INTERESTING, INVENTIVE MEXICAN CRAFT BREWERY."

CROSSING BORDERS

TO HAMMER THAT POINT HOME, GARCÍA HAS SLOWLY GIVEN CUCAPÁ A QUIRKY, BORDER-STRADDLING IDENTITY: ONE FOOT IN MEXICO, THE OTHER IN AMERICA. THE STRONG, SPICY LOWRIDER IS MEXICO'S FIRST BOTTLED RYE BEER. IMPERIAL STOUT LA MIGRA, NAMED AFTER THE IMMIGRATION POLICE, FEATURES A STERN-FACED BORDER AGENT ON ITS LABEL. GRASSY RUNAWAY IPA'S LABEL DEPICTS A SILHOUETTED FAMILY MAKING A BORDER BREAK. AND THAT BARLEY WINE? IT'S CALLED GREEN CARD. WHILE THIS CULTURAL KIDDING MAY PIQUE CURIOSITY, IT'S THE BEER'S UNIQUE MEXICAN QUALITIES THAT WILL CONVERT THE CRAFT-BEER CONSUMER. TO THAT END, GARCÍA IS CURRENTLY LOOKING TO SOURCE LOCAL INGREDIENTS (UP TO THIS POINT HE HAS HAD TO IMPORT ALMOST EVERYTHING SAVE FOR THE COLORADO RIVER WATER), SUCH AS MEXICAN WHEAT. BUT WHEN HE TRIED TO BUY OLD TEQUILA BARRELS IN WHICH TO AGE HIS BARLEY WINE, HE FOUND DISTILLERS WERE AS RELUCTANT TO PART WITH THEM AS A TODDLER WITH ITS FAVORITE BLANKET.

UNLIKE BOURBON BARRELS, WHICH ARE USED ONLY ONCE, GARCÍA DISCOVERED THAT DISTILLERS KEEP TEQUILA BARRELS UNTIL THEY DISINTEGRATE. "IT TOOK A WHOLE YEAR TO GET TEN BARRELS," GARCÍA SAYS, LAUGHING. BUT THE ENDEAVOR BORE FRUIT, RESULTING IN A BARLEY WINE REDOLENT OF CITRUS, MOLASSES, AND THE SWEET, LUSH AROMA OF TEQUILA. IT'S AN ENGLISH BEER BY WAY OF MEXICO, A CENTURIES-OLD STYLE GIVEN A NOVEL TWIST IN A NEW LAND.

"WE LOVE BEER, AND WE LOVE MAKING BEER," GARCÍA SAYS. "WE JUST HAPPEN TO BE IN MEXICO."

Into the Blend(er)

The thing about aging beer in barrels is that each barrel's contents are snowflake-unique. Some will age faster, others slower. Thus, brewers often blend batches to create a uniform flavor. Other times, brewers blend beer aging in different types of barrels—a few bourbon, perhaps, plus a half dozen brandy. The sum, they hypothesize, can be tastier than its parts. The trick is finding a delicious balance.

In 2005, Firestone's Brynildson embarked on an ambitious project in which he acted like an amateur winemaker. In honor of the brewery's tenth anniversary, he filled 80 bourbon, brandy, and fresh-oak barrels with barley wines, hyper-hoppy IPAs, and Russian imperial stouts. They aged for ten months in hopes of creating an ale that would be complex, beguiling, and as balanced as a ballerina. With local winemakers' input, ten components were "put together like a puzzle," Brynildson says, creating, well, 10.

"We broke the taboo that says you can't blend beers," the brewer says of his vanilla ice creamy libation, his first release in a continuing adventure. Building on the success of 10, which is part of the Quercus Alba series (the botanical name for white oak), Brynildson blends a new rendition each year (11, 12, 13, etc.), drawing from a rotating store of barrels in the brewery's cellar. Each release is unlike the last, producing a never-before-tasted beer. "It's amazing that the brewing industry has turned away from oak. It's their history," Brynildson says. "Now it's our future."

FIVE TO TRY

J SERIES LONG HAUL SESSION ALE
TWO BROTHERS BREWING COMPANY
ABV: 4.2%

ILLINOIS'S TWO BROTHERS OUTFITTED ITS BREWERY WITH AN ARRAY OF ROOM-DWARFING FRENCH OAK FOUDRES—BASICALLY, LARGE-SCALE BARRELS. THE FOUDRES IMPART A COMPLEX, WOODSY CHARACTER WITHOUT OVERWHELMING THE BEER AND SERVE AS THE BASIS OF THE BREWERS' NEW J SERIES. THE FIRST TWO RELEASES ARE RESISTANCE IPA AND LONG HAUL. IT'S A LIGHT, EASY-DRINKING ALE WITH SUCH A LOW ABV THAT YOU COULD GUZZLE A SIX-PACK WITHOUT GETTING BLITZKRIEGED, BUT IT HAS ENOUGH OAKY NOTES TO STAY INTERESTING.

HUMIDOR SERIES JAI ALAI IPA
CIGAR CITY BREWING
ABV: 7.5%

TAMPA, FLORIDA, IS HOME TO THIS SUPER BREWERY, WHICH TAKES INSPIRATION FROM THE TOWN'S CIGAR-ROLLING HISTORY FOR ITS HUMIDOR SERIES. THE BREWERY SPECIAL-ORDERS DOWELS OF CEDAR (THE WOOD USED FOR HUMIDORS), WHICH ARE THEN SOAKED IN ITS BREWS—MOST WINNINGLY, THE TROPICAL, RESINOUS JAI ALAI IPA—TO BESTOW SUBTLE, SPICY FLAVORS AND A DRY MOUTHFEEL. CIGAR CITY ALSO RUNS AN A-PLUS BARREL-AGING PROGRAM. IF YOU SEE A SPECIAL RELEASE, SNAG IT.

KENTUCKY BREAKFAST STOUT
FOUNDERS BREWING COMPANY
ABV: 11.2%

THIS MICHIGAN OUTFIT DESERVES BACK PATS FOR KBS, AN OUTRAGEOUS IMPERIAL STOUT CONSTRUCTED WITH ENOUGH CHOCOLATE AND COFFEE TO KEEP YOU AWAKE FOR WEEKS. AS IF THAT'S NOT ENOUGH, A HEAVY HOP BILL (HELLO, 70 IBUS) ADDS A BITTER STREAK THAT'S EVENED OUT BY A YEARLONG SIESTA IN OAK BOURBON BARRELS STORED IN A COOL CAVE. IT'S EXCESS PERSONIFIED. YOU'LL ASK FOR A REFILL.

NOTES OF VANILLA AND OAK, AUGMENTING, NOT OVERPOWERING, BEERS SUCH AS GOLDEN AND CRIMSON ALES, WHICH ARE SOLD IN WINE-SIZE BOTTLES. BY CONTRAST, THE SINGLE SERVE SERIES IS A WILDER AFFAIR, INCLUDING AMONG ITS OFFERINGS OAK-AGED GOLDEN AND BROWN ALES RUN THROUGH WITH WILD YEASTS, AND A BOURBON-BARREL STOUT. THEY'RE ALL WINNERS.

RASPBERRY TART/WISCONSIN BELGIAN RED
NEW GLARUS BREWING
ABV: 4%

I ENVY THE WISCONSINITES WHO DRINK DAN CAREY'S DIVINE NECTARS, SUCH AS SPOTTED COW FARMHOUSE ALE AND THE HEFEWEIZEN-PALE ALE MASH-UP CRACK'D WHEAT, BUT HIS OAKED FAB FRUIT DUO TAKE THE CAKE. RASPBERRY TART (WHICH IS SPONTANEOUSLY FERMENTED IN OAK) IS FRESH, CLEAN, AND FRUIT FORWARD, BUT WISCONSIN BELGIAN RED MAY BE A MASTERPIECE. WISCONSIN WHEAT AND MONTMORENCY CHERRIES ARE PARTNERED WITH AGED HALLERTAUER HOPS (TO LESSEN BITTERNESS), THEN LAGERED IN OAK. THE RESULT IS AN INTENSELY BUBBLY, CHAMPAGNE-LIKE ELIXIR WITH A SUPERB SWEET-TART EQUILIBRIUM.

WOODCUT AND SINGLE SERVE SERIES
ODELL BREWING COMPANY
ABV: VARIES

INSTEAD OF USING BOOZE-SEASONED OAK BARRELS FOR ITS WOODCUT SERIES, COLORADO'S ODELL OPTS FOR VIRGIN OAK CASKS WITH A LIGHT CHAR LICK. THEY PROVIDE MODERATE

Cask Ales

It's a breezy, blue-sky January afternoon in New Haven, Connecticut, and the mercury has sunk to eyeball-chilling low double digits. Despite the frigid weather, hundreds of revelers clad in wool caps and thick coats are swarming around the entrance to Brü Rm., the brewpub at BAR. These dedicated drinkers are waiting to sample dozens of beers that are anything but extreme: tepid, lightly fizzy, low-alcohol, cask-conditioned ales.

At 1 p.m., the doors to 2010's tenth annual Connecticut Real Ale Festival swing open and attendees stream into the expansive, high-ceilinged bar. Like kids at a candy shop, they grab sample glasses and flit from table to table, exchanging gray tickets for a pour of Victory Brewing Company's fresh, fragrant Hop Wallop or City Steam Brewery Café's strong, apple-scented Careless Love. Instead of throwing back beers, attendees swirl and sniff before taking dainty sips of the aromatic brews. If this seems more genteel than most rowdy, modern beer festivals, that's because cask ales are not modern, super-charged brews. "It's beer brewed as if it were the 1800s, not 2010," enthuses Jeff Browning, Brü Rm.'s brewmaster and festival founder.

Creating cask-conditioned (or real) ales is not complex. Add live yeasts and store any unpasteurized and unfiltered beer in a cask or firkin—a wood, plastic, or, more usually, stainless steel keg that holds 10.8 gallons—and it will develop a gentle, natural carbonation. (The same process applied to bottled beers is called bottle conditioning.) The beer is alive, developing and changing flavor every day, even after it has been tapped. Because firkins aren't pressurized, "beer engines" (usually hand pumps) or gravity must be employed to dispense the nectar, best savored at 55 degrees Fahrenheit, a temperature that accentuates its subtle aroma and nuanced flavor. Sample a draft of Green Flash Brewery's West Coast

IPA served chilly and highly effervescent alongside the same beer from a cask, and you'll find the cask ale's flavors mellower, with the astringent bitterness made smoother. "This is what real beer tastes like," Browning says.

While the tepid temperature is tough for some American drinkers to appreciate, cask ales have been making headway in the United States, slowly transforming over the past two decades from a cultish British import to an American craft mainstay. These days, microbreweries such as California's Lagunitas Brewing Co., Baltimore's Clipper City, Bell's Brewery in Kalamazoo, and Portland, Maine's Peak Organic have bought their own firkins in order to regularly offer cask varieties of their draft line. More taprooms are adding beer engines, buying their own firkins, and sourcing cask ale directly from breweries. And cask festivals have sprouted up from Patchogue, Long Island, to Westland, Michigan, to San Francisco, celebrating the pleasures of warm, lightly effervescent ales.

Hello, Old Friend

While America's embrace of real ale might seem novel, in many respects it's a return and an appreciation of the country's brewing past. At the turn of the twentieth century in America, "beer was cask ale by default. There was little refrigeration, and everything was served in wooden casks," says Brooklyn, New York's Alex Hall, an English expat, who, since relocating from Brighton to the United States in 1999, has become a leading real ale proselytizer. "But then along came Prohibition," Hall adds, causing the death of breweries—and cask ale before it could assume that moniker.

When beer making in America legally resumed, brewers moved away from real ale. It's a finicky product—hot or cold snaps ruin yeast, firkins are prone to leaking, and it has a short shelf life (five weeks unopened, three or four days once tapped)—so breweries changed their technique. They filtered and pasteurized the beer to halt the brewing process. This kept the flavor from changing and gave the beer a longer, more stable shelf life. But without yeast, beer won't develop carbonation, so breweries force-carbonated it with carbon dioxide. This new process permitted mass production and ensured uniform quality. Like a Big Mac, a Coors could taste the same from Colorado to North Carolina.

Across the Atlantic, the writing was on the bar in England. Breweries also began phasing out naturally carbonated milds and bitters in favor of gassier, pasteurized beer that, by comparison, was cold and flavorless. Displeased drinkers formed the grassroots organization Campaign for Real Ale (CAMRA) in 1971. The group agitated brewers to keep traditional English ale alive via aggressive lobbying and vocal boycotts of force-fizzed beer. Today, cask remains integral to British pub culture, and CAMRA (whose members now number more than 100,000) continues to champion its liquid cause. "They're the reason real ale still exists," Hall insists.

Feeling Festive

Around the time cask ale received a stay of execution in England, American drinkers were barely rustling from their macro-beer slumber. Enlightening consumers about cask ales first required hipping them to microbrews. "In this country, it's hard enough to build consciousness for craft beer, much less cask," says Steve Hamburg, who helped found the Chicago Real Ale Festival—America's first cask fest—in 1996. (Sadly, the festival is now kaput.)

"We thought, If you've been to a British pub and enjoyed the beers, wouldn't it be cool to enjoy the same beers in this country?" says Hamburg, whose dedication to cask ales was forged when he apprenticed as a London brewery's cellarman (the employee who taps and tends to casks) in the early 1990s. To prep for the fests, Hamburg imported serving equipment and cask-conditioned beer from Britain, and he had to jerry-rig standard kegs with hand pumps.

"Dispensing," Hamburg says, "was definitely an issue." Selling the event was simple. "It was easier to come here than it was to go to Britain," Hamburg says, laughing.

Early on, festivals were key to educating beer drinkers and creating demand for cask ales both British and, increasingly, American. In 1995, former *Beer Philadelphia* publisher Jim Anderson launched Philadelphia's Real Ale Rendezvous. (That year, Philadelphia's Dawson Street Pub purchased a beer engine and began serving local brewery Yards' Extra Special Ale on cask.)

Two years later, the volunteer-run Cask-Conditioned Ale Support Campaign launched the New England Real Ale Exhibition (NERAX), held every spring in Somerville, Massachusetts. In 1998, California's Pizza Port launched the San Diego Real Ale Festival, while that year also saw the first Friday the Firkinteenth at Philadelphia's Grey Lodge Pub. Building on the success of the Real Ale Rendezvous, Mike "Scoats" Scotese, Grey Lodge's "lodge master," concocted the event (it occurs every Friday the thirteenth) to attract attention to cask ales. "Because there's a learning curve to get people used to beer that's naturally carbonated, having a big event with a kitschy name helps," says Scotese. The Lodge served about seventeen gallons of cask during the first event. Now, Scotese says, "we do a good week's worth of business in one night"—about 240 gallons, or nearly sixteen standard kegs. Firkin fests have now spread nationwide. St. Paul, Minnesota's Happy Gnome hosts an annual spring bash, while Magnolia Gastropub & Brewery puts on a cask fest during San Francisco Beer Week. Ashley's Beer and Grill held the inaugural Michigan Cask Ale Festival in Westland in November 2009.

However, cask's most tireless cheerleader is undoubtedly Hall. As an agent for UK Brewing Supplies, which sells cask equipment, he installs and maintains beer engines at bars in New York. He also pens a cask column for *Ale Street News*. But most of his free time is spent curating real ale festivals both international (England's Glastonwick, launched in 1996 and now featuring nearly 70 casks) and stateside. Three times a year, Hall runs the Cask Head Cake Ale Festival at Brooklyn's Brazen Head, offering several dozen painstakingly sourced real ales. Hall acquires them by mailing empty firkins (from his personal stock of 54) to breweries nationwide that do not typically offer real ale. He also acquires imported British casks fresh off the boat.

Hall insists on serving fresh, rare casks because he sees each firkin as an opportunity to convert another drinker to the gently carbonated realm of real ale. "The point of a cask ale festival is to raise consciousness that cask can be wonderful," Hall says. "I want to create demand."

Earning a Place at the Pub

Festivals are definitely working, as cask ales are finding a place at the bar. Anchorage, Alaska's Midnight Sun Brewing Company trots out a firkin the first Friday of the month. Atlanta-based SweetWater Brewing hosts Brew Your Cask Off, in which more than 70 guest brewers create their own unique real ales. Events like these may be gimmicky, Chicago Real Ale Festival co-organizer Steve Hamburg says, "but they're instrumental in expanding the horizon of beer drinkers."

Cask ale is no novelty for an increasing number of breweries and bars. San Francisco's Toronado augments its hopped-up California ales with a quartet of rotating cask ales, and Portland, Oregon's venerable Horse Brass Pub pours a trio of real ales.

For Ted Sobel, a midlife crisis caused him to turn to cask ale. Nearing three decades as a software engineer, the Oakridge, Oregon, resident was burned out. He quit and traveled to England, where he visited the Lake District's Woolpack Inn, home of the adjoined Hardknott Brewery. There he sampled Hardknott's warm, flavorful bitters and took a brewery tour. In the fermentation tanks and firkins, Sobel, an avid homebrewer since he was 21, saw his future: to run Oregon's first pub brewing only cask ale.

Sobel first fell in love with real ale in 1991, when he and his wife spent a month hitchhiking around the United Kingdom. "I became hopelessly addicted to pubs and real ale right from the start," Sobel says. "In my mind, it's not only the flavors and mouthfeel that are expressed by a well-kept pint, but the environment in which it is consumed that makes it what it is."

To re-create the British pub experience, in August 2008 Sobel opened Brewers Union Local 180 in a renovated dive bar. The tavern's dark karaoke and poker den became the brewery, where Sobel crafts his smooth Wotcha bitter, Black Wooly Jumper dry Irish stout, and other English-style ales poured by the proper ten-ounce glass or twenty-ounce imperial pint. Upon opening, Sobel hedged his bets. Unsure how the outdoorsy town favored by mountain bikers would cotton to cask, he stocked a half dozen traditional drafts and ciders on tap. A year and a half into his experiment, "I sell two to five times as much cask as regular draft," he says. "People love the gentle carbonation, the full flavors, and the lack of gas." Chalk it up to creating a market—if you serve it, they will come. Making cask an everyday indulgence was certainly Greg Engert's goal when he devised the beer list for Washington, D.C.'s ChurchKey, settling on 500 bottled brews, 50 drafts, and five cask ales. Outside of a festival,

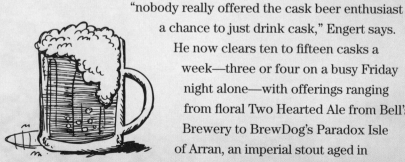 "nobody really offered the cask beer enthusiast a chance to just drink cask," Engert says. He now clears ten to fifteen casks a week—three or four on a busy Friday night alone—with offerings ranging from floral Two Hearted Ale from Bell's Brewery to BrewDog's Paradox Isle of Arran, an imperial stout aged in

wooden Scotch barrels. "We've been flying through the casks much quicker than I anticipated," Engert says.

But feeding demand poses several quandaries unique to cask ales: Modern mechanized draft and bottling lines aren't set up to fill firkins, which must be manually cleaned, filled, and primed with yeast. The extra effort means a 10.8-gallon cask can be as expensive as a 15.5-gallon keg. "It's a labor of love," says JT Thompson, the former cellarman and current media coordinator for Smuttynose Brewing Co. in Portsmouth, New Hampshire.

Greg Engert is the resident cask ale and craft-beer expert at Washington, D.C.'s ChurchKey.

Adding to the complexity, many microbreweries have not purchased their own vessels. At the New Haven festival, Thompson was pouring samples of nutty Old Brown Dog Ale from the *sole* firkin that Smuttynose owns. "Firkins have a habit of disappearing pretty easily," he says. That one vanished for more than a year before resurfacing, so the brewery instead fills empty casks loaned by distributors (such as New York's Union Beer, which purchased a stock of firkins) or by barkeeps like Engert.

To ensure a steady supply, the ChurchKey bought about forty

empty firkins—which cost roughly $150 to $200 each—that Engert pays to ship to breweries for filling. (The firkins are returned via normal distribution channels.) Still, this painstaking effort can pay delicious dividends: For instance, Avery Brewing fills Engert's firkins with its IPA, then adds to each batch a different variety of hops to alter the flavor. "Every firkin you get is a beer unto itself. It's a one-off," Engert says. "Serving casks is not profit driven. I'm reviving a tradition that's gone by the wayside."

Cleanliness Equals Quality

While it's encouraging to see real ale join beer lists, bars must go beyond simply installing a beer engine and tapping a firkin; they have an obligation to handle the rather finicky beer with care. "I'm always hesitant to order a cask ale," says Chicago's Hamburg, "because it demands more on the serving side. How long has it been sitting around? How has it been handled? Does the barkeep have any cellaring knowledge?"

In order to extend a cask's life span from three or four days to nine or ten, many bars use "cask breathers." It's a system for covering the beer with a blanket of carbon dioxide that, at low levels, does not impact flavor or add carbonation, but does inhibit oxidation and spoilage. While CAMRA shuns this practice, it's essential for many bars' bottom lines. "Bars that can't get through a cask in three days—that is, most of them—absolutely need a cask breather," Alex Hall says. "All it takes is one bad pint to turn off drinkers from trying cask again."

Cask ale's quality and flavor are also impacted by cleanliness. Because cask ales are served at a higher temperature, a beer engine's lines are much more prone to bacterial growth than those of its chilly kegged counterpart. When ChurchKey's barkeeps swap out a cask, they thoroughly clean the beer lines, too—even if it means interrupting service. However, this rigorous commitment to cleanliness is hardly industry standard. Education often lags behind enthusiasm.

These are lessons that will come in time. Like craft beer in the late 1990s, cask ale will undergo growing pains. But the good pints will eventually outweigh the bad. Britain has had hundreds of years to perfect—and protect—its cask ale tradition; America has had less than two decades. Soon, what is today a novelty can become a tradition. "Cask ale is a traditional beer," Hall says, "and tradition is never a novelty."

ON CASK: TIPS FOR SUSSING OUT A PROPER PINT

ASK WHEN A CASK WAS TAPPED. IF IT'S BEEN LONGER THAN THREE DAYS (AND A BAR DOES NOT USE A CASK BREATHER), THEN IT'S NOT WORTH DRINKING. THE BEER WILL BE AS DULL AS MY SEVENTH-GRADE SCIENCE TEACHER, AND IT MAY TASTE OF SULFUR OR VINEGAR. THAT'S A TELLTALE SIGN OF DYING YEAST.

REQUEST A SAMPLE. CASK ALE'S FLAVOR IS CONSTANTLY EVOLVING, AND IT CHANGES LICKETY-SPLIT AFTER A FIRKIN HAS BEEN TAPPED. THE BEER YOU LOVED LAST MONTH MAY BE A DIFFERENT BEVERAGE TODAY.

BEWARE BUYING BRITISH CASK ALE COME SUMMER. THE HEAT, COMBINED WITH THE WEEKS-LONG SHIPPING TIME, CAN SEVERELY SHORTEN A BEER'S LIFE SPAN AND WREAK HAVOC WITH FLAVOR.

UNFILTERED, YES; CLOUDY, NO. ALTHOUGH CASK ALE IS UNFILTERED, IT SHOULDN'T BE AS CLOUDY AS A ROTTEN FISH'S EYE. IDEALLY, A FIRKIN SHOULD BE ALLOWED TO SIT UNDISTURBED FOR AT LEAST 24 HOURS BEFORE IT'S TAPPED, LETTING FININGS (WHICH CLARIFY BEER) SINK TO THE BOTTOM.

PATRONIZE A BREWERY OR BREWPUB THAT PREPS ITS OWN FIRKINS. THE BREWERS HAVE COMPLETE CONTROL OVER HOW THE BEER IS CONDITIONED AND SERVED. YOU'LL GET THE BEST FLAVOR.

NO SPARKLER, PLEASE. SOME PUBS POUR CASK ALE THROUGH A SPARKLER—A NOZZLE WITH SMALL HOLES—WHICH AERATES THE BEER AND CREATES A THICK HEAD. SOME PURISTS COMPLAIN THAT SPARKLERS DULL REAL ALE'S FLAVORS AND AROMAS; MORE IMPORTANT, THE EQUIPMENT CAN

MASK THE FACT THAT THE BEER IS FORCE-CARBONATED OR DISPENSED VIA CARBON DIOXIDE. THOUGH YOU MAY SEEM LIKE A FUSSBUDGET, ASK THE BARTENDER TO REMOVE THE SPARKLER BEFORE POURING.

ASK IF THE BAR IS REALLY SERVING CASK. IT SOUNDS PERSNICKETY, BUT IMPOSTER BEER ENGINES CAN BE SET UP TO DISPENSE STANDARD KEGGED BEER VIA A HAND PUMP. ALSO, OCCASIONALLY, BREWERIES WILL LEAVE THEIR BEERS UNFILTERED WHEN FILLING KEGS, THUS CREATING "KEG-CONDITIONED" BEER THAT'S PUSHED OUT WITH CARBON DIOXIDE. THOUGH DOWNRIGHT TASTY, THIS IS NOT CASK ALE.

SPIC-AND-SPAN BEER LINES ARE CRUCIAL TO CASK ALE'S NUANCED FLAVOR. IDEALLY, A BAR SHOULD TIDY UP ITS BEER LINES AT LEAST TWICE A MONTH—AND EVERY TIME A CASK IS SWAPPED OUT FOR A NEW FIRKIN. WHEN IT COMES TO CASK ALE, CLEANLINESS IS NEXT TO DELICIOUSNESS.

FOUR

BACK TO THE LAND:

Breweries Are Harvesting a Whole New Crop of
Eco-Conscious Beer

FOR A MOMENT, PONDER THE OUT-OF-SEASON
supermarket tomato: pale and as flavorful as a balloon, this tomato
is no more natural than a stick of chewing gum. But a summertime
heirloom tomato, organically grown and as juicy
as a watermelon, is sublime. Provenance plus
careful production equals unparalleled flavor.

That's a lesson that craft brewers are taking
to heart. Driven to create beers as pure as they
are flavorful, eco-minded breweries have started
sourcing organic grains and hops. Taking that
concept to the next level, other breweries have
started acting like farmers, growing their own
barley and hops. The result is beers with singular
flavors that speak of the soil from which they've
risen. Winemakers may call this *terroir*. I call it
terrific beer.

Going Green Has Never Tasted So Good

In food circles, hormones, pesticides, and genetically modified crops have become as feared as the boogeyman, linked to a litany of diseases that, if I were to list them, might harsh your beer buzz.

In response, supermarkets and restaurants have been awash in grub touting words like *all natural*, *organic*, and *green*, adjectives that seem odd when applied to beer. "Foods like organic yogurt and granola are meant to be healthy, but beer is a guilty pleasure," says Mike Cadoux, a representative for Portland, Maine's Peak Organic, where his brother Jon is brewmaster. "How is organic beer supposed to be good for you?"

Previously, if you wanted a green beer, you waited until St. Patrick's Day, when bartenders doctored Guinness with a drop or two of food coloring. But the organic revolution has finally reached the six-pack. From Portland, Oregon's Laurelwood to Vermont's

Wolaver's and Bison Brewing in Berkeley, California, a budding crop of all-natural brewers are paying more than just lip service to sustainability. But be aware that this is not a new movement. Instead, it's a return to the pre-preservative era, in which every beer was natural.

Back in Time

A century ago, beer was organic by default. Those were simpler times, when Monsanto was a meaningless word, not a multinational biotechnology firm preaching the pesticide gospel. Over time, brewing's raw ingredients—malt, hops—became as chemical laced as waxy, mealy apples. The thing is, "brewers of quality beer don't need to use chemicals," says Steve Parkes, owner of the American Brewers Guild and former head brewer at Wolaver's Organic Ales, a Vermont brewery that's helped define all-natural beer since 1997. There's nothing eco-radical about how Wolaver's crafts its toothsome oatmeal stouts and smooth, tongue-tingling IPAs. The difference lies in the pedigree of the hops and wheat. To be organic, 95 percent of a beer's ingredients must be stamped organic by the U.S. Department of Agriculture (signaling they were grown without the use of pesticides, herbicides, or fungicides), and the brewing process must also pass USDA muster, meaning brewers cannot use synthetic ingredients such as silicone based antifoam agents. The results are unadulterated brews that "show beer drinkers that you don't have to sacrifice flavor to save the planet," Parkes says.

Ah, yes: somewhere along the line, consumers lumped organic beers into the same flavorless category as bean sprouts and rice cakes. But organic ales are hardly as bland as tap water. "We wouldn't even brew an organic beer if it wasn't any good," says Mike De Kalb, owner of Laurelwood Brewing Co. In 2002, Laurelwood became one of Oregon's first breweries to sell certified organic beer, brews like the roasty, chocolaty Tree

The tap lineup at Portland, Oregon's organic-focused Laurelwood Brewing.

Hugger Porter and coppery, hoppy Free Range Red. For De Kalb,
the decision to go organic was based on a belief "in the cycle.
We get the organic grains from the farmer, and we give back the
mash to the farm for feed. It's better for the environment—and
for our customers."

Hop Loophole

Becoming an organic brewery isn't as simple as ordering a big ol'
bag of pesticide-free barley. While organic brewers may aim for
100 percent natural ingredients, a USDA loophole allows up to 5
percent certain nonorganic ingredients to be used when there's no
feasible organic substitute. Malts are not on the list, so breweries
stay committed to buying organic malts, ensuring that thousands of
acres of grains are grown pesticide-free. For brewers, the exception

is mainly used for hops, which are on the list and are so light as to fit within the 5 percent threshold.

For hop farmers, chemical applications are commonplace. The delicate plants sprout from stubs to twisting bines in two weeks, offering insects a tender, irresistible feast. Moreover, hops are also susceptible to fungi and mildew, which makes it tough to grow them pesticide-free in the cool, wet Pacific Northwest. Few American-grown organic hops are available, and the majority of organic hops hail from New Zealand, where hop-hungry pests have yet to reach. But "why should we have to look to New Zealand for hops?" says Cadoux, whose brewery is working with farmers in Washington State to grow domestic organic hops.

In addition to the problem of finding sufficient inventory of organically grown hops, there is also the issue of flavor. "The first couple batches of Chinook hops I tasted weren't equal to the nonorganic version," says Daniel Del Grande, owner and brewmaster of Berkeley, California's Bison Brewing. He held high hopes for organic Mount Hood and Willamette hops, but "they weren't all that flavorful. They were more muted."

Restrict yourself to only organic hops, and it's a bit like running a restaurant with half a spice cabinet. On the other hand, Del Grande says, "that makes me unique. While brewers started adopting Amarillo"—seriously citric, bordering on orange—"I've never brewed with it. My beers taste different from anyone else's on the market."

The different flavor of organic hops may soon be a moot point: In October 2010, the National Organic Standards Board voted to remove hops from the exemption list as of January 1, 2013, meaning that brewers will no longer be able to use nonorganic hops and continue to label their beer as organic.

What's the source?

One of the ways in which organic brewers are setting themselves apart is by focusing on unorthodox flavors. In Santa Cruz, California, Uncommon Brewers operates under the California Certified Organic Farmers' stringent guidelines, which state that every ingredient must be 100 percent organic. Uncommon brews off-kilter elixirs such as Golden State Ale, which is made with toasted poppy seeds, and Siamese Twin Ale, a Belgian-influenced beer with a Thai twist, thanks to the addition of organic Kaffir lime leaves and lemongrass. "We're not making spiced beer; we're making beer with spices," explains Uncommon cofounder Alec Stefansky.

However, relying on kooky organic ingredients can sometimes backfire. In 2010, Uncommon's Kaffir stock ran low because the suppliers' harvest was quarantined due to an insect infestation. Also, when he first brewed his Bacon Brown Ale, which is made with cured pork, he was unable to use the organic label. "Even though it's technically organic, the farm we want to work with isn't certified organic," Stefansky says. "I can't make the full organic claim." Bison hit a similar snag with its Honey Basil Ale. The herbs were easily sourced from a farm south of Berkeley; however, the honey must be imported from Brazil, due to stringent USDA regulations that require organic honey to be harvested from bees that feast only on organic flowers.

Even if supply problems are solved, brewers still need customers to purchase their organic suds, a product not considered "macho," Cadoux says. In America, he adds, "You still sell beer through T&A. As a company, this is an ongoing challenge." Plus, there's the question of consumer knowledge. While Bison may work in eco-friendly California, "when I talk about organics in South Carolina, I get these blank stares, like, What are you talking about?" Del Grande says. Then there's cost. Since organic malts run two to three times the cost of conventionally farmed grains, and hops double, brewers' margins are pin thin.

"I have to charge more for the beer," Del Grande says. "In California, it's $9.99 a six-pack, and that's as low as I can go. I have to hope that consumers understand that an organic product costs more."

Toast to the Future

High costs. Crop availability. Thin margins. These sound like insurmountable hurdles for organic beer. However, eco-friendly brews are hardly circling the drain. In 2009, organic beer sales reached $41 million, more than doubling 2005's $19 million, according to the Organic Trade Association.

Increased sales have led to a domino effect on the growers' end, with more acreage of organic American hops being planted at farms such as Oregon's vaunted Goschie Farms and Oregon Hophouse. (Owner Pat Leavy's smiling face can be found on a bottle of Wolaver's Pat Leavy's All-American Ale.) The increased bounty means brewers like Bison's Del Grande can finally release double IPAs, a hop-intensive style that he could never brew due to availability and cost. Even more telling, organic beer's marquee event, Portland, Oregon's annual North American Organic Beer Festival, has grown from, in De Kalb's words, "a couple of breweries gathered around a parking lot" to a celebration attracting upward of 20,000 attendees and dozens of breweries.

More than ever, Mother Earth is not the only reason to crack an organic beer. "You might get a customer the first time with the organic seal, but they're not going to come back a second time unless the beer is good," Cadoux says. "We're making delicious beer that just happens to be organic."

NINE TO TRY

ORGANIC FARMER SERIES
WOLAVER'S ORGANIC BREWING
ABV: VARIES

THE VERMONT BREWERY'S ORGANIC FARMER SERIES IS A LIQUID COMMITMENT TO LOCALLY SOURCED PRODUCE. FOR INSTANCE, SUMMER'S GOLDEN, ORANGE PEEL-SPICED BEN GLEASON'S WHITE ALE, CONTAINS ORGANIC WHEAT, ROLLED OATS, AND BARLEY FROM GLEASON'S FARM, LOCATED ABOUT TEN MILES FROM THE BREWERY. FIFTEEN MILES AWAY, IN SHOREHAM, THE GOLDEN RUSSET FARM'S PUMPKINS HELP CREATE WILL STEVENS PUMPKIN ALE. THIS BALANCED FALL SEASONAL OFFERS FLAVORS OF NUTMEG, CINNAMON, AND BROWN SUGAR.

ESPRESSO AMBER ALE
PEAK ORGANIC BREWING COMPANY
ABV: 7%

WHILE THE AVERAGE BREWER INCORPORATES GROUND COFFEE— EITHER STEEPED OR ADDED DURING BREWING—INTO STOUTS AND PORTERS, PORTLAND, MAINE'S PEAK OPTS FOR A ROBUST, FAINTLY FRUITY ALE INFUSED WITH FAIR TRADE-CERTIFIED SOUTH AMERICAN JAVA. THE RESULT IS A TAWNY TREAT BURSTING WITH ESPRESSO BITTERNESS THAT'S BALANCED BY A SWEET MALT BACKBONE. BLAME ME IF ESPRESSO BECOMES YOUR NEW MORNING BEVERAGE.

FREE RANGE RED
LAURELWOOD PUBLIC HOUSE & BREWERY
ABV: 5.9%

TOO OFTEN, AMBER ALES RUB ME WRONG; ALL THAT OVERBEARING MALT SWEETNESS IS A BIG OL' ICK. BUT PORTLAND, OREGON'S LAURELWOOD MADE ME AN AMBER BELIEVER WITH FREE RANGE, A COPPER-HUED BEAUTY OF THE FIRST ORDER. BREWED WITH A BOATLOAD OF CASCADE HOPS, RED SMELLS OF JUICY CITRUS, WITH TOASTED BREAD LURKING IN THE BACKGROUND. FLAVOR FOLLOWS AROMA, AND THE MEDIUM BODY MEANS AN EASY DRINKER AS SMOOTH AS A MONDAY-MORNING SHAVE.

CHOCOLATE STOUT
BISON BREWING COMPANY
ABV: 6.1%

THOUGH SOME STOUTS ARE THICK ENOUGH TO SLICE WITH A KNIFE, THIS OFFERING FROM BERKELEY, CALIFORNIA'S BISON IS LIGHT AND NIMBLE. IT'S NOT A DEFECT. CHOCOLATE POURS ASPHALT BLACK, AND ITS BOUQUET IS A MIXTURE OF COFFEE, ROASTED GRAINS, AND FUDGE; THAT'S DUE TO A DOSE OF COCOA. THANKFULLY, THE STOUT IS MORE BITTERSWEET THAN SICKLY

SWEET, WITH SOME ASSERTIVE BITTERNESS SEALING THE DEAL.

HOPWORKS IPA
HOPWORKS URBAN BREWERY
ABV: 6.6%

TO CONVERT AN ORGANIC SKEPTIC TO ALL-NATURAL BEER, STEER THE CYNIC TO THIS PORTLAND, OREGON, BREWPUB. FROM THE ESPRESSO-KISSED SURVIVAL "SEVEN-GRAIN" STOUT TO THE SMOOTH, FLORAL CROSSTOWN

PALE ALE, HUB'S ALL-ORGANIC BREWS ARE SO GOOD IT'S HARD TO SINGLE ONE OUT. HOWEVER, I ADORE THE NAMESAKE IPA. THE GOLDEN ALE IS REDOLENT OF CITRUS AND PINE SAP, CAUSING PALATES TO COME CLOSE TO BITTER, RESINOUS OVERLOAD.

SOLSTICE
PISGAH BREWING COMPANY
ABV: 9.5%

NORTH CAROLINA'S PISGAH CONCOCTS SOME OF AMERICA'S BEST ORGANIC BEERS, FROM THE BELGIAN YEAST-BALTIC PORTER HYBRID COSMOS TO HELLBENDER BARLEYWINE, MADE WITH CENTENNIAL HOPS AND BROWN SUGAR. STILL, I'M A BIG FAN OF THE BUBBLY GOLD SOLSTICE TRIPEL, WHICH HAS A SPICY, YEASTY SCENT WITH HINTS OF FRUIT. WHEN SIPPING, YOU'LL NOTICE APPLES, PEARS, LEMONS, AND A SUBTLE HOP BITE.

ORGANICALLY PRODUCED LAGER BEER
SAMUEL SMITH OLD BREWERY
ABV: 5%

THIS ICONIC ENGLISH BREWERY IS KNOWN FOR ITS NUT BROWN ALE AND OATMEAL STOUT, BUT IT ALSO PRODUCES QUALITY ORGANIC BEER. FRUIT LOVERS SHOULD LOOK TOWARD THE FINE CHERRY-, RASPBERRY-, OR STRAWBERRY-INFUSED BREWS. ME? I LIKE THE OLD-FASHIONED LAGER. THE CLEAR, GOLD BEER SMELLS OF EARTH, GRAIN, AND HOPS, WHILE IT SLIDES DOWN TART, SLIGHTLY MALTY SWEET, AND AS BRISK AS SELTZER. MORE, PLEASE.

TRIPLE EXULTATION
EEL RIVER BREWING COMPANY
ABV: 9.7%

AS AMERICA'S FIRST CERTIFIED ORGANIC BREWERY, CALIFORNIA'S EEL RIVER CONCOCTS PALATE PLEASERS LIKE THE ENGLISH-STYLE IPA AND INTENSE RAVEN'S EYE IMPERIAL STOUT. THESE ARE GREAT BEERS, BUT I RECOMMEND TRIPLE EXULTATION. TYPICALLY, THIS RICH, SWEET, BRITISH-STYLE BEER GOES EASY ON THE HOPS. HOWEVER, EEL RAN WILD WITH 'EM, CREATING A FULL-BODIED POTABLE DRESSED UP IN DARK FRUITS, VANILLA, AND BITTERNESS. TRIPLE'S BOOZY WARMTH WILL KEEP YOU TOASTY COME WINTER.

SIAMESE TWIN
UNCOMMON BREWERS
ABV: 8.5%

NEXT TIME YOU ORDER AN INCENDIARY THAI CURRY, PAIR IT WITH THIS SANTA CRUZ, CALIFORNIA, OUTFIT'S TIPPLE. THE BELGIAN DUBBEL (A RICH AND MALTY ALE) IS DOCTORED WITH THAI CUISINE'S TRADEMARK FLAVORS (LEMONGRASS AND KAFFIR LIME LEAVES), WHICH PROVIDE A FLORAL HERBACEOUSNESS THAT'S SUITED FOR THE BREADY MALT PROFILE. TASTE-WISE, SIAMESE HAS A TOUCH OF CARAMEL SWEETNESS, BUT THERE'S A ZESTY LIME KICK TO KEEP TWIN GROUNDED—AND DOUSE FIVE-ALARM FIRES IN YOUR MOUTH.

Tiny Terroir

For brewers, 2007 was a terrible year. Hops, the aromatic flowers that flavor beer, were as scarce as a subway seat during rush hour. The shortage was caused by a perfect storm of misfortune. The previous year, a fire incinerated a Yakima, Washington, hops warehouse, while drought, disease, and floods decimated crops from America to Europe.

Nationwide, brewers were forced to pay double, quadruple, or even ten times the typical price for the scattered remaining hops, or rein in the amount used in each batch. That meant fewer IPAs as bitter and sticky as fresh-sliced grapefruit. "That would've broken our hearts," says Brett Joyce, the president of Rogue Ales in Newport,

Harvesting hops at the Rogue Farms Micro Hopyard in Independence, Oregon.

Oregon. "It was our desire to never have to tell our head brewer to cut back his hop usage." Since the hops cupboard was bare, the brewery decided to eliminate the middleman and grow its own.

"The project was born out of necessity," Joyce explains of the brewery's partnership with venerable hop growers Coleman Farms. They created Independence, Oregon's Rogue Farms Micro Hopyard, the proud producers of seven varieties of hops: Freedom, Revolution, Independent, Liberty, Alluvial, Newport, and Rebel. The first brew born of this partnership was the grassy, piney, incredibly fresh-tasting Independence Hop Ale, released in 2008. You might say those flavors were Independence expressing its terroir.

While the concept of terroir—the unique characteristics that soil and climate give agricultural products—is typically reserved for coffee, tea, and wine, in recent years, brewers have begun laying claim to the term. They're planting barley fields, inoculating beers with native yeasts, and using hops that, more often than not, were grown specifically for—or by—the brewery. The result is singular beers that, pint for pint, are as idiosyncratic and region specific as the finest Sonoma County cabernet.

"People get confused and think that beer is an industrial product," say Bill Manley, the communications director for Sierra Nevada Brewing Company. "Beer is just as much an agricultural product as wine."

Land Rush

Long before the hops shortage, when the phrase *quality American beer* was pretty much an oxymoron, there was Chico, California's Sierra Nevada. Since 1980, Ken Grossman has been a brewing pioneer, releasing bitter pale ales in a lager-dominated land.

Sierra Nevada became one of the first breweries to experiment with planting its own hops. The farming experiment was spurred by Grossman's long drives across the California countryside. He noticed towns with names like Hopland, a reminder of the region's prominence as a hotbed of hop growing. "The thought was, 'People used to grow hops here. Why can't we?'" Manley says.

In 1996, the brewery began planting test batches of hops. There were plenty of missteps. "We planted some English-style hops, but those didn't take too well," Manley says. "It's really hot in Chico. It gets to 112 degrees in the summertime, which is not the climate of the English countryside." By 2003, Sierra was ready to plant an experimental hop yard in a field beside the brewery. They focused on hop varieties that could thrive in the northern California climate, such as Centennial, Cascade, and Chinook. Five years later (hop bines typically take around three years to mature), Sierra Nevada

Plucking hops at Sierra Nevada's California farm.

was ready to release its Chico Estate Harvest wet-hop ale, a beer emphasizing the fresh, green flavors of their homegrown yield. "Agriculturally, you get a lot more in touch with beer," Manley enthuses. "This is what the craft-beer movement is all about."

Hops-wise, the concept is catching on countrywide. Once upon a time, Virginia was one of the country's largest producers of hops. Afton's Blue Mountain Brewery has helped resuscitate this tradition by cultivating more than 200 hop bines at its adjoining farm. Left Hand Brewing Co. in Longmont, Colorado, has also tried its, well, hand at growing hops, with some of the annual yield going into releases such as the Warrior IPA. It's a fresh-hop beer made with 100 percent Colorado-grown hops.

While not every brewery can afford to plant production hop fields, other breweries are taking the next best step and working with local farmers. In Black Mountain, North Carolina, the all-organic Pisgah Brewing Company has contracted with a nearby farmer to grow hops for the brewery. "I hope that, for a month and a half every fall, we'll be able get fresh hops every Friday and brew a different batch of beer with them," says Pisgah cofounder and head brewer David Quinn. Beyond hops, Quinn also crafts the Pisgah Pub Ale, an English-style ale made with locally harvested Haw Creek wildflower honey. "Whenever possible, we try to brew with local ingredients," Quinn says.

All on Your Own

Tossing homegrown hops and local-pedigree honey into the brew kettle is terrific, but that alone does not create terroir for beer. To rival wine's pedigree, beer's four main components—hops, water, barley, and yeast—must originate from the same source or region. For Sierra Nevada, that became possible when the company purchased a sprawling parcel of land near the brewery. Ostensibly, the transaction was for the property's rail spur, which would permit

Sierra to receive deliveries. But the spur took only fifteen acres, leaving wide swaths of extra land. On a whim in fall 2008, the brewery decided to plant barley. By spring, the crop was ready to be harvested (by the combines of Chico State University, with whom the brewery has a partnership).

Fields of barley growing at Sierra Nevada's farm.

The barley, along with local water and Sierra's hops and yeast, became the Estate Homegrown Ale. Smooth, biscuity, and seriously citrus oriented, it's a beer that speaks volumes of soil, climate, and the brewers' commitment to changing drinkers' perceptions of beer.

It's a template that Rogue, too, decided to follow. Buoyed by its hop fields' success, the Oregonians expanded into barley production. "We thought, If we're crazy enough to farm hops, we can farm barley," Joyce says. The problem is, Oregon's climate isn't suited for barley farming. "The maltsters"—the people who roast malt—"were skeptical," Joyce says. "They went out and kicked the soil and decided we could not grow barley fit for brewing beer."

Rogue gambled, planting more than 100 acres of barley at a farm near Tygh Valley, Oregon. Rogue won the bet. "The plump"— kernel plumpness, which is a signifier of quality—"and protein content came out just right," Joyce says of the barley varieties,

Rows of Rogue's Dare and Risk barley grown in Oregon.

named Dare and Risk. The grain, combined with the brewery's proprietary Pacman yeast, locally grown hops, and coastal water, became the basis for Chatoe Rogue. It's a brand built on the notion of GYO—grow your own.

The GYO releases have included the crisp and roasty Dirtoir black lager, smooth Single Malt ale, and OREgasmic Ale, whose lurid name denotes that every ingredient hails from Oregon. "We're proud of being from Oregon, and the flavor of our beers reflects on our region," Joyce says.

Trouble Brewing

For wineries, it's easy to tout their varietals' terroir. Many wineries double as vineyards, growing their own grapes, then plucking, pressing, and fermenting them into intoxicating fruit juice. From ground to glass, it's terroir in action. That's not how breweries operate. The grains, hops, and yeast arrive via a patchwork of suppliers, from far-flung quadrants of the country and the globe. To be fair, numerous wineries also buy grapes from far and wide, but it's the brewing process that gets branded as industrial. Terroir can be a tough row to hoe.

Though Milwaukee's Lakefront Brewery does not own farmland, it uses 100 percent Wisconsin-grown barley and hops in its Local Acre Lager. President Russ Klisch loves how "there's more flavor coming through in the malt, and there's a different type of floral aroma that occurs with the hops—it's a little cleaner flavor." The beer was originally released in late 2009, and Lakefront had trouble keeping it on the shelves for two reasons: the public's thirst for quality, locally crafted beer and a severe shortage of raw materials.

"Hops take three years to grow and get good production," Klisch says. "It's very limiting." Then there's cost, which is an issue for Sierra Nevada. Communications director Manley estimates that Sierra hops' free-market price is an eye-popping $170 a pound, compared to perhaps $2 a pound. That's because the brewery has a lower yield than farms in, say, Washington's Yakima Valley, and "the people harvesting are our well-paid brewery employees," he says. Rogue's employees aren't picking hops, but the brewery has assumed all economic risk for its farms. If there's a bad yield or crop failure, the brewery takes a fiscal bath.

More than money, though, there's the larger hurdle of getting drinkers to accept a wine term to describe beer. "We got backlash by calling our beer *estate* or using words like *terroir*. People thought it was pretentious," Manley says. To short-circuit any claims of pretension, Rogue pokes fun at its efforts by intentionally misspelling *chateau*. "We spell Chatoe like how it sounds, not how it's spelled," Joyce jokes. "We come from a blue-collar town of nine thousand, and we can't spell things fancy like that."

So will breweries be forced to cloak terroir in different terminology? Perhaps. Or it might be a matter of time. Look at wine: In the 1960s, the top-selling brand in the United States was the rotgut better known as Thunderbird. Wine consumers (aka winos) would have laughed long and hard, glinting their red-stained teeth, if you dared discuss the ineffable qualities of soil, climate, and place.

Manley and Sierra Nevada are happy to take their lumps if it means altering people's perception of their carbonated beverage. "We're willing to take a knock on the pretentious scale," Manley says, "so we can get people to start thinking about beer as an agricultural product again."

TEN TO TRY

Local Acre Lager
LAKEFRONT BREWERY
ABV: 7%

IN THE LATE NINETEENTH CENTURY, WISCONSIN WAS ONE OF AMERICA'S TOP HOP-PRODUCING STATES, UNTIL DOWNY MILDEW WIPED IT OUT IN THE 1920S. TODAY, MILWAUKEE'S LAKEFRONT IS HELPING REVIVE THE HUMBLE HUMULUS LUPULUS WITH ITS LOCAL ACRE, MADE WITH SIX-GRAIN BARLEY AND HOPS GROWN WITHIN A HUNDRED-MILE RADIUS OF THE BREWERY. PALE AND CLOUDY, LOCAL HAS A DOUGHY, SLIGHTLY PEPPERY NOSE AND HINTS OF CITRUS AND CORN. DESPITE THE 7 PERCENT ABV, LOCAL IS AWFULLY DRINKABLE.

Chatoe Rogue Series
ROGUE ALES
ABV: VARIES

THE ESTATE BEERS ROTATE SEASONALLY, BUT THEY'VE COUNTED BEAUTIES SUCH AS THE BRACINGLY FLORAL WET HOP ALE AND DIRTOIR BLACK LAGER, WHICH HAS ROASTED-COFFEE FLAVORS, A LIGHT BODY, AND A PRESENT BITTERNESS. I LIKE THE TAWNY-ORANGE OREGASMIC ALE, FEATURING 100 PERCENT OREGON INGREDIENTS, A PINEY AND FRUITY NOSE, AND A SPICY, PEPPERY TANG.

Full Nelson Virginia Pale Ale
BLUE MOUNTAIN BREWERY
ABV: 5.9%

SITUATED IN VIRGINIA IN THE SCENIC BLUE RIDGE MOUNTAINS, THIS BREWERY PLANTED A COUPLE

HUNDRED CASCADE HOP BINES THAT
ARE NOW USED IN BLUE'S FLAGSHIP,
THE FULL NELSON. THE COPPER
CREATION'S BREADY MALT BACKBONE
IS SIMPLY A STAGE FOR THE
CASCADE HOPS TO SING: THEY SMELL
BRIGHT AND FLORAL, WHILE MAKING
CRISP, SPICY FULL NELSON BITTER
ENOUGH TO PLEASE ANY MOUTH-
PUCKERING FAN.

ESTATE HOMEGROWN ALE
SIERRA NEVADA BREWING CO.
ABV: 6.7%

THIS WAS THE
COUNTRY'S FIRST
ESTATE BEER AND
IT CONTINUES TO
PLEASE. THE HOPS AND
BARLEY ARE GROWN
ON SIERRA'S SUNNY
HOMESTEAD, RESULTING
IN AN ALE THAT
SPEAKS RESOLUTELY
OF THE BREWERS AND
THE SOIL. BISCUITY
ESTATE IS INTENSELY,
PLEASINGLY CITRIC—
GRAPEFRUIT, LEMON,
AND PINE, OH MY. BUT
IT DRINKS SMOOTH AND
IS AS BALANCED AS
A TEETER-TOTTER,
CLOSING WITH A WELCOMING,
ENDURING BITTERNESS.

BOHEMIAN PILSNER
RED HILL BREWERY
ABV: 5.9%

RUN BY HUSBAND-AND-WIFE AUSSIES
KAREN AND DAVID GOLDING, RED HILL
BREWERY HAS ITS OWN ON-SITE HOP
YARD. SINCE THE GROWING CYCLE IS
FLIPPED DOWN UNDER, THE HOPS ARE
PLUCKED IN MID-MARCH (INSTEAD OF
AUGUST AND SEPTEMBER, LIKE IN THE
UNITED STATES). THE FLOWERS FLAVOR
BEERS SUCH AS THE SPICY, LIGHTLY
SWEET BOHEMIAN PILSNER, WHICH
GETS ITS FLORAL KICK THANKS TO HOPS
STEEPED IN THE CONDITIONING TANK.

HUNDRED YARD DASH FRESH HOP ALE
BRAU BROTHERS BREWING COMPANY
ABV: 6.8%

FOR THESE FAMILIAL MINNESOTA
BREWERS, THE MEASUREMENT
REFERS TO THE DISTANCE BETWEEN
THE BREW KETTLE AND THE HOP
YARD, HOME TO ELEVEN DIFFERENT
VARIETIES. THIS ENGLISH-LEANING
ESTATE ALE'S MÉLANGE OF JUST-
PLUCKED CENTENNIAL, CASCADE, MT.
HOOD, NUGGET, AND STERLING HOPS
IS A GRASSY, PINEY PLEASURE, WITH
NOTES OF TOAST AND CARAMEL.

ST MARTIN BRUNE
BRASSERIE DE BRUNEHAUT BREWERY
ABV: 8%

THIS 120-YEAR-OLD BELGIAN
CONCERN FOCUSES ON TRADITIONAL
WITBIERS, ABBEY-STYLE ALES, AND

ORGANIC BEERS. THE PRODUCT LINES' COMMON THREAD IS THAT BRUNEHAUT USES ITS OWN LOCALLY GROWN AND HARVESTED BARLEY AND WHEAT, WHICH IS MASHED WITH WATER DRAWN FROM THE BREWERY'S WELL. STANDOUTS INCLUDE THE FRUITY, GOLDEN BRUNEHAUT BLOND AND MY PICK, ST MARTIN BRUNE. IT SMELLS OF DARK FRUITS AND LICORICE AND TASTES OF CARAMEL, MALT, AND BROWN SUGAR.

DEVIL'S KRIEK
DOUBLE MOUNTAIN BREWERY
ABV: 9+%

BESIDES RUNNING HOOD RIVER, OREGON'S DOUBLE MOUNTAIN (HOME TO THE EXCELLENT HOP LAVA IPA), BREWMASTER MATT SWIHART HAS HIS OWN CHERRY ORCHARD. COME HARVEST SEASON, HE DEVISES HIS STANDOUT DEVIL'S KRIEK. STARTING WITH A BASE OF PERHAPS A STRONG GOLDEN ALE OR A STURDY BROWN ALE, SWIHART ADDS BING CHERRIES, THEN A MEASURE OF BRETTANOMYCES AND OTHER YEAST STRAINS, SUCH AS KÖLSCH AND BELGIAN ALE. THE RESULT? TART, FRUITY PARADISE.

COLD SMOKE SCOTCH ALE
KETTLEHOUSE BREWING COMPANY
ABV: 6.5%

GOOD THINGS ARE BREWING IN MISSOULA, MONTANA, WHERE KETTLEHOUSE BREWING LEANS ON LOCALLY GROWN BARLEY. THE LIGHT, FRESH BONGWATER PALE ALE HAS A NUTTY CHARACTER DUE TO THE ADDITION OF HEMP SEEDS, DUDE, WHILE THE COLD SMOKE SCOTCH ALE DRINKS BIG AND HEARTY, WITH NOTES OF SMOKE AND COFFEE AND AN IDEAL BALANCE BETWEEN BITTER AND SWEET.

HORSENECK GOLDEN IPA
JUST BEER
ABV: 5.9%

EACH YEAR, MASSACHUSETTS'S JUST BEER (MAKERS OF THE FRAGRANT MOBY D ALE AND JUICY, WHEATY GOLDEN FLOUNDER) EXCLUSIVELY USES CASCADE HOPS FROM WASHINGTON'S SEGAL RANCH. THE FARM'S TERROIR HELPS HORSENECK STAND APART FROM THE HERD. THE ALE POURS LIKE HAZY SUNSHINE AND SMELLS LIKE LEMONS ROLLED IN CREAM. HORSENECK'S PINE-TREE BITTERNESS CURLS AROUND THE BACK OF YOUR TONGUE LIKE A CAT. DEPENDING ON THE HARVEST, THE IPA WILL DIFFER EACH YEAR.

FiVE

DRINKING SEASON:

From Spring to Summer, Fall to Winter, Flipping the Calendar's Pages Brings a New Beer to Embrace

WHEN I WAS A YOUNG COLLEGIATE KNOW-NOTHING,
I drank the same dirt-cheap domestic lager year-round. No matter
if it were 90 degrees or 9 below, I'd wrap my hands round a can
of something crappy and cold. It was equal parts routine and
bullheaded ignorance.

While I wasted my weekend nights sipping Natural Ice and
Busch Light, I spent Saturday morning shopping at southeastern
Ohio's superb Athens Farmers Market. A die-hard cook since
childhood, I followed the harvest with a religious zeal. In the spring,
I sautéed asparagus with freshly trimmed garlic scapes. During
summer, I made cooling cucumber salads and roasted corn. Fall was
reserved for cauliflower curries and roasted pumpkin.

What I later discovered is that beer also follows its own
distinct seasonal rhythms. Though spiced Christmas ales have long
been earmarked for winter, and cloudy, banana-scented German
hefeweizens have a toehold in summertime, craft brewers have

begun broadening the definition of seasonal beer by either creating new brew styles or taking a shine to an old beer. These days, summer is perfect for the saison, a Belgian farmhouse ale typically brewed during the winter to be ready for hot-weather quaffing. A snowy December night is the ideal time to sip a sweetly potent, hopped-up American barley wine. Fall is fit for grassy, aromatic ales made with freshly harvested hops, or perhaps a pumpkin beer that tastes like pie. No matter the month, a beer is always in season.

Spring

Witbier

Too often, I'm harsh on global brewing giants who've sacrificed taste for a fat bottom line. But once in a blue moon, I'll give conglomerates credit for a beer brewed well—in this case, Blue Moon.

In a macrobrew industry mired in an endless slump, the Blue Moon witbier is MillerCoors' brightest beacon. I'd wager its success on a simple fact: Blue Moon doesn't taste half bad. The cloudy, unfiltered brew is spiced with coriander seeds and orange peel, resulting in a lightly sweet, orangey treat that's fit for a sunbaked afternoon or an easygoing eve.

It's a witbier with real mass appeal. And its existence is due to the efforts of a milkman named Pierre Celis. He lived in the Belgian village of Hoegaarden. For centuries, the region was lauded for its witbier ("white beer"). These were gentle, graceful beers made with wheat, oats, and barley and doctored with dried orange peels and coriander. But by the mid-1950s, Hoegaarden's last brewery had closed. Witbiers weren't seen again until 1966, when Celis exchanged milk bottles for beer bottles and founded Brouwerij Celis.

A DISASTROUS SUCCESS

His witbiers took off like wildfire—but it was fire that doomed him. After a blaze decimated his brewery in the mid-1980s, Celis accepted an investment from Stella Artois in order to rebuild. Stella merged with another firm to form Interbrew, which later becoming big, bad InBev. Quality diminished. Angry at how the recipe was changing, Celis divested himself of his shares. "I sold my brewery, but not myself," Celis once said.

To capitalize on American interest in witbiers, he moved to Austin, Texas, started Celis Brewery, and made Celis White according to the original Hoegaarden recipe. It was a hit. But his investors wanted a bigger return on their bucks. To buy them out, he sold a company stake to Miller. The brewing giant skimped on ingredients, nixing imported Czech hops. Again, quality suffered. As time passed, Celis had the opportunity to reacquire company shares, or sell the brewery outright to Miller. He sold. Since Celis wasn't very profitable, Miller eventually shuttered the brewery, and the brand was pawned off to the Michigan Brewing Company. It still makes Celis White today, but sadly, it ain't the same.

While Pierre Celis was, pardon my French, screwed by big business, his legacy is that witbiers have survived and thrived. In Cleveland, Great Lakes Brewing Company's Holy Moses White Ale gets an additional fragrant nudge from chamomile, while Japan's Hitachino Nest White Ale gets a hit of nutmeg. Then there's cloudy, spicy Allagash White from Portland, Maine, and light, subtly tart Witte Ale from Brewery Ommegang in Cooperstown, New York, neither of which need a lemon squeeze—there's already plenty of citrus pop in the bottle.

While drinkers can shoot for the Moon, they'd be happy to sip these stars of craft brewing.

FOUR TO TRY

(512) WIT
(512) BREWING
ABV: 5.2%

THE 512 DENOTES THE AREA CODE FOR THIS AUSTIN, TEXAS, BREWERY, WHERE OWNER KEVIN BRAND HAS WON OVER TEXANS WITH HIS TERRIFIC LINEUP. CHOCOLATY, PITCH-BLACK PECAN PORTER IS BREWED WITH LOCALLY HARVESTED NUTS. THE IPA IS AN APRICOT-KISSED, DRY-HOPPED DREAM. BUT I'M WILD ABOUT THE HAZY WIT. THE BLEND OF BARLEY, OATS, AND WHEAT IS SPICED WITH CORIANDER AND GRAPEFRUIT PEEL, CREATING A TART, CRISP DRINKER THAT'S ACES DURING THE HOT TEXAS SUMMER.

MOTHERSHIP WIT ORGANIC WHEAT BEER
NEW BELGIUM BREWING COMPANY
ABV: 4.8%

COLORADO-BASED NEW BELGIUM'S MOTHERSHIP IS A TERRIFIC RIFF ON THE ZESTY BELGIAN CLASSIC. KOWTOWING TO STYLE, MOTHERSHIP POURS CLOUDY AS ALL GET-OUT, RELEASING SUBLIME NOTES OF CORIANDER, ORANGE, AND BANANA—POTPOURRI FOR A BEER GEEK. THAT SOUR TANG IS A NICE TOUCH TOO.

HITACHINO NEST WHITE ALE
KIUCHI BREWERY
ABV: 5.5%

THE WISP OF BITTERNESS IN THIS JAPANESE WITBIER (ABOUT 13 IBUS), IS COMPLEMENTED BY A TON OF FLAVOR THANKS TO CORIANDER, ORANGE PEEL, NUTMEG, AND EVEN A SPLASH OF ORANGE JUICE. THE ALE GOES DOWN AS EASY AS WATER.

ST. BERNARDUS WITBIER
BROUWERIJ ST. BERNARDUS
ABV: 5.5%

WITBIER SAVIOR PIERRE CELIS HELPED DEVELOP THIS SPECIMEN, WHICH IS EVERY BIT AS EXCELLENT AS YOU'D EXPECT: THE HAZY GOLDEN BREW HAS A WHITE HEAD LIKE SANTA'S BEARD, AND A PERFUME OF CORIANDER, CLOVE, AND LEMON—TEXTBOOK WITBIER. A SECONDARY BOTTLE FERMENTATION ENSURES THAT THE BEER'S CARBONATION IS CRISP AND NEARLY ENDLESS.

Summer

Saison

Thirsty field workers, combined with a lack of refrigeration,
helped foster one of Belgium's singular refreshments. In southern
Belgium's French-speaking Wallonia region, pastoral grain farms
dot the countryside. Local farmers typically double as brewers,
but not during summer—brewing during hot weather increases the
risk of blemished beer, thanks to yeasts and microbes run amok.
Hop-packed batches of saison (French for *season*) brewed in the
winter were stored until summer, when the tart, earthy, low-alcohol
beer served as potable drinking water for toiling farmhands.
(Saisons are also called farmhouse ales.)

"Saisons couldn't have been sweet and cloying," says Steven
Pauwels, head brewer at Kansas City, Missouri's Boulevard Brewing
Co. "If you're working your butt off, you don't want a beer that's
sweet and aromatic. You want a beer that's dry, thirst-quenching, and
flavorful." That's where the guidelines for making saison end.

Rustic, bottle-conditioned saison remains open to creativity
and interpretation. The varieties range from dry and hoppy to
sweet and spicy, from the color of pale straw to burned amber.
"It's like, here's a big bucket where you can add in any ingredient
you want," says Pauwels, who crafts several Champagne-corked
saisons at Boulevard—a fresh, well-hopped rendition and one
spiked with funky, barnyard-like *Brettanomyces* yeast. "Saisons
already have earthy, musty characteristics," Pauwels says. "Adding
Brettanomyces just makes that beer even earthier."

INSPIRED ELIXIRS
Pauwels is hardly the only brewer doing as he pleases. For instance,
Long Island's Southampton Ales & Lagers fashions its Cuvée des

Fleurs with edible flowers and the tropical fruit–like Saison Deluxe, while Pennsylvania's Bethlehem Brew Works makes Space Monkey Raspberry Saison. But experimentation only partly explains saison's resurgence. More important, "If you're not into extreme beers, the average saison is not going to shock you," says Brian Strumke, the founder and brewmaster of Baltimore's Stillwater Artisanal Ales (*see page 205*). When creating batches of what has become his flagship brew, the Stillwater Stateside Saison, he used friends as guinea pigs. "Even if they didn't like craft beer, I'd be like, 'Hey, try some of my saison.' Every time they were, 'Wow, this is *really* good,'" the brewer recalls.

Dose it with funky yeast, ferment it with blueberries—Pauwels couldn't care less about particulars. "You can do whatever you want to it," Pauwels says. What's more important, he says, is that "we're reviving one of brewing's grand old styles."

FOUR TO TRY

HENNEPIN
BREWERY OMMEGANG
ABV: 7.7%

HOUSED ON A FORMER COOPERSTOWN, NEW YORK, HOP FARM, BREWERY OMMEGANG IS ONE OF AMERICA'S FOREMOST BELGIAN-INSPIRED BREWERIES. THERE'S NARY A MISS, INCLUDING THE ELEGANT AMBER RARE VOS, PLUM- AND LICORICE-LIKE ABBEY ALE, AND—BE STILL MY HEART—THE HENNEPIN. EQUALLY IDEAL FOR QUAFFING ON A 90-DEGREE DAY OR AT DINNER, THIS LIVELY TONIC IS FANTASTICALLY FLAVORFUL, FILLED WITH SWEET GRAPES, LEMON ZEST, AND A SPICY, BITTER FINISH.

TANK 7 FARMHOUSE ALE
BOULEVARD BREWING COMPANY
ABV: 8%

NAMED AFTER THE BREWERY'S MALFUNCTIONING FERMENTATION TANK, THE HAZY, STRAW-HUED TANK 7 REEKS OF GRAPEFRUIT AND ORANGES, THANKS TO SIMCOE, TRADITION, AND AMARILLO HOPS. BUT WHEN SIPPED, THE HOP BITTERNESS RELENTS TO SWEET MALT, LIVELY PEPPER, AND SPICY YEAST. TOSS IN A DRY FINISH, AND TANK'S A TREAT.

FANTÔME SAISON
BRASSERIE FANTÔME
ABV: 8%

BASED IN SOUTHEASTERN BELGIUM'S WALLONIA REGION, FANTÔME HAS MADE SAISON ITS FLAGSHIP BREW. IT HAS A VIVIDLY CITRIC FRAGRANCE TEMPERED BY SWEET MALT AND A BIT OF BARNYARD. CONSIDER THE FLAVOR CHAMELEONIC: SERVED COLD, IT'S SNAPPY AND BRACING AND HAS A FLAVOR OF MUTED CLOVES AND FRUIT. WHEN WARM, THE FLAVORS BECOME FULLER AND MORE PRONOUNCED, COATING YOUR PALATE. IT'S A CLASSIC.

SAISON DUPONT
BRASSERIE DUPONT
ABV: 6.5%

OPERATING SINCE 1844, THIS FARM-BASED BELGIAN BREWERY USES SPRING-WATER AND PROPRIETARY YEAST STRAINS TO MANUFACTURE THE MARVELOUS SAISON DUPONT. ITS VIBRANT LEMON-HONEY HUE IS PARTNERED WITH A BOUQUET OF CLOVES AND PEARS AND ENERGETIC CARBONATION. TAKE A SIP, AND SEMITART APPLES SEGUE INTO BANANAS, WITH A DRY, CRACKLING FINISH. IT'S THE STYLE'S STANDARD-BEARER.

Kölsch

"If you tell people they're sipping a kölsch, it's meaningless to most beer drinkers," says Brock Wagner, cofounder of Houston's Saint Arnold Brewing Company. "Instead, we just tell people they're drinking our Lawnmower Beer—Fancy Lawnmower beer, that is."

Still, calling kölsch "Lawnmower Beer" may be a minor slander. Hailing from Cologne, Germany, this light, elegant beer is a study in balance, restraint, and pinpoint craftsmanship. To develop gentle, fruity flavors, the beer is fermented at warmer temperatures before cold lagering rounds out the sweet malts and subdued hop bitterness. The pretty, pale result is traditionally served in a narrow, cylindrical glass called a stange. (At bars in Cologne, kölsch is delivered in specially designed trays by brusque waiters called Köbes, who wear blue shirts and long aprons. They'll keep bringing you kölsch until you put a coaster over your glass.)

Since kölsch possesses such mild flavors, it's tricky to craft. Any off notes will shine through, ruining the brew. (That's why brewers often favor IPAs and stouts, which are flavorful enough to masquerade defects.) Style-wise, kölsch inhabits a wide spectrum. Some are as innocuous as a baseball-stadium light beer, while others are well hopped, but their commonality is drinkability: "Beers don't have to be big to be great," Wagner says.

Restrained Charm

In the rush to create burlier beers, the subtle pleasures of kölsch are often overlooked. But since this easy-sipping style is so summertime friendly, it's become an increasing favorite of brewers searching for an unusual hot-weather seasonal. "I didn't want to do a typical golden ale or a corn ale," says Josh Brewer, the appropriately named brewmaster at Mother Earth Brewing in Kinston, North Carolina. To fit the bill, he created Endless River, a kölsch that is crisp,

refreshing, and highlighted by a gentle grassy bitterness. "I wanted something with a little more flavor."

But, just like the Fancy Lawnmower, the new crop of kölsch beers often doesn't bear the umlaut-topped moniker. Instead, snag a stange and search for the beer named after summer. Geary's Summer Ale is a mellow, citrus-hinted treat, as is Harpoon Summer Beer and the Alaskan Brewing Co.'s Alaskan Summer Ale. Savor them as long, lazy afternoons dissolve into evening. "If you're thirsty, a kölsch is mellow enough to sip several of them," Wagner says. "Kölsch is the anti-extreme beer."

FOUR TO TRY

ENDLESS RIVER
MOTHER EARTH BREWING
ABV: 4.9%

LOCATED IN EASTERN NORTH CAROLINA'S BBQ COUNTRY, MOTHER EARTH MAKES BEERS EVERY BIT AS TASTY AS THE REGION'S FAMOUS PULLED PORK. THE SISTERS OF THE MOON IPA IS A FLORAL AND CITRIC HOP BOMB, WHILE ENDLESS RIVER IS AS GOLDEN AS A POLISHED WEDDING BAND. IT SMELLS OF FRESH-CLIPPED FLOWERS DRIZZLED WITH HONEY, AND DRINKS AS CRISP AS PERRIER. YOU'LL SAVOR THE GRASSY HOP BITE.

GEARY'S SUMMER ALE
D.L. GEARY BREWING COMPANY
ABV: 6%

DAVID AND KAREN GEARY'S PIONEERING PORTLAND, MAINE, BREWERY RELEASED ITS FIRST—AND FLAGSHIP—BRITISH-STYLE PALE ALE IN 1986. SINCE THEN, GEARY'S HAS BECOME A NEW ENGLAND MAINSTAY, WITH ITS ROASTY LONDON PORTER, TOASTY HAMPSHIRE SPECIAL ALE, AND THE GOLDEN SUMMER ALE. THE KÖLSCH-STYLE SIPPER BOASTS BREAD MALT, A HINT OF HOPS, AND A CRISPNESS THAT'S LIKE BITING INTO A FRESH APPLE.

YELLOWTAIL PALE ALE
BALLAST POINT BREWING COMPANY
ABV: 5%

WHILE THE SAN DIEGO BREWERY IS KNOWN FOR ITS RESINOUS IPAS, IT SHOWS A DEFT HAND WITH THIS PALE ALE, WHICH IS MODELED ON KÖLSCH. THE GOLDEN YELLOWTAIL SMELLS LIGHTLY MALT SWEET AND, WITH RESTRAINED NOTES OF GRASS, CITRUS, AND FRUIT, DRINKS AS EASY AS A SUNDAY MORN.

GAFFEL KÖLSCH
PRIVATBRAUEREI GAFFEL BECKER & CO.
ABV: 4.8%

CRACKING A BOTTLE OF THIS BREW FROM COLOGNE, GERMANY, RELEASES A BOUQUET OF HONEYSUCKLE, PLUM, AND GRAPEFRUIT. REFRESHINGLY BRISK CARBONATION LEADS TO FLAVORS OF BREADY YEAST AND EARTHY HOPS, BEFORE CLOSING WITH A TWIST OF LEMON PEEL.

Fall

Fresh-Hop Beer

How many freshly harvested hops can fit inside a Honda Element? A few late summers back, Ben Love answered that question by driving out to Goschie Farms, one of Oregon's top hop producers. Harvest season was in manic, 24-hour-a-day mode, with the air perfumed with the pungent, earthy scent of the bines' ripe flowers. Love stuffed his car with four burlap sacks—each about four feet tall and two feet around and containing about 100 pounds of whole-cone hops—and hustled back from Silverton, Oregon, to his head-brewing gig at Portland's Hopworks Urban Brewery. Every minute counted.

"Those hops were in the beer within three hours of me leaving the field," says Love, who created a batch of fall's new fleeting brew delicacy: Parsec Pale, a fresh-hopped beer. Typically, the moist, just-plucked hops go straight from the bine to the kiln, thus preventing spoilage. That's because hops are like cut grass. Initially, the smell is superb, but it quickly goes rotten. Hence, fresh hops (also called wet hops) are best used within 24 hours of their plucking and ideally in a pale ale—instead of a mouth-puckering IPA—which permits the flowers' flavors to shine. Done right, "you get that lovely, green hop character that's very delicate," says Jamie Emmerson, executive brewmaster at Full Sail, which crafts the draft-only Lupulin Fresh Hop Ale and Hopfenfrisch Fresh Hop Lager.

THE FRESH START

The seasonal style's inception can be traced to Sierra Nevada Brewing Co. The California brewery kicked off the fresh-hop movement with its Harvest Ale, dosed with Washington State's fresh Cascade and Centennial hops. However, it is Pacific Northwest breweries such as Oregon's Deschutes, Ninkasi, and Pelican that have helped popularize fresh-hop ales, so much so that "it's becoming something of a Pacific Northwest style," Emmerson says.

That's partly due to the breweries' locations near the hops fields of Oregon and eastern Washington's Yakima Valley, where three-quarters of America's hop crops are grown. When harvest-time hits, it's no hassle to send a brewer to nab four or five burlap sacks of sticky, aromatic hops. Still, this style isn't region specific. In Easton, Pennsylvania, Weyerbacher Brewing Company makes its Harvest Ale with Cascade hops culled from brewery founder and president Dan Weirback's farm. Founders Brewing Co. in Grand Rapids, Michigan, uses both West Coast hops and some hops harvested from employees' homes to create its Harvest Ale. Still, if a brewery is far from a farm, sourcing hops can cause a migraine.

"Getting the hops here is a logistical nightmare," says Brian Dunn, owner of Denver's Great Divide Brewing Company. "We contract a truck and put two drivers on it, so they drive straight through from Washington to Denver." Once the hops are hours from arrival, Great Divide starts brewing. When the hops arrive, they're unpacked and immediately dumped into the brew kettle. The painstaking effort pays dividends upon first sip of their Fresh Hop Pale Ale: "Fresh, grassy, and crisp, it's such an amazing beer," Dunn says. "I wish we could brew it more than two or three days a year."

But fresh-hop beers' brief season is what makes this style such a September–October treat. "They're like beaujolais nouveau—enjoy the drinking season, and when it's gone, it's gone," Emmerson says. "The magic in these beers is that they're so fleeting."

FIVE TO TRY

HARVEST ALE
WEYERBACHER BREWING COMPANY
ABV: 6.2%
WHEN HOPS HARVEST SEASON HITS, THIS PENNSYLVANIA BREWERY NEEDS NO OUTSIDE SUPPLIER FOR ITS STINKY GREEN CONES; INSTEAD, WEYERBACHER SOURCES CASCADE HOPS GROWN ON FOUNDER AND PRESIDENT DAN WEIRBACK'S FARM. THE RESULTING WET-HOP IPA BURSTS WITH BRIGHT AND ENTICING AROMAS OF LAWNMOWER-CUT GRASS AND JUST-PEELED CITRUS, WHILE THE BITTERNESS REMAINS PRESENT YET RESERVED. EVEN HOPS HATERS SHOULD ADORE THIS ALE.

FRESH HOP PALE ALE
GREAT DIVIDE BREWING CO.
ABV: 6.1%
WHOLE-CONE HOPS CULLED IN THE PACIFIC NORTHWEST ARE OVERNIGHTED TO DENVER, WHERE BREWERS DUMP THE HOPS INTO A BREW KETTLE ON THE DOUBLE. THE RESULT POURS SUNSET ORANGE AND PACKS A GENTLE HOP WALLOP—A GRAPEFRUIT AROMA LEADS TO GRASSY FLAVORS CUT WITH A HINT OF PINE NEEDLES. THERE'S BALANCE, NOT TONGUE-WHIPPING BITTERNESS.

HOP HARVEST ALE
BRIDGEPORT BREWING CO.
ABV: 6.56%
OREGON'S OLDEST CRAFT BREWERY CHERISHES ITS PROXIMITY TO AREA HOP FIELDS, SOURCING FRESHLY PLUCKED HOPS, WHISKING 'EM TO THE BREWHOUSE, AND DUMPING THEM INTO A PRE-PREPARED BATCH OF BEER— ALL WITHIN AN HOUR. THE RESULT, IN THIS CASE 2010'S CENTENNIAL HOP-BASED OFFERING, IS TRANSCENDENT: A SWEET, CITRUS-FLORAL SCENT AND A HARMONIOUS FRAMEWORK OF FULL-BODIED MALT.

HIGH TIDE FRESH HOP IPA
PORT BREWING COMPANY
ABV: 6.5%
EACH BATCH OF HIGH TIDE IS STUFFED TO THE GILLS WITH 180 POUNDS OF FIELD-FRESH HOPS, SUCH AS CENTENNIAL OR

CHINOOK. THOUGH THE RECIPE IS TWEAKED ANNUALLY DEPENDING ON CROP AVAILABILITY, EXPECT THE IPA TO HAVE A DANK AROMA OF WET GRASS, GRAPEFRUIT, OR PINE RESIN; A DOUGHY SWEETNESS; AND A STICKY MOUTHFEEL.

Halcyon Green Hop Harvest
THORNBRIDGE HALL COUNTRY HOUSE BREWING COMPANY
ABV: 7.7%

TO FASHION THE FRESH VERSION OF ITS HALCYON IMPERIAL IPA, U.K.-BASED THORNBRIDGE DRY-HOPS EACH FALL'S SELECTED CROPS (TYPICALLY TARGET, THOUGH THE BREWERY MAY EXPERIMENT WITH OTHER ENGLISH VARIETIES) FOR TWO WEEKS, THEN LAGERS THE BEER UNTIL AT LEAST APRIL. THE PROCESS CLARIFIES THE UNFILTERED, SHARPLY BITTER ALE, CREATING A HAY-COLORED LOOKER SCENTED WITH PINE RESIN AND PINEAPPLE. FLAVORS VARY ANNUALLY.

Pumpkin Ales

During the early days of America, colonial brewers had a problem: there was barely enough malted barley to go around. The grain was imported from England, a costly and lengthy undertaking. In order to make their grain supply last, brewers turned to readily available indigenous fermentables such as spruce, Jerusalem artichokes, molasses, and pumpkins.

"When I see everyone replicating the beers of the past, I kind of laugh," said Bob Skilnik, author of *Beer & Food: An American History*, in an interview with the *Contra Costa Times*. "What most people don't know is there was some pretty foul stuff passing for beer in colonial America."

While these early American beers may not have been palate pleasing, brewers' necessity led to an interesting discovery: pumpkin is a darn fine fermentable. But over time, as Americans learned to cultivate barley, the use of pumpkins in brewing beer faded.

RETURN TO THE PATCH

In recent years, brewers have rediscovered the gourd, spurring the birth (or perhaps rebirth) of a singular, thoroughly American fall delight: pumpkin beer.

Stylistically speaking, these beers inhabit a broad flavor spectrum. Some pumpkin brews are pie sweet, spiced with clove, nutmeg, ginger, and cinnamon, while others trade sweetness for a bitter streak. Stouts, saisons, even sours—name the style, and you can likely use pumpkin.

One of the first breweries to craft pumpkin ale was Buffalo Bill's Brewery in Hayward, California. While reading a brewing book, founder Bill Owens happened upon the tidbit that George Washington once brewed a beer featuring squash. That brainstorm

led, in 1986, to the creation of Pumpkin Ale, an amber-tinted brew made with roasted pumpkins, cinnamon, cloves, and nutmeg. (The brewery later introduced the stronger, similarly spiced Imperial Pumpkin Ale, incorporating brown sugar.)

The vegetable-based beer became a big hit for the brewery. Since then, hundreds of breweries have released their own pumpkin brews, typically in the fall. Shipyard Brewing Co. in Portland, Maine, offers sweet, strong Smashed Pumpkin, while Dogfish Head Craft Brewery makes its Punkin Ale with brown sugar, allspice, cinnamon, and nutmeg.

SILLY FOR SQUASH

However, one brewer stands apart in his pumpkin dedication. Over the last decade, Dick Cantwell, the cofounder and head brewer at Seattle's Elysian Brewing Company, has devised more than *twenty* different gourd-based beers, each one odder and more innovative than the last. The wheaty Hefe-Pumpkin was spiced with cinnamon and cloves. PK-47 was a pumpkin-based malt liquor. The Great Gherkin starred, along with the pumpkin mash, cucumber and chai spices, including Sichuan peppercorns and cardamom.

"Our devotion to pumpkin ales shows both how serious and how ridiculous we can be," says Cantwell. "It's like the fortune cookie thing, where you add 'in bed' to the message to make it funny. We add 'with pumpkin' to everything to give it a new comic twist, but it still has to be a fabulous and engaging beer."

Elysian's pumpkin journey began in 1998, when the brewery wanted an offbeat beer to serve at its Halloween bash. Markus Stinson, now Elysian's lead brewer and production coordinator, developed a pumpkin beer recipe, with Cantwell contributing his thoughts. That first beer, dubbed Night Owl, featured every bit of the pumpkin, right down to seeds, both roasted and green. The eight kegs were consumed in 48 hours. "We didn't think it would be as good or as popular as it was," Stinson recalls.

The following year, production doubled. The beer disappeared on the double. The next year, the same result. "People are into the pumpkin," says Cantwell, whose brewery now sells three bottled pumpkin-based fall seasonals: Night Owl, imperial-style Great Pumpkin Ale, and pumpkin stout Dark o' the Moon. Moreover, in 2005, Cantwell and Elysian launched the Great Pumpkin Beer Festival. The two-day event features dozens of different pumpkin beers, as well as the showstopper: beer served straight from an enormous hollowed-out pumpkin, where it's undergone a secondary fermentation.

"There's no limit to the beers that can be made with pumpkin, or the things you can do with pumpkins in connection with making and serving beer," says Cantwell, who sees the style as America's homegrown version of Oktoberfest lagers, Germany's classic fall

Tapping a brew-filled gourd at Elysian Brewing's annual Great Pumpkin Beer Festival.

seasonal. "People's faces light up when you talk about pumpkin beer—except maybe Germans, at first. I've talked about pumpkin beers with quite a few German brewers. At first, as a rule, they're horrified. Putting pumpkin in beer? Outrageous! Then they laugh. Then they ask if they can have some."

FIVE TO TRY

PUMKING IMPERIAL PUMPKIN ALE
SOUTHERN TIER BREWING COMPANY
ABV: 8.8%

THIS WESTERN NEW YORK BREWERY RAIDS THE SPICE CABINET'S SUPPLY OF GINGER, CINNAMON, AND NUTMEG TO CONSTRUCT PUMKING, WHICH IS A BIT LIKE BOOZY PUMPKIN PIE. THE COPPER-ORANGE ELIXIR HAS A TERRIFIC NOSE OF RUM AND VANILLA, AND A TONGUE-STICKING SWEETNESS THAT CEMENTS PUMKING AS A DESSERT BREW.

PUMPKIN IMPERIAL SPRUCE STOUT
ROCK ART BREWERY
ABV: 8%

IF YOUR TASTES RUN TOWARD SAVORY, TRY THE VERMONT BREWERY'S SLOW-DRINKING STOUT BREWED WITH PUMPKIN AND PLENTY OF SPRUCE TIPS. THEY SUPPLY A PINEY, FRESH-FROM-THE-FOREST FLAVOR AND, JUST LIKE HOPS, A BOLT OF BITTERNESS.

DARK O' THE MOON
ELYSIAN BREWING COMPANY
ABV: 6.5%

PUMPKIN TAKES ON A SINISTER TINT IN DARK O' THE MOON, A FULL-BODIED STOUT MADE WITH ROASTED

PUMPKIN SEEDS, PUMPKIN FLESH, AND A SPRINKLING OF CRUSHED CINNAMON. THE OUTCOME IS A CREAMY, CHOCOLATY INDULGENCE WITH A CINNAMON-SPICY SCENT AND LONG, ROASTY FINISH.

FROG'S HOLLOW DOUBLE PUMPKIN ALE

HOPPIN' FROG BREWERY
ABV: 8.4%

THIS AKRON, OHIO, BREWERY IS KNOWN FOR ITS BIG, FULL-BODIED BEERS, SO IT'S NO SURPRISE THAT FROG'S HOLLOW IS A WEIGHTY BREW. THE ORANGE-COLORED ALE SMELLS

STRONGLY OF PUMPKIN MEAT, CLOVES, AND NUTMEG. DESPITE THE STRENGTH, THE WELL-CARBONATED BEER IS SMOOTH AND NOT SUPER-SWEET.

PUMPKIN ALE

SMUTTYNOSE BREWING CO.
ABV: 5.6%

THE HARVEST-SEASON ALE INCORPORATES A HEAP OF PUMPKIN FLESH AND PLENTY OF NUTMEG AND CINNAMON. THE RESULT IS A SPRIGHTLY, MEDIUM-BODED BREW WITH A SPICY NOSE THAT VERGES MORE TOWARD PUMPKIN'S VEGETAL SIDE, WITH A LIGHTLY BITTER END.

Winter

Barley Wines

Don't let barley wine's name throw you for a loop: The beer style has little in common with fermented grapes — except for an alcohol content that can hit double digits. That explains why the thick, sometimes fruity, always strong belly-warming ale has become one of winter's signature sips. But to suss out the style's genesis, we need to turn to eighteenth- and nineteenth-century Britain.

Back then, many farmhouse breweries around the British Isles and Europe used a process called parti-gyle brewing to produce multiple beers from a single grain mash. (Today, one grain mash makes one beer batch.) The first running, or wort, contained the most fermentable sugars—the fuel that yeasts require to create alcohol. The second running created "common" beer and, if there were enough residual sugars left for a third batch, "small" beer. (Fun fact: Parti-gyle brewing was also common in Belgium, creating the styles now known as tripel, dubbel, and blond.)

The less-potent beers were quickly consumed, but the stronger first runnings were often stored to be sipped later, as the beers' higher ABVs kept them from spoiling. What happened next is debatable: perhaps to better preserve their ales, or maybe to one-up fellow beer makers, British brewers kept boosting their strong beers' alcohol content. Accomplishing that required elbow grease. Since yeasts don't thrive at elevated alcohol levels, brewers would jostle them into action by occasionally rolling barrels of beer around the brewery or pumping oxygen through the brew to revive the essentially drunken yeast. The longer fermentation process made barley wines mellower and more multifaceted, adding intricate layers of flavor.

In the 1800s, these potent aged brews (which were sometimes blended with weaker beers to provide complexity) went by several aliases—strong ales, stock ales, winter warmers, old ales—or, quite commonly, they were simply marked by three Xs or Ks branded into a wooden barrel. Not all were what you'd consider a barley wine, but they *would* knock your socks off. In fact, the term *barley wine* wasn't used commercially until 1903, when what is now Bass Brewers Limited released its Bass No. 1 Barley Wine.

AN AMERICAN RESURGENCE

Over time, barley wines in Britain were marketed more for their booziness than for their flavor. The style fell out of favor. In America, few beer drinkers had ever heard of barley wine until 1975, when San Francisco's Anchor Brewing released Old Foghorn Barleywine Style Ale, which was (and still is) substantially hopped with flowery Cascade hops. And there began the divide. While England offered more balanced, less liquored-up barley wines, American brewers used a heavy hand with the hops and ratcheted up the alcohol content.

For example, Rogue Ales's XS Old Crustacean boasts more than 100 IBUs and an 11.5 percent ABV (*see page 244 for a tasting note*); Great Divide Brewing's Old Ruffian annually offers more than 85 IBUs and 10 percent ABV. And while the namesake barley wine of Farmville, North Carolina's Duck-Rabbit Craft Brewery registers 11 percent ABV, "it's not bitter enough to really be an American barley wine," says Paul Philippon, the brewery's philosopher turned founder, who brews some of America's finest dark brews. At the same time, "it's too bitter to be an English barley wine, and it uses American hops." As for a definition, he says, "I tell people that it's a Farmville-style barley wine—and we're the only brewer in Farmville." (The burgeoning wheat wine variant incorporates a large percentage of wheat, which creates a soft, rich mouthfeel.)

That's the thing about modern-day barley wines: While it'd be nice to set them in a nice, tight box, they're as mutable as the big ol' strong beers of yore. Some are warming and a smidgen spicy, like Real Ale Brewing Company's rye-infused Sisyphus Barleywine Style Ale. By contrast, the Flying Mouflan, from Pennsylvania's Tröegs Brewing Company, is ruby-brown and IBU'd up the wazoo with Warrior, Chinook, and Simcoe hops. Flying Mouflan is released in the spring, which makes sense: The brewers recommend cellaring the barley wine for four months, letting the hops and alcohol mellow, thus making it ready to serve as a toasty respite in the cold heart of winter.

You can age most barley wines (*see page 234*), but these dark, powerful beers are also excellent fresh, which is why Duck-Rabbit's Philippon releases his in January. "We make it with the intention that it should be enjoyed right away," Philippon says. "I always feel like beer is for drinking, not saving."

FIVE TO TRY

CORPS MORT
MICROBRASSERIE À L'ABRI DE LA TEMPÊTE
ABV: 9%

SINCE THIS QUEBEC BREWERY SITS ON ONE OF THE ISLANDS OF THE ÎLES DE LA MADELEINE ARCHIPELAGO IN THE GULF OF ST. LAWRENCE, ITS LOCALLY SOURCED BARLEY IS LICKED BY A SEA BREEZE THAT IMPARTS A SLIGHTLY SALTY PROFILE. FOR CORPS MORT ("DEAD MAN"), THE BARLEY IS SMOKED, RESULTING IN A BEER THAT SMELLS LIKE SPICY, PEATY SCOTCH. STICKY-SWEET CARAMEL AND TOFFEE COME INTO PLAY ON THE TONGUE, WITH A SALINIC UNDERPINNING. IT'S SINGULAR.

OLDE GNARLYWINE
LAGUNITAS BREWING COMPANY
ABV: 10-12%

AN AMERICAN-STYLE BARLEY WINE BUILT FOR THE LONG HAUL, THIS ALE BEGINS LIFE WITH MOUTH-BENDING HOP BITTERNESS OF PINEAPPLE AND PINE. GIVE GNARLYWINE TIME AND THE BITTERNESS WILL RECEDE AS THE MALTS ASSERT THEMSELVES, LENDING FLAVORS OF TOASTED BREAD, TOFFEE, AND CARAMEL.

BARLEYWINE ALE
THE DUCK-RABBIT CRAFT BREWERY
ABV: 11%

A HEFTY LOAD OF AMARILLO HOPS GIVES THIS MAHOGANY, NORTH CAROLINA-BREWED BARLEY WINE PLENTY OF SWEET, TROPICAL FRUIT AROMAS, PLUS A BITTERNESS THAT VERGES FROM CITRUS TO PINE. THE HOPS SERVE AS A COUNTERPOINT TO THE TOFFEE-MALT PRESENCE, WHILE THE SMOOTH, SILKY MOUTHFEEL WILL KEEP YOU SIPPING.

ARCTIC DEVIL BARLEY WINE
MIDNIGHT SUN BREWING CO.
ABV: 13.2%

NAMED AFTER THE WOLVERINE THAT HAUNTS ALASKA'S WOODS, THIS ENGLISH-STYLE BARLEY WINE IS A MALTY MONSTER. TO TAME IT, THE BREWER LETS THE BEER SPEND MONTHS HIBERNATING IN OAK BARRELS THAT HAVE BEEN PREVIOUSLY USED TO AGE PORT, WINE, OR WHISKEY BEFORE BEING BLENDED AND BOTTLED. EACH ANNUAL VINTAGE IS UNIQUE, BUT EXPECT A ROBUST, COMPLEX BREW WORTHY OF A SNIFTER GLASS AND A SEAT BY THE FIRE.

Nils Oscar Barley Wine
THE NILS OSCAR COMPANY
ABV: 9.5%

HAILING FROM SWEDEN, THE "SWEDISH BARLEY WINE STYLE ALE," AS IT'S CALLED, SKEWS TOWARD THE SWEET SIDE. FLAVOR-WISE, IT OFFERS LOADS OF DARK FRUIT AND A LIGHT BITTERNESS, INSTEAD OF OFF-THE-CHARTS IBUS. IT'D BE DIVINE FOR DESSERT. THE BEER WON GOLD IN SWEDEN'S NATIONAL HOME BREWING COMPETITION IN 1993.

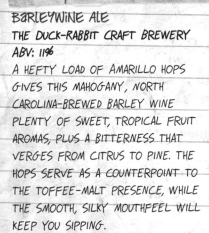

INTERNATIONAL SPOTLIGHT: NORWAY'S NØGNE Ø

TO PUT IT MILDLY, NORWAY IS NOT KNOWN FOR ITS BEER.

IN THAT FRIGID SCANDINAVIAN LAND OF REINDEER JERKY AND SMOKED SALMON, MORE THAN 90 PERCENT OF THE COUNTRY'S QUAFFS ARE LIGHT LAGERS AND NEUTERED PILSNERS. MOREOVER, MANY NORWEGIAN BARS POUR JUST ONE TAP BEER, PROVIDING DRINKERS AS MUCH CHOICE AS VOTING IN A DICTATOR'S ELECTION.

"NORWEGIANS," LAMENTS BEARDED GIANT KJETIL JIKIUN, COFOUNDER AND BREWMASTER OF THE MICROBREWERY NØGNE Ø IN GRIMSTAD, NORWAY, "DON'T KNOW MUCH ABOUT CRAFT BEER." CONSIDER JIKIUN AN EXCEPTION. SINCE LAUNCHING NØGNE Ø ("NAKED ISLE," TAKEN FROM A POEM BY HENRIK IBSEN) IN 2002, THE GREGARIOUS, BESPECTACLED NORWEGIAN HAS BEGUN TRANSFORMING HIS COUNTRY'S CARBONATED LANDSCAPE. WITH AN ARTISAN'S TOUCH AND MISSIONARY ZEAL, HE CRAFTS BOLD, FLAVORFUL PORTERS,

Nøgne Ø brewmaster Kjetil Jikiun (far right) discussing his delicious Scandinavian brews.

STOUTS, INDIA PALE ALES, AND HERB-PACKED ODDITIES MORE IN LINE WITH EXPERIMENTAL AMERICAN MICROBREWS THAN NORWAY'S WEAK SWILL.

NORWEGIANS WEREN'T ALWAYS CONTENT TO CONSUME SIMPLE LAGERS. SEVERAL HUNDRED YEARS AGO, THE GOVERNMENT MANDATED THAT FARMERS MUST GROW HOPS AND BREW BEER. IF FARMERS REFUSED, THEY WERE FINED OR COULD LOSE THEIR LAND. SPECIAL BREWS WERE CRAFTED TO HONOR DECEASED NORWEGIANS. "YOU COULDN'T BURY THE BODY UNTIL THE BEER WAS READY," EXPLAINS NØGNE Ø MANAGER KJELL EINAR KARLSEN. "IN THE SUMMERTIME, THIS COULD BE A PROBLEM."

AS IN AMERICA, THE TEMPERANCE MOVEMENT, TAXATION, AND BIG BREWING KILLED TRADITION. ENTER JIKIUN. AN AIRLINE PILOT, HE SAMPLED SUDS WHEREVER HE LANDED, DEVELOPING AN AFFINITY FOR RELEASES FROM STONE BREWING AND DOGFISH HEAD. HE BEGAN HOMEBREWING, USING AMERICAN CRAFT BREWERS AS HIS MUSE. BIG MISTAKE.

"I BREWED WHAT I THOUGHT WAS MY BEST IPA EVER," JIKIUN SAYS OF HIS RIFF ON HOPPY, WEST COAST ALES. "I ENTERED IT IN A HOMEBREW COMPETITION—ONLY TO RECEIVE THE SECOND-LOWEST SCORE OF ANY IPA." TO THE JUDGES, JIKIUN'S BREW WAS AS ALIEN AS THOSE SAUCER-EYED ROSWELL CREATURES. STILL, "EVERYBODY ELSE I SERVED MY HOMEBREWS TO LIKED THEM, SO I THOUGH THERE'D BE A MARKET," JIKIUN SAYS. HE STARTED NØGNE Ø WITH MORE OPTIMISM THAN MONEY. "OUR FIRST THREE YEARS, WE WERE ABOUT TO GO BANKRUPT EVERY MONTH," JIKIUN SAYS, LAUGHING. IN NORWAY, BREWERS PAY TAXES COMMENSURATE WITH THEIR BEER'S ALCOHOL PERCENTAGE: A HIGHER ABV EQUALS HIGHER TAXES.

"OUR BEERS ARE MORE EXPENSIVE IN NORWAY THAN IN AMERICA," SAYS JIKIUN, WHOSE BEERS OFTEN FLIRT WITH AN EYE-SPINNING 10 PERCENT ABV. A SECOND FACTOR IS THAT THE GOVERNMENT RESTRICTS SALES OF BEERS STRONGER THAN 4.75 PERCENT ABV (COMPARABLE TO BUD) TO SPECIALLY LICENSED SHOPS OR STATE-RUN CHAIN VINMONOPOL—UNSURPRISINGLY, IT TRANSLATES TO "WINE MONOPOLY." EVEN NUTTIER IS THAT NØGNE Ø WAS BARRED FROM PUBLICIZING ITS BEER ONLINE. "THE GOVERNMENT SAID, 'IF YOU DON'T CLOSE DOWN THE SITE IMMEDIATELY, WE'RE GOING TO CLOSE IT DOWN,'" JIKIUN RECALLS. THE GOVERNMENT'S DECREE WAS AS STRANGE AS ITS SOLUTION: THE BREWERY COULD TOUT ITS BEER PROVIDED THE COPY WAS WRITTEN IN THE LANGUAGE SPOKEN IN NØGNE Ø'S EXPORT MARKETS—ENGLISH. "AND NORWEGIANS SPEAK ENGLISH," JIKIUN SAYS, LAUGHING.

'TIS THE SEASONAL FOR SUCCESS

DESPITE MOUNT EVEREST ODDS, JIKIUN REFUSED TO COMPROMISE HIS MISSION TO CRAFT UNFILTERED, UNPASTEURIZED, AND BOTTLE-CONDITIONED BREWS. NØGNE Ø FOUND SUCCESS WITH YULETIDE ALES SUCH AS THE SPICED UNDERLIG JUL ("PECULIAR CHRISTMAS"), WHICH IS INSPIRED BY MULLED WINE GLØGG, AND STRONG, CARAMEL-SWEET GOD JUL (CALLED "WINTER ALE" IN THE UNITED STATES). NOW THE BREWS ARE FOUND ON AMERICAN SHORES (AND EVEN IN AUSTRALIA AND JAPAN), ARMED WITH FLAVOR PROFILES THAT RESONATE WITH FANS OF CRAFT BEER.

NØGNE Ø'S INDIA PALE ALE IS SIMILAR TO A CALIFORNIA HOPS BOMB; BOLD AND RICH, THE BEER'S MALT-SWEET FOUNDATION KEEPS THE BITTERNESS FROM GOING OVERBOARD. THE SAISON IS A FUNKY SUMMERTIME REFRESHMENT REDOLENT OF PEARS AND APPLES. THE OIL-THICK IMPERIAL STOUT PACKS A COFFEE AND BITTERSWEET-COCOA FLAVOR PUNCH, MAKING IT PERFECT FOR BROWNIE PAIRINGS. STILL, THE STANDOUT IS #100, A BEER ORIGINALLY UNINTENDED FOR PUBLIC CONSUMPTION.

"WE WANTED IT TO BE BEER FOR THE BREWERS," JIKIUN SAYS. "NOT MANY BARS IN NORWAY WANTED CRAFT BEER—BUT THEY WANTED THIS ONE." UNDERSTANDABLY SO: THE BARLEY WINE–LIKE BREW POSSESSES A SPICY AROMA COMPLEMENTED BY CARDAMOM AND A LOVELY, LINGERING BELLY WARMTH OWING TO ITS 10 PERCENT ABV. IT TASTES FAMILIAR, YET DISTINCTLY FOREIGN.

"WE'RE INVENTING A SCANDINAVIAN BREWING IDENTITY," JIKIUN SAYS.

100
BARLEY WINE-STYLE ALE

Six

ON THE MAKE:

Collaborators, Amateurs, Semipros, Small-Fries, Gypsies: Inside the Men—and Women—Behind Your Beer

SOME INDUSTRIES ARE TOUGH NUTS TO CRACK. TO become an NFL player or a nuclear physicist, you better be a freakish physical specimen—a Mensabrain or megabrawn. Brewing doesn't require such genetic luck. Buy a sack of grain, a handful of hops, yeast packets, and a couple of pots and carboys (a vessel suited for fermentation), and you too can brew. The first couple of experiments may be overcarbonated catastrophes. In time, though, the ratios make sense. Results improve, from drinkable to delectable. Your beer might be just as good—or better—than suds served at the bar. What next?

In the past, brewers eager to go pro may have apprenticed or worked for a brewery, or decided to open their own operation, a laborious, debt-ridden undertaking. Now the path to a brewing career, and the definition of a brewer, isn't so clearly defined. Beer making's ranks have swelled with small-scale nanobrewers, rootless gypsy brewers, collaborators and conspirators, and homebrewers who straddle the amateur-professional divide—men and woman alike. Today's homebrewer might easily be tomorrow's brewing star.

Getting It Together: Brewery Collaborations

Let's pretend I own a factory manufacturing, oh, sneakers. It's a frenzied Friday afternoon on the assembly line and, lo and behold, I discover that I'm short shoelaces. My suppliers have clocked out. Work has halted. Deadlines are imminent. I need those laces—and the only person with any is my closest competitor. I'd be screwed. Why help a rival?

That's not the case for craft beer. Though breweries battle for the same bucks, the industry is driven less by competition than by kinship. "The brewing industry is collegial in nature," says Paul Gatza, the director of the Brewers Association. "Brewers are friends with their competitors. You often hear conversations like, 'Hey, do you have some Cascade hop pellets? I'm short this week.' That wouldn't happen in any other industry."

Further demonstrating their bonhomie, droves of brewers have teamed up to concoct collaboration beers. This is less a style than a phenomenon in which two (or three or six) breweries combine forces to create a singular beer. Sometimes brewers commingle to exchange ideas. Other times, it's to avoid a lawsuit. Back in 2001, Avery Brewing and Russian River Brewing Company discovered they both made beers named Salvation. Instead of calling lawyers, they ganged up in 2008 to release the now-annual Collaboration Not Ligation Ale, a combination of the two beers. It's 50 percent Avery's Belgian golden ale, 50 percent Russian River's Belgian strong ale—and 100 percent delicious.

Blending two batches is pretty extreme. Normally, brewers concoct a single recipe, one that lets their freak flags fly. Each year, Georgia's Terrapin Beer Co. and Colorado's Left Hand Brewing manufacture a madcap Midnight Project beer. (The 2010 release was Oxymoron, an American IPA brewed with a large portion of German malts and hops and Left Hand's proprietary lager yeast.) Chicago's Half Acre Beer Co. joined with Michigan's Short's Brewing in 2010 to make Freedom of '78, an IPA brewed with 1,000 pounds of guava fruit. Seattle's Elysian Brewing Company and Colorado's New Belgium create the Trip series, oftentimes crossing hopped-up West Coast ales with Belgian flair.

Two great breweries, one great beer. Teamwork never tasted so good.

TWO COLLABORATIONS TO TRY

BROOKLYNER-SCHNEIDER HOPFEN-WEISSE
BROOKLYN BREWERY AND PRIVATE WEISSBIERBRAUEREI G. SCHNEIDER & SOHN
ABV: 8.5%
BROOKLYN BREWMASTER GARRETT OLIVER AND HIS GERMAN COUNTERPART, SCHNEIDER'S HANS-PETER DREXLER, COLLABORATED ON THIS STRONG, HOPPY, LIMITED-RELEASE WHEAT BEER, WHICH THEY BREWED IN EACH OTHER'S BREWERIES. THOUGH BOTH BREWERIES SHARE THE LABEL, EACH VERSION DIFFERS SLIGHTLY IN THE DRY-HOPPING: DREXLER OPTED FOR AMERICA'S CITRIC AMARILLO AND FLORAL PALISADE HOPS, WHILE OLIVER WENT FOR GERMANY'S ZESTY HALLERTAUER SAPHIR (HIS VERSION IS SCHNEIDER-BROOKLYNER HOPFEN-WEISSE).

SIGNATURE SERIES
DE PROEF BROUWERIJ
ABV: VARIES
TO CREATE THE REVOLVING SIGNATURE RELEASES, MASTER BELGIAN BREWER DIRK NAUDTS PARTNERS WITH DIFFERENT AMERICAN BREWERS TO CREATE AN ALE THAT EMBODIES BOTH BREWERIES. FOR EXAMPLE, LES DEUX BRASSEURS (BREWED IN CONJUNCTION WITH ALLAGASH BREWING'S JASON PERKINS) WAS FERMENTED WITH EACH BREWERY'S BRETTANOMYCES STRAIN, WHILE VAN TWEE USES SOUR CHERRY JUICE FROM MICHIGAN—HOME TO BELL'S BREWER JOHN MALLET.

Professional Homebrew

Every couple of months, I become a tour guide. In New York, this is a commonplace profession: tourism is a bedrock of our economy, with pretty pennies to be earned escorting visitors to the Statue of Liberty and Times Square. That's not my bag. I'm a journalist and a beer lover, not necessarily in that order.

Thus, I lead a homebrewers tour. I escort suds fans to apartments and lofts, where we sample brewmasters' liquid bounty.

Yes, that's me.

Offerings run from the expected (inky stouts, citric IPAs) to the unexpected (Earl Grey tea–infused pale ales, peanut butter porters), with the commonality being the beer's quality: "I never expected homebrew to taste this good," two or three attendees will utter each tour. I'll smile, watching misconceptions burst like beer bubbles.

"I judge homebrew contests, and in every competition I find half a dozen beers that make me think, *That* could be a professional beer," says Paul Gatza, director of the Brewers Association. At its

Look at the happy hosts and attendees on my homebrew tour.

core, homebrewing is beer making's minor leagues, where liquid chefs perfect techniques and recipes before turning pro. When done properly, a pint of homebrew can be just as satisfying as anything poured at a corner saloon. In fact, that homebrew might be poured at a corner saloon.

Breweries such as Baltimore's Clipper City Brewing Co. and the Boston Beer Company sponsor competitions in which the winner's recipe is brewed, bottled, and sold. Other microbreweries, such as Widmer, collaborate with homebrewers to craft their suds, then distribute them. Building on that concept, Portland, Oregon's Green Dragon brewpub allows homebrewers to run its small, in-house brewing system—with the delicious results dispensed on draft. The line between amateur and professional brewers is growing as fuzzy as a barfly's eyes at last call.

GREAT AMERICAN BEER FESTIVAL PRO-AM COMPETITION

EACH SEPTEMBER, DENVER HOSTS THE GREAT AMERICAN BEER FESTIVAL, WHICH I LIKEN TO U.S. CRAFT BREWING'S SUPER BOWL. HUNDREDS OF MICROBREWERIES BRING THOUSANDS OF STOUTS, IPAS, AND BARREL-AGED ODDITIES TO THE MILE-HIGH CITY, HOPING TO WIN A MEDAL THAT COULD FOREVER ALTER THEIR FORTUNES. SAME GOES FOR HOMEBREWERS.

IN 2006, THE BREWERS ASSOCIATION AND THE AMERICAN HOMEBREWERS ASSOCIATION LAUNCHED THE GABF PRO-AM COMPETITION. "WE WANTED TO KEEP IN EVERYONE'S MIND IN THE INDUSTRY THAT PROFESSIONAL BREWERS COME FROM THE HOMEBREWING RANKS," BREWER'S ASSOCIATION DIRECTOR PAUL GATZA SAYS. IN THE CONTEST, BREWERIES PARTNER WITH HOMEBREWERS TO RE-CREATE THEIR AMATEUR RECIPES. BUT THIS IS NO MAKE-A-WISH EVENT: EACH TEAM IS EQUALLY INVESTED, WITH MEDALS AWARDED TO BOTH PROFESSIONAL AND AMATEUR—WHO MAY, IN TURN, BECOME TOMORROW'S PROFESSIONAL.

LAST CALL
9:45 PM

LAST POUR
9:50 PM

Yes, the Great American
Beer Festival is really
THAT much fun.

(Not) Fighting the Law

The legalities surrounding selling homebrewed beer are as clear as Bud Light. When President Jimmy Carter legalized homebrewing in the late 1970s, he allowed folks to brew up to 100 gallons of beer a year. Many brewers slosh over the threshold, but it's unlikely that cops will come a-knocking. That would happen only if homebrewers sold their tipples. "There's a defining line between amateurs and professionals: Are they selling their beer and paying their taxes?" Gatza says.

Vending beer means hacking through a tangled web of regulations wrapped around the three-tier system, in which breweries sell to distributors, which then peddle to stores and bars. Taxes are collected at every step. Plus, there's the cost of acquiring a federal permit from the Alcohol and Tobacco Tax and Trade Bureau. It's a pain in the butt to sell a pal a growler.

However, no law prohibits a brewery from producing a semipro's recipe. Each spring, San Diego's Stone Brewing Co. hosts a homebrewing competition, in which the winner's brew, such as Ken Schmidt's Aloha Plenty Porter in 2009, becomes the basis for a Collaboration Series release created with other breweries. In this case, Schmidt teamed up with Stone and Maui Brewing Co. to create Kona Coffee Macadamia Coconut Porter.

For its annual homebrewing battle, Baltimore's Clipper City Brewing Company, the maker of Heavy Seas beers, bestows the winner with the Letter of Marque—a document that once branded a pirate a professional privateer. "We're making a homebrewer a legitimate professional," says Clipper City founder Hugh Sisson.

The Letter of the Marque, which is released in Heavy Seas' strong-beer Mutiny Fleet Series, was born from Sisson's "enormous respect for people who homebrew on a really high level," he says. "People who are able to overcome the challenge of making beer with stockpots and other equipment that wasn't designed to make beer, and still focus on learning the process and craft, deserve to be commended."

Winning brewers are invited to Heavy Seas, where they discuss their recipe—say, a hoppy rye porter—with the brewmaster, then help craft the beer. "This is about passion, which is driving the craft beer industry. You don't get any more passionate than homebrewers."

More critically, if it weren't for homebrewers, America wouldn't have so many breweries. "When we started back in the eighties, homebrewers were nourishing the craft-brewing movement," says Boston Beer president Jim Koch, whose first batch of Sam Adams was concocted on his stove in 1984. In order to "keep the connection between craft brewing and homebrewing alive," Koch says, the Boston Beer Company launched the Samuel Adams LongShot American Homebrew Contest in 1996, soliciting recipes from brewers nationwide. Of the 800-plus annual entries, the top two,

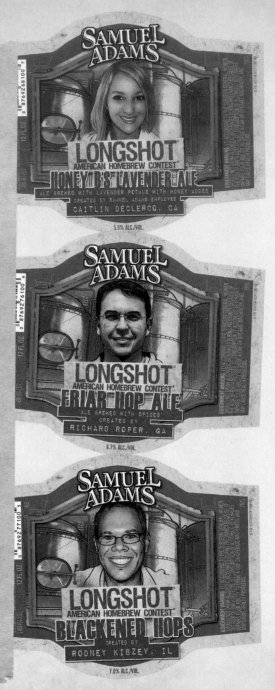

along with a Boston Beer employee's best brew, are scaled up and sold as the LongShot six-pack.

"As a professional brewer, the quality of LongShot beer reminds me that the line between a talented homebrewer and a professional is largely arbitrary and unrecognizable," Koch says of the winning beers, among which have counted a potent barley wine, a lemon-pepper saison, and a cranberry wit. After more than 25 years in the business, "I still learn from tasting homebrews," Koch says. "Some of the best brewers in this country are homebrewers."

Beer Today, Here Tomorrow

By and large, these amateurs-gone-legal beers are one-off

releases to be savored and never sipped again. Sometimes, though, a homebrew beer is so good a brewery can't say good-bye. In Portland, Maine, Peak Organic brewer Jon Cadoux was so smitten by pal Tim Broderick's IPA recipe that it inspired Peak's floral and citric ale—one of its biggest sellers. One of Boston Beer's LongShot winners leapt into regular rotation, with Ken Smith's Boysenberry Wheat becoming the basis for the Blackberry Witbier. "Homebrewers' experimentation can lead to a commercial product," Koch says.

That sentiment is understood in Portland, Oregon, home to Widmer Brothers Brewing Co. In the late 1990s, cofounder Rob Widmer says, homebrewers had limited access to the eclectic yeast strains now available. "Unless a guy was cultivating his own, the only yeast strain came from a packet of dried brewers' yeast, which was infinitely horrible stuff," he says.

To aid the Oregon Brew Crew, a homebrew club, Widmer Brothers began giving members the brewery's yeast strain. In return, Widmer Brothers asked for bottles of the resulting batch, helping the brewery better understand its yeast's properties. "Some of the beers they brought back were so good," Widmer recalls, that in January 1998 the brewery launched its annual Collaborator competition.

The rules are as simple as they are groundbreaking. Widmer Brothers foots the ingredient bill for the homebrewers to craft their beers. The resulting brews are entered into a contest. The winners (there could be one or four; nothing's set in stone) are invited to Widmer to help formulate and brew a large-scale batch of the victorious beer or beers, which then hits the local marketplace. To date, Widmer has released more than 30 Collaborator beers, from a bright and fresh kölsch to a smoked porter. Pop into Widmer's Gasthaus Pub or a fine Portland taphouse, and you'll likely find a Collaborator on draft. But of all the releases, it was the very first Collaborator—a milk stout, released in summer 1998—that was too tasty to let disappear from the draft line.

Collaborator Stout was so successful that it was selected in 1999 as the American Homebrewers Association's Big Brew recipe for National Homebrew Day, in which homebrewers nationwide use the same recipe. Then, in 2004, Widmer again boosted Collaborator Stout to the big leagues. The recipe served as the basis for Snowplow Stout, which ran for four years as the brewery's winter seasonal. Oh, and that year at the Great American Beer Festival? Snowplow won gold in the British stout category. Not a bad feather in a homebrewer's cap, indeed.

Think Your Homebrew Is Up to Snuff? Try Entering These Amateur-to-Pro Competitions

Contest	Sponsor	Qualifying Entrants	Prize
Samuel Adams Patriot Homebrew Contest	The Boston Beer Company samueladams.com/promotions/PatriotHomebrew	Open to homebrewers in ME, NH, VT, MA, RI, NY, CT	Winner will have their brew served at Gillette Stadium for the coming pro football season
Samuel Adams LongShot American Homebrew Contest	The Boston Beer Company samueladams.com/promotions/LongShot	Open to U.S. homebrewers	Two grand champions will have their beers included in the LongShot variety pack, available nationwide
Heavy Seas Letter of Marque	Clipper City Brewing Company Check hsbeer.com for details and announcements	Open to U.S. homebrewers	The winning brewer will work with Clipper City to brew the beer, available in most states east of the Mississippi River

Contest	Sponsor	Qualifying Entrants	Prize
Brew It Forward	LoneRider Brewing Company loneriderbeer.com/brew-it-forward	Open to North Carolina homebrewers	Winning brewer will work with LoneRider to brew the beer, sold in North Carolina
Big Batch Brew Bash	Kuykendahl Gran Brewers Homebrew Club (KGB) in conjunction with Saint Arnold Brewing Company thekgb.org/BigBatchBrewBash/CurrentNews.aspx	Open to U.S. homebrewers; each year's competition focuses on a predetermined style	The winning recipe serves as inspiration for a Saint Arnold Divine Reserve single-batch series release; sold in Texas
Stone Brewing's AHA March Madness Rally	Stone Brewing Co. stonebrew.com (check the website for special contest announcements)	The American Homebrewers Association Membership Rally is open to members residing in San Diego, Los Angeles, Orange County, San Bernardino, and Riverside counties in California	The winning brewer teams up with Stone and another brewery to create a Collaboration Series version of their recipe; available nationwide
The Bruery's Commemorative-Batch Contest	The Bruery thebruery.com (check the website for special contest announcements)	Open to members of the American Homebrewers Association	Winning brewer will work with the Bruery to brew the beer, sold nationwide

Meet Me at the Homebrew Pub

When people take my homebrew tour, the main attraction is the beer. Yet an equally important, if less acknowledged, lure is the voyeuristic thrill of entering a stranger's home. There's their toothbrush, their laundry basket, their cigarette-stained couch. Initially, attendees are awkward— until the second or third beer. Then the homey setting creates the kind of casual intimacy I wish existed at every bar. Strangers

The Elizabeth Street Brewery (above) and Richard Brewer-Hay crafting a batch of backyard beer.

talk. Relationships bloom. It's like a roving house party, which is a lovely thing.

That's what makes San Francisco's Elizabeth Street Brewery so wonderful. Back in 2003, eBay employee Richard Brewer-Hay began cooking five-gallon batches of beer on his stove. Richard's interest in brewing grew, but his home did not. His wife, Alyson, contacted the TV show *While You Were Out*, and the program transformed the couple's storage room into a speakeasy-like den decorated with a dartboard and beer bottles galore.

If it were up to me, I'd make this the ultimate man cave. Instead, Richard turned his den into what he dubs a "homebrew pub." "I've always been the one throwing the party," Brewer-Hay explains. "I had a huge mailing list, so I started inviting friends over to have beers." Maybe once a month, he and Alyson send out the word on Twitter (and their rather professional website), setting a time frame during which curious drinkers can stop by for free samples of his creamy Daddy's Chocolate Milk stout, hopped-up Auntie Ben's IPA, and namesake Elizabeth Street Bitter.

While it's a leap of faith to open his home and taps to strangers ("We once had more than a hundred people in our basement, and people were opening beers that were still fermenting," Richard says), by and large, "the kind of person who goes into someone's home is good people." To meet demand, Brewer-Hay now brews ten-gallon batches of beer, and he won't open his door unless he has at least fifteen gallons available. Adding to the bounty, local homebrewers often bring by beers to be poured on tap. In a way, he says, "we're providing a community service, by bringing the community together in almost a town-square setting."

If you're wondering how this is legal, it's because Elizabeth Street Brewery doesn't charge. People can provide donations, but there's no requirement. "We're like a nonprofit homebrewery," Brewer-Hay says. "We're not making any money, but we're not losing

that much, either." That may change. In 2010, Richard collaborated with Shaun O'Sullivan, of local brewery 21st Amendment, to create Imperial Jack, a souped-up ESB that won gold at the World Beer Cup. The success has started Brewer-Hay thinking about opening a legal brewpub. Still, he's hesitant to go pro.

"What we have going is as good as it's ever going to be, as far as an emotional reward. I don't have to deal with taxes, or regulations—but I do have to go to work," he says. If the pub happens, he wants to do it on his terms, in his neighborhood. "Everything has been very organic, from the growth of our fan base to the growth of my hobby," he says. "I don't want to force the next level."

Step Right Up to the Tap

If you're not lucky enough to hit Brewer-Hay's home, or visit Pat Wlodarczyk's Reno, Nevada, barn converted into the community-centric Woody's Nano Brewery, or have friends that brew, how else

BACK 30

1. Rogue Root Beer $2.50
2. Black 15 Cascadian Dark
3. Black Diamond Amber
4. Black Diamond IPA
5. Black Diamond Saison
6. Black Diamond Winter Dubbel
7. GREEN DRAGON FINALLY! IPA LIMITED
8. Widmer "Brrr"
9. Silver Moon "Hoptober Fresh"
10. Bayern Oktoberfest
11. Cascade "Autumn IPAnox"
12. Beer Valley "Black Flag" fresh hop hop Stout 8oz.
13. Ft. George "Co-Hoperative" fresh hop Belg
14. Mad River "Serious Madness" 8 oz.
15. Dogfish Head "Punkin" Ale

16. Alameda "Papa Noel"
17. New Belgium "Hoptoberfest"
18. 4th St. Lager
19. Oakshire Amber
20. Full Sail "Wassail"
21. Hopworks Urban Brewery ESB
22. Double Mountain "Hop Lava" IPA
23. Southern Oregon Brewing Porter
24. 7 Brides "Oatmeal Elle" Stout
25. Caldera Imperial Stout 8 oz.
26. Upright "Fresh Hop of Bel Air"
27. Eugene City Tracktown 200m IPA
28. Rogue "Si Rogue" Red
29. Laurelwood "Oktoberfest"
30. Lompoc NITRO Problematik Red
$2.75 for Pints-unless marked as 8 oz. pour.

GREEN DRAGON
FINALLY! IPA
release...
w/ 29 new taps~!

Above: Part of the tasty tap selection at Portland, Oregon's Green Dragon, where homebrewers' craft beer is served on site—check out No. 7.
Below: The Green Dragon's tap handle.

can you taste homebrew? Let's head back to the Oregon Brew Crew. While Widmer has been kind to the OBC, the club's beers are hardly exclusive to the brewery. In 2009, the OBC began a collaboration with Portland's Rogue Ales–owned Green Dragon Bistro & Brewpub.

Dubbed the Green Dragon Project, this unique union lets club members use the pub's single-barrel brewing system—equipment originally used by Rogue head brewer John Maier—to craft 20- to 22-gallon batches. Just messing around on Maier's system might be reward enough for some brewers, like an amateur ballplayer swinging Babe Ruth's bat. But Green Dragon goes one step beyond, offering each OBC beer as one of its 50-odd eclectic drafts.

"We've gotten a great response from the beer-drinking public," says OBC communications chair Josh Blender of the beers, which have included porters, dark and hoppy IPAs, and a farmhouse-style French ale partly aged in a

Rogue Dead Guy Ale whiskey barrel. "Each release"—there's a new one every few weeks—"usually only lasts a couple days."

On several levels, this project is an ideal educational tool. First, the OBC gets to act like a full-fledged, if small-scale, brewery. While Green Dragon supplies the brewing license and pays taxes, members of the Green Dragon Project Committee select and refine recipes, source ingredients (Rogue foots the bill), and shepherd the brew from conception to tap, including naming the liquid creation. Can I interest anyone in a pint of 5-Point Exploding Palate Technique or Golden Dragon Ale?

Second, and in some respects more crucial, this project educates consumers, breaking down barriers and drawing the connection between breweries, homebrewers, and bargoers. Most nights, a consumer can see firsthand "the amazing quality of beers that can come from homebrewers," Blender says. It's one thing to have someone praise a pint of homebrew in a basement, but it speaks volumes to pony up cold, hard cash.

Does this make it professional? Is it still amateur? Why make distinctions? No matter a beer's label, its quality boils down to a matter of taste.

Nanobreweries

Sometimes, a nasty recession can be a blessing. Just ask northern New Hampshire's Bill Herlicka. A couple of years ago, with the economy freefalling, Herlicka read the writing on the wall at his Fortune 500 firm. "I knew I was facing an impending layoff," Herlicka says.

Instead of panicking, he assessed his situation. Since 1994, this resident of teensy Hooksett (population: about 13,000) had been a passionate homebrewer, cranking out Belgian tripels, bold and complex Russian imperial stouts, and oak-aged English barley

White Birch founder Bill Herlicka doing what he does best.

wines. "I loved beer and brewing"—he even built a beer cellar to study how brews age and evolve—"and people seemed to enjoy what I made," he explains. As for the job, "I realized I hadn't been happy with what I'd been doing. I thought, You only live once. Let's see how you can make a brewery work."

In June 2009, Herlicka launched the artisanal White Birch microbrewery—extra emphasis on the *micro*. White Birch Brewing began as a one-man operation, with Herlicka brewing, bottling, labeling, and distributing his robust, nuanced line of limited-edition barley wines, sour ales inoculated with wild yeasts and bacteria, and Belgian-inspired brews. Emphasis on *limited*. When he started, Herlicka brewed only one barrel (about 31 gallons) at a time, meaning that each release comprised just a couple hundred 22-ounce bottles.

"My only goal for 'production' is to grow organically in a way that doesn't burden me with huge debt and does not make me feel I have to cut a corner to meet an arbitrary goal," Herlicka says.

In recent years, the global beer industry has consolidated. Behemoths such as Anheuser-Busch and InBev, as well as Miller and Coors, have combined to gobble market share. Conversely, many microbreweries are growing itsy-bitsier. Nowadays, homebrewers who are eager to turn pro yet keep their operations intimate and expand as demand necessitates are opening nanobreweries: a small-scale, do-it-yourself brewery typically run by one or two people on a threadbare budget *and* operating on a three-barrel system or smaller.

"My son is my only employee—and I don't pay him," jokes Jim Jamison, owner of Foggy Noggin Brewing in Bothell, Washington. In his spare time, he produces half-barrel batches of English-style ales, distributing beer to neighbors, folks who drive up to his garage brewery, and outlets around Seattle. "I like getting to know the people that drink my beer."

Back to Brewing's Roots

Consider this a revival of the concept of the village brewer. During the early days of the twentieth century, America was dotted with breweries rooted in the community, whose beers slaked townsfolk's thirst. Too bad Prohibition, combined with America's push toward industrialization, wiped aside these unique lager makers. This Bud's for you—and you, and you, and you.

No longer. Hyperlocal nanobreweries are bringing craft beer to the community level. On Long Island, Blind Bat Brewery's Paul Dlugokencky fashions three-barrel batches of flavorful artisanal ales, such as the Long Island Potato Stout, made with locally grown organic potatoes. On the other coast, Northern California attorney Kevin McGee spends his weekends running Healdsburg Beer Company, concocting brews like the English-style IPA Alexander Cask. And in Northwood, Iowa (a town of about 2,000 located on the Minnesota border), brewer Peter Ausenhus's Worth Brewing Company (he is partners with wife Margaret Bishop) is turning out ten-gallon batches of spicy saison and the malty, hazy, well-hopped Dillon Clock Stopper.

When it comes to brewing delicious beer, size doesn't matter.

Dollars and Sense

When making the professional leap, brewers need a business plan as excellent as their beer. After factoring in the costs of securing space, equipment, and licensing fees (not to mention grains and hops), the funds needed to open a brewery easily crest $100,000—and often go much, much higher. Then there's the issue of selling enough six-packs or kegs to start repaying the loan. Debt can doom even the best brewer.

Nonetheless, brewers don't need six figures of seed money to make and sell quality beer. In Seattle, Schooner Exact Brewing Company began in June 2006, when homebrewers Heather and Matt McClung wanted to increase their production capacity to brew beer for their pending nuptials. They found a used pilot system for about $1,500 and, along with pal Marcus Connery, decided to purchase it. When the men were retrieving the system, Heather told MSN.com, the men looked at each other and mused, "Wouldn't it be cool if we decided to go pro?" That idle thought became Schooner Exact, makers of beers like the assertively hopped 3-Grid IPA and the summery Gallant Maiden Hefeweizen.

Whereas Schooner Exact waded into the waters of a city with a thriving craft-beer scene, Peter Ausenhus opted to make a splash in a small town. Ausenhus caught craft-beer fever back in the 1990s, when he worked for Minnesota's Northern Brewer supply shop, then put in time at St. Paul's Summit Brewing. In 1998, he and his wife, Margaret Bishop, relocated across the Iowa border to a farmstead in Worth County's Northwood. Bishop launched a successful engineering firm.

A decade later, in 2007, Ausenhus decided to turn his passion into a profession. He bought downtown's historic Peoples Gas and Electric Building and rechristened it Worth Brewing. Perhaps a better name would have been Cross Your Fingers Brewing. "Our main concern was, 'Are these people going to take to craft beer?'"

Worth Brewing's Peter Ausenhus picking through a pile of hops.

Ausenhus recalls. "Most of the residents were Bud and Miller drinkers, who hadn't tried any craft beer."

Working in his favor was the low barrier to entry—since Iowa liquor licenses are based on a percentage of a population, his cost about $250 annually—a modest ten-gallon brewing setup, and no payroll. Ausenhus decided to serve as brewer and bartender, pouring a pale ale, lightly hopped brown ale, and an easy-drinking cream ale. "I thought, I better have one more on the mild side," he says, laughing. To his surprise, his brown ale took off, as did business. "When we were imagining this and thinking how many pints we needed to sell a day, we thought, 'Can we sustain it?'" Ausenhus says. "I thought, 'Well, I'll do this part-time.' Very quickly it went full-time."

Encouraged by consistent sales, Ausenhus started expanding his beer selection. Now among his six taps you can find a wet-hopped ale, Smoked Kellerbier, and even a Belgian Grand Cru. "We're attracting people from thirty miles around," Ausenhus says. "It's nice to feel like I'm a productive member of the community."

No Compromising Taste

For brewers, one of the benefits of running a nanobrewery is creative control. With no boss to demand they make a double IPA or, say, a Christmas ale, brewers can indulge their creative muse and craft the beers they crave. "I have twenty-three different beers fermenting in the brewery, as well as several wild ales that might not see the light of day for two or three years," says White Birch's Herlicka, who also has beers aging in oak barrels once used for bourbon, whiskey, and wine. "The ability to be creative and actually call it a business—what can be better than that?"

That's what drives McMinnville, Oregon's Rick Allen. After more than two decades as a homebrewer, the Oregonian founded Heater/Allen Brewing in 2007 with a focus that's rarely found on the hop-mad West Coast: classic, German-style beers such as his effervescent Pils.

"There was this huge hole in Oregon," Allen explains of concentrating on German-style beers. His decision was both aided and hindered by the quality of imported German beer. "So much of what we get on the West Coast is stale," Allen says. "It works in my favor because people say, 'Wow, this is really fresh.' On the other hand, people don't want to try German beers because what's available is stale or pasteurized."

To ensure his beer met his exacting standards, Allen embraced a kind of obsessive-compulsion common to restaurant chefs and professional brewers. "In 2006, I started brewing the same things over and over. I brewed fifteen consecutive batches of my pilsner.

My main concern was getting brewhouse procedures down and to understand the ingredients."

Likewise, Foggy Noggin's Jamison also noticed an underserved niche in the Northwest beer-drinking scene. "No one was doing any classic British beers," he says. Unlike prevailing Pacific Northwest styles such as IPAs and imperial IPAs, whose alcohol percentage can hit double digits, Jamison's flagship, the Bit o' Beaver bitter, registers 3.4 percent ABV. "It's a beer you can drink two or three of," he says proudly.

A loyal Foggy Noggin customer.

Since he brews only on a half-barrel system, Jamison could quickly face the problem of demand outstripping output. "I'd rather have my fear be 'People can't have enough beer' than worry about trying to pay back a loan or employee expenses," he says. "I don't have any debt—and I want to keep it that way."

Trouble in Paradise

Freedom. Creative control. What's the catch? Well, running a brewery by the seat of your pants can have its drawbacks too. With few, or no, employees, a helping hand can be hard to find. "In my head, I knew I was going to be working a lot of hours, but it's different once you're actually *working* the sheer number of hours," Worth's Ausenhus says. However, he has no qualms about brewing; as the only employee, it's pouring beer that drives him batty. "I'd rather be on the other side of the bar drinking the beer," he says, laughing.

When you go it alone at a nanobrewery, you're forced to assume every role: beer maker, custodian, distributor, and, most crucially, salesman. "You've got to be comfortable selling beer, because that's at least fifty percent of the job," explains Heater/Allen's Rick Allen. He first released his beer in bottles but found shelf space tough to come by in competitive Portland, Oregon. "It would've been smarter to have been in kegs first," because people are more willing to try a draft beer, Allen says. With bottles, "it's difficult to increase your volume in the market."

But with a push toward kegs, Heater/Allen is growing: In 2010, he produced 428 barrels of beer, inching toward his goal of about 575 a year. Allen has even hired his first employee: his daughter, who has been able to help with the increased brewing, kegging, and cleaning.

Small, measured growth is a fact of life for many nanobreweries. When you're brewing such small quantities, there's nowhere to go but up. Build your brand, create demand, and very quickly a nanobrewery can become a small craft brewery. In 2009, Plains, Pennsylvania, pals Chris Miller and Mark Lehman turned Miller's garage into Breaker Brewing Company. On a wood-lined one-and-a-half-barrel system, they created liquid tributes to the area's mining past, such as the coffee-y Olde King Coal Stout. A bit more than a year into the endeavor, the duo increased production to four barrels and will soon relocate to a former church they'll convert into a brewpub. White Birch is now brewing up to seven-barrel batches (and operates an apprentice program for young brewers), while Schooner Exact has upgraded to a fifteen-barrel system.

But for some brewers, staying itty-bitty suits them just fine. "There's no guarantee that I'd make more money if I expanded," Ausenhus says. "Being small, I have total freedom."

TEN NANOBREWERIES TO TRY

BARRIER BREWING CO.

OCEANSIDE, NEW YORK

BARRIERBREWING.COM

"BREWING FOR QUALITY, NOT QUANTITY" IS THE MOTTO OF EVAN KLEIN'S SINGLE-BARREL BREWERY LOCATED ON THE SOUTH SHORE OF LONG ISLAND. HE SPECIALIZES IN AROMATIC, HOP-FORWARD BREWS SUCH AS THE SPICY RUTHLESS RYE IPA, GREENROOM PALE ALE, AND THE CARDAMOM-SPICED BEECH ST. WHEAT. BARRIER BEERS ARE SOLD ON DRAFT AT BARS IN LONG ISLAND AND NEW YORK CITY AND BY THE GROWLER AT THE BREWERY.

LAWSON'S FINEST LIQUIDS

WARREN, VERMONT

LAWSONSFINEST.COM

VETERAN HOMEBREWER SEAN LAWSON SPECIALIZES IN SMALL-BATCH CURIOSITIES SUCH AS MAPLE TRIPPLE, A STRONG ALE BREWED ONCE A YEAR DURING SUGARING SEASON WITH MAPLE SAP INSTEAD OF WATER, AND RED SPRUCE BITTER, A COLD-WEATHER SEASONAL SPICED WITH CINNAMON AND INFUSED WITH SPRIGS FROM RED SPRUCE TREES. DRAFT AND BOTTLE DISTRIBUTION IS LIMITED TO VERMONT'S MAD RIVER VALLEY.

OYSTERHOUSE BREWING COMPANY

ASHEVILLE, NORTH CAROLINA

OYSTERHOUSEBEERS.COM

LOCATED INSIDE ASHEVILLE'S LOBSTER TRAP RESTAURANT, OYSTERHOUSE

BREWING USES A HALF-BARREL SYSTEM TO CRAFT TASTY BREWS SUCH AS UPSIDE DOWN BROWN (MADE WITH BROWN SUGAR) AND MOONSTONE STOUT. EACH BATCH INCLUDES FIVE POUNDS OF OYSTERS, SHELLS INCLUDED, WHICH IMPARTS A SLIGHTLY SALINIC CHARACTER. FIND THE BEER AT THE BREWERY.

THE BLIND BAT BREWERY
CENTERPORT, NEW YORK

BLINDBATBREWERY.COM

BAD VISION INSPIRED THE NAME OF ILLUSTRATOR PAUL DLUGOKENCKY'S PART-TIME OPERATION, BASED ON THE NORTH SHORE OF LONG ISLAND. USING A THREE-BARREL SYSTEM (A STEP UP FROM HIS ONE-THIRD-OF-A-BARREL BEGINNINGS), DLUGOKENCKY CREATES IDIOSYNCRATIC SMOKED BEERS SUCH AS HIS CAMPFIRE-FLAVORED HELLSMOKE PORTER AND BELGIAN-ESQUE BEACHED BLONDE, JAZZED UP WITH CARDAMOM AND CORIANDER. FIND HIS BEERS ON DRAFT AND IN BOTTLES ON LONG ISLAND AND IN NEW YORK CITY.

HESS BREWING
SAN DIEGO, CALIFORNIA

HESSBREWING.COM

MIKE HESS AND HIS WIFE, LYNDA, RUN SAN DIEGO'S FIRST LICENSED NANOBREWERY, WHICH IS AMONG THE CITY'S SMALLEST. HESS, WHO BOASTS MORE THAN A DECADE OF HOMEBREWING EXPERIENCE, CHURNS OUT 1.6-BARREL BATCHES OF BEERS INFLUENCED BY EUROPE (GOLDEN CLARITAS KÖLSCH),

Merry drinkers mingling at San Diego's Hess Brewing.

MEXICO (GRAZIAS VIENNA CREAM ALE), AND THE WEST COAST (WILDLY HOPPED AMPLUS ACERBA SAN DIEGO PALE ALE). BUY HESS AT SAN DIEGO PUBS AND AT THE BREWERY.

LEFTY'S BREWING COMPANY

BERNARDSTON, MASSACHUSETTS

LEFTYSBREW.COM

FORMER ROOFER BILL "LEFTY" GOLDFARB RUNS THIS TWO-BARREL BREWERY. HE HAND-BOTTLES AND HAND-LABELS EACH BREW, INCLUDING CHOCOLATE OATMEAL STOUT, COFFEE PORTER, AND ROBUST PALE ALE WITH A FULL-ON FLORAL AROMA. LEFTY'S IS SOLD AT SELECT BARS AND STORES IN NORTH-CENTRAL MASSACHUSETTS.

CRAFT BREWING COMPANY

LAKE ELSINORE, CALIFORNIA

CRAFTBREWINGCOMPANY.COM

WITH MORE THAN 50 YEARS OF BREWING EXPERIENCE AMONG THEM, A QUARTET OF HOMEBREWERS TOOK THEIR PASSION TO A PROFESSIONAL LEVEL IN MARCH 2010. THE DEPENDABLE, WAY-DRINKABLE OFFERINGS INCLUDE SILKY, VANILLA-HINTED RAVEN STOUT AND LIGHTLY HOPPED OBADIAH POUNDAGE PORTER. SWING BY THE BREWERY FOR A GROWLER FILL.

FOGGY NOGGIN BREWING

BOTHELL, WASHINGTON

FOGGYNOGGINBREWING.COM

IN MARCH 2010, JIM JAMISON TURNED HIS GARAGE INTO A TRADITIONAL ENGLISH-STYLE BREWERY, FEATURING MILDS AND BITTERS CONCOCTED IN HALF-BARREL BATCHES. COME WEEKENDS, YOU CAN PULL UP TO HIS HOUSE AND FILL A GROWLER, OR HIT UP ONE OF THE NUMEROUS WASHINGTON PUBS CARRYING HIS BRITISH BREWS.

VERTIGO BREWING

HILLSBORO, OREGON

VERTIGOBREW.COM

A WAREHOUSE SERVES AS THE HEADQUARTERS FOR MIKE HAINES AND MIKE KINION'S VERTIGO BREWING. THE TWOSOME BREW OFFBEAT FRUIT BEERS, SUCH AS CRISP APRICOT CREAM ALE AND REFRESHING RAZZ WHEAT, MADE WITH MORE THAN TWELVE POUNDS OF RASPBERRIES PER BARREL. VERTIGO BEGAN WITH A SINGLE-BARREL SYSTEM BUT HAS SINCE UPGRADED TO A SEVEN-BARREL SYSTEM. SAMPLE THEIR BEERS ON DRAFT AT BARS AROUND WESTERN OREGON.

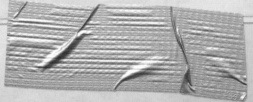

NATIAN BREWERY

PORTLAND, OREGON

NATIANBREWERY.COM

A PART-TIME OPERATION RUN BY NATALIA LAIRD AND IAN MCGUINNESS, NATIAN—A MASH-UP OF THEIR FIRST NAMES—USES A 1.3-BARREL SYSTEM TO BREW BEERS SUCH AS DESTINATION HONEY RED (MADE WITH OREGON HONEY), THEIR BALANCED EVERYDAY IPA, AND LUMBERJANE STOUT. FIND NATIAN'S BEERS ON TAP AT PORTLAND BARS.

Natian founders Natalia and Ian.

Nomadic Brewers

For Baltimore's Brian Strumke, the party was coming to an end. The techno DJ and producer had long made a living performing in Europe. But gigs were growing scarcer. Boredom had set in. "I needed a creative outlet," Strumke says.

Looking to channel his restless energy into a new hobby, he borrowed a brewing kit from his friend and started making batches in his kitchen. Like a piano-playing child prodigy, Strumke showed a savant-like knack for formulating flavorful, innovative beers such as a cabernet sauvignon lambic and a Belgian ale flavored with molasses and ginger. On a lark, he entered them into Samuel Adams LongShot and Holiday Homebrew competitions, as well as the American Homebrewers Association's National Homebrew Competition. He won. "I thought it was a mistake at first," Strumke says.

That wasn't Strumke's big break. It came one day in 2009, when Belgian-beer writer Charles "Chuck" Cook convinced Brian Ewing, owner of Brooklyn's 12 Percent Imports, to sample Strumke's beers. Ewing was wowed at first sip, both by the brews and by where they were manufactured. "Brian was amazed that I brewed this stuff in my basement and backyard," Strumke says. Ewing struck up a deal to distribute Strumke's beers, starting with Stateside Saison, under the label Stillwater Artisanal Ales. Only there was one problem: He needed a production facility, and his backyard wouldn't do.

Luckily, Strumke had a friend who used to own DOG Brewing Co., located in nearby Westminster, Maryland. He approached DOG

Stillwater's zesty Stateside Saison.

about brewing on-site, under a relationship called an alternating proprietorship. They bit. "We had a contract drawn up within twenty-four hours," he says. And so, Stillwater was born—without a brewery to call its own.

Follow the Money

Building a production brewery from the ground up is insanely expensive. Costs can spiral into hundreds of thousands—if not millions—before suds enter a keg. For many brewers, alternating proprietorships are an appealing middle ground between paying someone to brew your beer (contract brewing) and investing in infrastructure. It's a relationship that's beneficial to both brewer and brewery owner due to a simple fact: Like an airplane, a brewery should be running full-time, at 100 percent capacity. If there's extra capacity, it behooves the brewery owner to rent time on its brewing system.

These relationships aren't always advertised, but look closely, and you'll see them. In Asheville, North Carolina, the Biltmore Brewing Company brews its British-style Cedric's ales at the local Highland Brewing Company, while Erie, Pennsylvania's Lavery Brewing Company leases equipment at Brewerie, a local brewpub.

Start Me Up

Dann Paquette has been a professional brewer since 1992, tending to kettles and fermentation tanks across the Northeast and England. By 2008, he was ready to be his own boss. So, along with his wife, Martha Holley-Paquette, a scientist at MIT, he decided to launch Pretty Things Beer and Ale Project. While they had boundless ideas and enthusiasm, they had precious little capital.

"The paradox for a brewer is that, if you've been brewing for any length of time, you don't have enough extra money," Dann says. "Doing it on your own is out of the question." Luckily, Dann, now based in Cambridge, Massachusetts, had colleagues at Westport's Buzzard's Bay Brewing, located about 70 miles away. The brewery had extra capacity. Pretty Things found a place to hang its shingle. "I treat it like it's my own brewery," Dann explains. "I get there five hours before anyone else does."

Pretty Things' do-it-all duo Martha Holley-Paquette and Dann Paquette.

Untethered to loan payments, Dann is able to explore whatever catches his fancy. One week, he'll do a hopped-up Belgian Tripel, the next, a vintage British mild that clocks in at nearly 10 percent ABV. Even his flagship brew, Jack D'Or saison, goes against convention, created with a trio of yeast strains and a quartet of hops. "I have complete creative control," Dann says. "Having worked for so many breweries for so many years, I can tell you what most did wrong. It's always the same problem: You are desperate to make your money back quickly. I'll never take a dime of anyone else's money."

Restless Brewers

The term *nomadic brewer* may be a bit misleading. By and large, most brewers are crafting their IPAs and stouts at a single location. It's a stable relationship. Copenhagen's Mikkel Borg Bjergsø doesn't care for that kind of stability. Since the part-time schoolteacher launched Mikkeller in summer 2007, he's developed a cult following with his offbeat beers. His Beer Geek Brunch Weasel coffee stout is made with Vietnamese beans that have been fed to and then "harvested" from the droppings of the civet cat (the referenced "weasel"), said to add a "certain something" to the

Mikkeller's genius gypsy brewer, Mikkel Borg Bjergsø.

flavor of the beans. Meanwhile, the abundantly bittered 1000 IBUs is enough to make you OD on hops.

Even more interesting than the beers is where Bjergsø—whose illustrated bearded image graces every bottle—brews them: *everywhere*. He'll make ox-strong stouts at Norway's Nøgne Ø, then craft barrel-aged ales and IPAs at Belgium's De Proef Brouwerij and collaborate on a tripel at San Diego's Stone Brewing. Making matters easier, the breweries usually source the ingredients, and an importer picks up Bjergsø's beer and distributes it. "I get to have all the fun," he says, "and I don't have to clean up."

This brand of international beer making also appeals to Strumke. In addition to brewing in Maryland, his importer arranged for him to create beers at smaller breweries in Belgium. "Brian [Ewing] said, 'Let Brian brew this batch, and I'll buy this from you, cash in hand.'" So Strumke headed to a small brewery in Beerzel, Belgium, to make his Of Love & Regret saison, featuring chamomile, dandelion, and lavender, and A Saison Darkly, which incorporates rose hips and hibiscus.

"Belgium is my testing ground," he says. "It's definitely a unique endeavor—an American going over to Belgium to create a beer for the American market." The former DJ also enjoys the itinerant lifestyle. "I was used to traveling for music, and I took that business model and pumped it over to the beer world."

Too Small for Their Britches

For many brewers, running their fledgling operation as an alternating proprietorship is a great way to get off the ground. However, this relationship can be as tenuous and troubling as it is beneficial.

In 2008, veteran Nebraska brewer Zac Triemert was looking to branch out. He left his head-brewer position at Omaha's Upstream Brewing to launch the Lucky Bucket Brewing Company. Instead of buying equipment, he hooked up with the SchillingBridge Winery & Microbrewery, located in Pawnee City, just south of Omaha. It seemed like a great fit: "It allowed us to launch our brand," Triemert says. Nebraskans were soon snapping up his light, aromatic lager. A good thing, right?

"It feels so naïve to look back now, but I originally thought that I would be working at this alternating proprietorship for three years," Triemert says. "After three months, it became apparent that we were going to run out of capacity." Triemert scrapped his business plan and began building his own brewery. His team worked quickly, cobbling together used brewing equipment. They weren't fast enough. "Our contract with the brewery ended a little early, so our production went dry for six weeks," Triemert recalls.

Such are the pitfalls of working on another brewery's schedule. If product demand increases, or if there's a special beer brewed that ties up the fermentation tanks, then the brewery renting space loses out. "You're leaving your whole company and brand in the hands of someone else's business," Triemert says. "If you're not in control of the equipment, you could really suffer. If I'm running a business, I wouldn't put an alternating proprietorship as part of my business plan."

Even if a brewery has excess capacity, that's not an open invitation. "Most breweries I know wouldn't let someone come in and start brewing on their equipment," Pretty Things' Dann Paquette says. "If someone were to say, 'I've got this business and I've been homebrewing for ten years,' 99.9 percent of the time the answer would be no. The brewery would be like, 'You're not touching our $250,000 brewing system.'"

Plus, there's the public perception that sometimes accompanies this unusual arrangement. "When I started in Denmark four years ago, people looked at me like I wasn't a brewer because I didn't have a brewery," Bjergsø says. "You can be a great clothing designer without owning your own factory." Now breweries in Denmark are following his lead. Excess capacity is tougher to find.

Would Bjergsø consider starting his own full-scale production brewery? He'd be able to set his own brewing schedule, travel less, perhaps spend more time with his daughter. No, thanks, he says. "I'm opening a bar instead."

THREE TO TRY

BABY TREE
PRETTY THINGS BEER
AND ALE PROJECT
ABV: 9%

FOR AN EVERYDAY GUZZLER, I FAVOR PRETTY THINGS' JACK D'OR SAISON, WHICH DRINKS DRY AND PEPPERY, WITH A HINT OF HOP BITTERNESS AND A MOUTHFEEL AS PRICKLY AS A CACTUS. HOWEVER, WHEN STEPPING UP TO THE BIG LEAGUES, I OPT FOR BABY TREE. THE DARK, STRONG BELGIAN BREW (THE NAME IS INSPIRED BY A FRIEND'S TREE FILLED WITH DIRTY, DISCARDED BABY DOLLS) IS PACKED WITH DRIED PLUMS, CREATING A VELVETY, CARAMEL— SWEET SIPPER WITH A CHARACTER THAT RECALLS FRUITCAKE.

BEER GEEK BREAKFAST

MIKKELLER

ABV: 7.5%

RISE AND SHINE WITH A BIG OL' GLASS OF BEER GEEK BREAKFAST. WHAT ABOUT COFFEE? NOT NECESSARY, THANKS TO GEEK'S INFUSION OF EVERYONE'S FAVORITE MORNING STIMULANT. BUT THE GRAIN BILL (CHOCOLATE MALTS, OATS, ROASTED BARLEY) GIVES GEEK A FULL BODY, MOUTH-COATING CREAMINESS, AND AN AROMA THAT EVOKES MILK CHOCOLATE. YOU HAVE MY PERMISSION TO START DRINKING BEFORE NOON.

CELLAR DOOR AMERICAN FARMHOUSE ALE

STILLWATER ARTISANAL ALES

ABV: 6.6%

THERE'S NOTHING DARK AND DREARY ABOUT CELLAR DOOR, STILLWATER'S SUMMERY SAISON. THE BEER'S BACKBONE IS GERMAN WHEAT AND PALE MALTS, WHICH MAKES CELLAR AS CRISP AS A PRESSED SHIRT AND AS CLOUDY AS SEATTLE. THE AROMA AND FLAVORS COME FROM STERLING AND CITRA HOPS, WHICH MEAN TONS OF TANGERINE AND A GRASSY CHARACTER. OH, AND THAT EARTHY ACCENT? THAT'S SAGE.

Women in Brewing

If you pay a trip to Westport, Massachusetts, where Dann Paquette and Martha Holley-Paquette toil at Pretty Things, you'll notice little division of labor. While Dann may be head brewer, Martha is just as likely to heft 55-pound grain sacks, mill malt, wash and fill kegs, paint tap handles, and formulate recipes. Oh, and she handles the accounting too.

"I love everything about working in a brewery," Holley-Paquette says. As a woman, she's not alone. While brewing may be male dominated, a growing league of ladies has made inroads into the craft-beer industry. The Pink Boots Society—only women in brewing can join—counts more than 500 members, from managers to sales representatives to brewers mashing grain.

This isn't unusual; this is *normal*. For thousands of years—stretching from Sumerians to Egyptians, from Vikings to colonial Americans—women were tasked with brewing, mainly at home. But according to the historian Alan Eames, this practice declined around the end of the eighteenth century. Blame money. Men saw they could turn a buck from beer. Industrial breweries blossomed. And, just like that, women were relegated to the sidelines of brewing.

No longer. Women have been vital to the resurgence of American craft beer. In the mid-1980s, Jim Koch's right hand was Rhonda Kallman, who was instrumental in growing Sam Adams from a fledgling lager to an international brand. In 1987, Carol and Ed Stoudt founded Stoudt's Brewing Company, with Carol serving as brewmaster. Down in Mississippi, Leslie Henderson brews Lazy Magnolia Brewing Company's beers, such as Jefferson Stout, made with sweet potatoes. Up in Oregon, Tonya Cornett is Bend Brewing Co.'s brewmaster, cranking out the medal-winning Cherry Baltic Porter and Black Diamond Dark Lager. And the brewer list stretches on, counting Denise Jones (Moylan's Brewery in Novato, California), Jenny Talley (Utah's Squatters Pubs & Beers), and Barbara Groom (Lost Coast Brewery in Eureka, California).

But for women, brewing may be just the beginning. Recent studies have shown that when judging beer, women may have more

Lazy Magnolia brewmaster Leslie Henderson and her husband, Mark.

acute senses of smell and taste than men. "Females often are more sensitive about the levels of flavor in beer," Barry Axcell, SABMiller's chief brewer, told the *Wall Street Journal*. Underscoring that, every year SABMiller runs an international competition among its 2,000 beer tasters to uncover the company's best taste buds. In 2010, three of the six finalists were women, and the winner was Poland's Joanna Wasilewska.

Men, your days may be numbered.

FIVE TO TRY

8-BALL STOUT
LOST COAST BREWERY
ABV: 5.5%

FOUNDED IN 1990 BY WENDY POUND AND BARBARA GROOM, NORTHERN CALIFORNIA'S LOST COAST FOCUSES ON ENGLISH-LEANING ALES SUCH AS THE DOWNTOWN BROWN NUT BROWN ALE AND 8-BALL. LEADING WITH A SCENT OF CITRIC HOPS AND HOT COCOA, THE OATMEAL STOUT DRINKS CREAMY AND NIMBLE, HIGHLIGHTING FLAVORS OF COFFEE AND BITTERSWEET CHOCOLATE.

HOP-HEAD IMPERIAL IPA
BEND BREWING CO.
ABV: 9.2%

BREWER TONYA CORNETT'S IMPERIAL IPA IS A SYMPHONY OF EXCESSIVE IBUS, FEATURING A NOSE OF TROPICAL FRUITS, JUICY MELONS, AND PINE. UNLIKE SO MANY IMPERIALS, HH KEEPS THE SWEET MALT DIALED BACK; DESPITE THE SHARP, BITTER BLAST, IT STILL TIPTOES ACROSS YOUR TONGUE.

Chasing Tail GOLDEN ALE
SQUATTERS PUBS & BEERS
ABV: 4%

HEAD BREWER JENNY TALLEY'S SUMMERTIME SIPPER DECANTS A TRANSLUCENT GOLD, SPORTING A MALTY BOUQUET THAT'S A BIT EARTHY AND FRUITY—THANK YOU, U.K. HOPS. CHASING TAIL STARTS OFF WITH LIGHT HONEY SWEETNESS, THEN GOES GRASSY. IT'S A CLEAN AND QUENCHING GULPER.

GOLD LAGER
STOUDT'S BREWING COMPANY
ABV: 4.7%

TO COMPETE WITH CZECH PILSNERS, GERMANS BREWERS IN THE 1800S CREATED THE HOPPIER GOLDEN LAGER CALLED MUNICH HELLES (GERMAN FOR BRIGHT). CAROL STOUDT'S TAKE (ONE OF THE COUNTRY'S BEST) POURS THE COLOR OF SUNSHINE, WITH A LIGHT BODY, A MORSEL OF SWEET MALT, AND A HOP SNAP.

SOUTHERN PECAN NUT BROWN ALE
LAZY MAGNOLIA BREWING COMPANY
ABV: 4.5%

HUSBAND AND WIFE MARK AND LESLIE HENDERSON (SHE'S THE BREWER) HEAD LAZY MAGNOLIA, MISSISSIPPI'S FIRST CRAFT BREWERY. SHE FOCUSES ON SOUTHERN INGREDIENTS, IN THIS CASE, ROASTED PECANS, WHICH GIVE THE AMBER-TONED ALE A SMOOTH, NUTTY CHARACTER. IT'S AN ALL-AFTERNOON DRINKER.

Women's Taste

One day in 2006, Suzanne Woods was tending bar at a Philadelphia Belgian-beer haunt. It was a slow afternoon, so perhaps that's why Woods, who began her suds-based career as a rep for Boston Beer, paid such close attention to the ladies who strolled in and ordered doppelbocks, a mocha porter, and other specialty brews. Since there were few customers, Woods spent time talking beer with the women, an experience that lit her lightbulb: "It got me excited about the idea of ladies tasting beer together," says Woods, who soon thereafter founded the women's beer-tasting club In Pursuit of Ale.

More or less twice a month, Woods (a writer better known as the Beer Lass and a sales rep for Sly Fox Brewing Company) organizes a meeting at a different Philadelphia bar serving at least six craft beers. Each IPA meeting focuses on educating attendees about subjects such as styles of beer (not just bitter IPAs, a common misconception due to the group's acronym), food-beer pairings, hops, and homebrewing, all accompanied by copious liquid research. Since 2006, IPA has welcomed more than 600 craft-curious women, nannies, personal trainers, and lawyers, experts and neophytes included.

"It's great to see younger women embrace craft beer," says Woods, whose club has company countrywide. In San Francisco, there's Women Who Like Beer, while Boston has Women in Beer; Girls Pint Out features chapters in Indiana, Arizona, Texas, and Illinois. In early 2011, brewer and Pink Boots Society founder Teri Fahrendorf launched Barley's Angels, a global network of beer-education chapters for women. While these are women-focused gatherings, the opposite sex isn't always excluded. "I'm just as excited to share a beer with a guy as a girl," says Woods, whose group hosts four male-female mixers annually, including a killer Christmas shindig. "I'm not a woman who likes to drink beer," Woods says. "I'm a person who likes to drink beer."

SEVEN

NICE PACKAGE:

Craft Beer Has Found a Happy New Home in Cans and Growlers

ONCE UPON A TIME, YOU COULD JUDGE A BEER ON looks alone. Cheap, crappy quaffs were found in aluminum cylinders that, when empty, you could flatten beneath your feet—or against your forehead. Craft beer sat inside comparatively elegant 12- or 22-ounce bottles, or perhaps Champagne carafes sealed with a cork. Why slum it in cans? Because they might be the best container for beer, brewers are discovering. Combine that with a resurgence of the refillable glass jugs dubbed growlers, and you have totally new options for toting craft beer.

Can It

Jeff Gill's journey to canned beer started with a phone call. On the other end of the line was an avid drinker of Gill's Tallgrass IPA, one of the flagship brews crafted at his Manhattan, Kansas, brewery.

The drinker had no quibbles with the quality of the bold, complex ale. Instead, the problem was the twenty-odd cases of empty glass bottles hunkering in his garage.

"Can you pick up the bottles to reuse them?" the caller asked. He was located in western Kansas, hours from the brewery. It was too far for the Tallgrass employees to travel.

"Why don't you just recycle the glass and cardboard?" Gill offered.

No local recycler, the man replied. In that case, the empty bottles would enter a landfill. This bugged Gill, a former environmental geologist. He started researching, discovering the serious waste associated with paper six-pack holders and glass bottles—craft beer's go-to packaging. More than 75 percent of bottles ended up as a landfill fodder, a statistic that stuck in his craw.

"I started looking at the different facets of the issue," recalls Gill. He pondered shifting his packaging line from bottles to cans, which are recycled at a 50 percent–plus clip. "In November [2009], I started talking to my wife. It took a day and a half to convince her," Gill says, adding, "which is when I knew I should do it. It took me a month and a half to convince her to let me name my milk stout Buffalo Sweat." By spring 2010, the canned switchover was complete. Tallgrass beers were now sold in four-packs of sixteen-ounce cans adorned with colorful, carnival-esque artwork. "We're trying to change the perception that you can't have classy beer in a can," Gill says.

For many serious beer quaffers, *can* is a four-letter word. The aluminum cylinders are seen as down-market, synonymous with mass-market brewskis sold by the 12-, 18-, 24, or 30-pack—quantity, not quality. But over the past decade, the maligned package has quietly made inroads into the craft-beer world.

Now the canned-beer craze has caught on at more than 100 breweries nationwide, from big boys such as Brooklyn Brewery, New Belgium, and Bell's (which offers five-liter mini kegs of brands such as Two Hearted Ale) on down to teensy start-ups including Maine's Baxter Brewing and Italy's Bad Attitude. This is no fly-by-night fad. Besides being environmentally beneficial and going where bottles can't tread (backpacking, the lake, the beach, stadiums), cans keep beer fresher and more flavorful. When it comes to canning, there *is* accounting for taste.

Big Bucks and Stinky Skunks

Traditionally, canning has been a high-volume process, with filling machines cranking out tens of thousands of cases of beer daily, says Ray Daniels, director of the Cicerone Certification Program. "You don't buy that sort of equipment—with price tags in the multiple millions of dollars—unless you can run it full-time and make the investment pay," he says.

Since some small craft brewers distribute fewer than 10,000 cases a *year*, the economics didn't add up. Brewers made do with bottling, a process not without its flaws. Squirting suds into bottles is messy business, with "beer getting squirted everywhere," Gill says. "As a brewer, all that waste made me cringe."

Then there's the issue of the bottles themselves. They're fragile and prone to breakage. The caps are not always sealed properly, letting carbonation and beer leak out. Plus, beer is a photosensitive foodstuff. Whether the glass is brown, green, or clear, every bottle lets in UV light, which can cause beer to smell skunky. That's because of the presence of hops, which, when boiled, release isohumulones. When light strikes these chemicals, they create chemical compounds found in skunk spray.

Canned beer prevents such ailments. And that tinny taste? It's long gone, due to water-based polymer linings that prevent beer from coming into contact with the aluminum. Yes, there's a bit of cancerous boogeyman BPA in a can's epoxy-resin lining, but you'd need to drink more than 450 cans of beer to exceed the daily recommended dose, according to the EPA. And I doubt you're *that* thirsty. This is all good news. Now, if only craft brewers could find a cost-effective way to can their beers.

Just the Fax, Ma'am

America's canned-beer resurgence couldn't have happened without a Canadian firm. In 1999, Calgary-based Cask Brewing Systems developed a two-container, hand-canning system for smaller breweries. A few years later, Cask sent a fax touting its invention

to Dale Katechis, owner of Oskar Blues Brewery in Lyons, Colorado, which crafts uncompromising brews such as the ferociously hopped Dale's Pale Ale and Old Chub, a tar-tinged Scottish-style ale packing a smoky punch. "We laughed hysterically for six months," Katechis recalls of receiving the fax. "Then one day I stopped laughing."

Beyond the obvious benefits, Katechis realized that cans were ideal for Oskar's hiker/ fisherman fan base. It was far easier to pack beer in—and out—without the added weight of glass. In November 2002, the hand-canning began. The

results were delicious and, oddly, therapeutic. Letters poured into Oskar about men drinking canned beer without feeling any shame. To meet demand, the company switched to Cask's automated canning machine. The "canned-beer apocalypse," as Katechis likes to call it, had befallen craft brewing.

"We get a great deal of joy out of handing a nonbeliever a can of our beer and watching their head spin around," Katechis says. "They just experienced something they'll remember for the rest of their lives."

Problems in Aluminum Paradise

By now, canned beer's benefits are well documented. But we live in an image-based society where looks often rule the roost—at the expense of common sense. "Consumers prefer bottles, plain and simple," Ray Daniels says. "They have a better image and a better reputation, whether deserved or not."

Tallgrass Brewing's Gill echoes that sentiment. When he tried selling his canned brews to restaurants, bars, and other on-premise locations, a typical response was, "We don't want a can in here. We're a classy place, and we want a bottle," Gill says. It's an irrational prejudice, sure, but you can understand why some consumers would be loath to embrace a container you can crush against your forehead. When the craft-beer movement kicked off, brewers turned to brown bottles, in part to separate their products from green-bottled foreign imports (Heineken, Grolsch) and market-dominating macrobrews. Compared to a squat, utilitarian can of Coors, a bottle of Sierra Nevada Pale Ale looks as elegant as a luxury sedan. Craft beer may not resonate the same way when packaged in an aluminum container.

"In the early days, there might have been sideways glances from people who consider themselves beer geeks, but we've found the craft-beer drinker is more than willing to embrace the cans," says Bryan Simpson, the media relations director for New Belgium Brewing in Fort Collins, Colorado. Since the brewery's 1991 inception, it has built a business model on innovative ales and environmental stewardship.

Thus, it was a no-brainer when New Belgium decided to can some of its flagship Fat Tire Amber Ale in summer 2008. The familiar product in an unfamiliar package "immediately sold ahead of forecast," Simpson says. In fact, canned Fat Tire was such a hit that New Belgium expanded its canning efforts to include its summery Sunshine Wheat and Ranger IPA.

Chicago's Half Acre Beer Company also opted to make the switch to cans in 2010, moving its Daisy Cutter Pale from 22-ounce bottles into 16-ounce cans sold by the four-pack. "We decided to go the sixteen-ounce route because these beers are truly made to be poured into a glass," explains PJ Fischer, the director of sales and marketing at Half Acre, which also cans its Gossamer Golden Ale and hoppy brown Over Ale. "This allows the beer to breathe, and then the consumer also gets the beer's aroma. It is a proven fact that most of what we taste actually comes from smell." Besides, he adds, "pouring a sixteen-ounce can into a pint glass just looks so much better than a twelve-ounce can."

Canned Revelry

Every month seems to bring news of another brewery beginning to can. Avery, Harpoon, Santa Fe Brewing, Redhook Brewery—with so many craft breweries electing to can, it's now possible to stock a bar serving dozens of different canned craft beers. That's the idea behind Full Circle Bar, in Williamsburg, which opened in fall 2009 with a mission to become New York's finest canned-beer bar. While drinkers roll rounds of Skee-Ball at one of three bleacher-flanked games (the saloon is home to Brewskee-Ball, the "first-ever national Skee-Ball league," as the owners like to call it), they can slurp more than twenty different canned barley pops, including Butternuts Beer and Ale's Moo Thunder Stout and 21st Amendment's Back in Black IPA. For its first anniversary party, Full Circle celebrated by hosting Candemonium, a weekend-long festival featuring more than 40 canned beers.

It's an all-aluminum gala that has been embraced by Oskar Blues Brewery, which hosted the Burning Can Beer Festival (a riff on the Nevada desert's artsy Burning Man bash) in its hometown of Lyons, Colorado. Additionally, there's the annual Canfest, in Reno, Nevada, which began in 2009. "It's a celebration of the can," says festival cofounder Doug Booth, whose Reno-based Buckbean

Brewing Company sells its Original Orange Blossom Ale, Black Noddy Lager, and Tule Duck Red Ale by the sixteen-ounce can. "This was our way of announcing to the world, 'You don't only drink beer out of a bottle.' We want to show that great beer comes out of a can." The first year, there were more than thirty breweries represented, with awards bestowed in categories that included pale ales and IPAs, dark ales, and lagers. For the future? "My goal is to have a canned beer from every single state," Booth says. "In the next ten years, that may be possible."

ELEVEN TO TRY

DAISY CUTTER PALE ALE
HALF ACRE BEER COMPANY
ABV: 5.2%

POWERED BY A FIVE-PRONGED HOP ASSAULT (WARRIOR, COLUMBUS, CENTENNIAL, SIMCOE, AMARILLO), DAISY IS A HAZY ORANGE BEAUTY, PERFUMED TO THE HILT WITH PINE, CITRUS, AND TROPICAL FRUIT. IT DRINKS EASY AND CLEAN, ALL DAINTY GRASSY BITTERNESS AND SWEET MALT.

RED RACER PALE ALE
CENTRAL CITY BREWING CO.
ABV: 5%

CENTRAL CITY MAY BE LOCATED IN BRITISH COLUMBIA, BUT ITS PALE ALE IS A QUINTESSENTIAL AMERICAN HOP BOMB. RED RACER IS A BUBBLY GOLDEN BEAUTY WITH A FLOWERY, CITRUSY TANG AND AN EVEN KEEL OF MALT SWEETNESS.

HELL OR HIGH WATERMELON WHEAT BEER
21ST AMENDMENT BREWERY
ABV: 4.9%

AMONG THESE SAN FRANCISCANS' MANY CANNED DELIGHTS (BREW FREE OR DIE IPA, MONK'S BLOOD BELGIAN DARK ALE), I LIKE THEIR SUMMERTIME SPECIALTY BEST. IT'S FERMENTED WITH RIPE, RED WATERMELON PUREE, CREATING A STRAWBERRY-BLONDE SIPPER THAT'S CRISP AND TART.

HAPPY CAMPER IPA
SANTA FE BREWING
ABV: 6.6%

AMONG THE CANNED TREATS FROM NEW MEXICO'S OLDEST CRAFT BREWERY (FREESTYLE PILSNER, OKTOBERFEST), I'M MOST SMITTEN BY THE HAPPY CAMPER. IT HAS A BIG OL' MALTY BODY, AND A SWEET AND STURDY FRAMEWORK THAT CAN WITHSTAND THE HOP ASSAULT. HAPPY IS ZESTY. HAPPY IS FLORAL. HAPPY IS GRAPEFRUITY. HAPPY IS HEAVEN.

TEN FIDY IMPERIAL STOUT
OSKAR BLUES BREWERY
ABV: 10.5%

AS THE INSTIGATORS OF THE SELF-PROFESSED "CANNED-BEER APOCALYPSE," THIS COLORADO CONCERN SELLS BEERS ONLY BY THE ALUMINUM VESSEL. MAMA'S LITTLE YELLA PILS MAY BE A SUMMER REFRESHER, BUT I LIKE CRACKING THIS CANNED MONSTER STOUT. THOUGH THE DENSE, CREAMY STOUT ROCKS A LUDICROUS 98 IBUS, THE BITTERNESS IS SWADDLED BY THE FLAVORS OF GOOEY BROWNIES, ESPRESSO, AND CARAMEL.

MODUS HOPERANDI INDIA PALE ALE
SKA BREWING
ABV: 6.8%

IF YOU ADORE A STINKY, MOOD-ALTERING GREEN HERB, THIS GRASS-COLORED CAN FROM DURANGO, COLORADO-BASED SKA CONTAINS YOUR PERFECT POTION. MODUS HOPERANDI IS A 65-IBU ODE TO HOPPY EXCESS, FLAUNTING AROMAS OF GRAPEFRUIT AND PINE TREES POWERFUL ENOUGH TO DOUBLE AS PERFUME. MODUS GOES DOWN LIKE RESIN, PAINTING YOUR PALATE WITH A STICKY BITTERNESS BACKED BY A BALANCING SPRINKLE OF MALT SWEETNESS. THIS ISN'T AN IPA FOR LILY-LIVERED DRINKERS—OR, PERHAPS, LAW ABIDERS.

COCONUT PORTER
MAUI BREWING CO.
ABV: 5.7%

TO MAKE ROBUST COCONUT PORTER, HAWAII'S MAUI BREWING HAND-TOASTS COCONUT FLESH, THEN INCORPORATES IT WITH SIX KINDS OF BARLEY AND A COUPLE OF TYPES OF PACIFIC NORTHWEST HOPS. THE SWEET, NUTTY COCONUT STRUTS ITS STUFF ON THE NOSE, AS WELL AS ON THE FIRST

MAUI BREWING CO.

CoCoNut PorTeR

...LIKE HOT CHICKS ON THE BEACH

SILKY SWIG. THE BREW ALSO REVEALS FLAVORS OF CHOCOLATE, ALMOST LIKE A LIQUID MOUNDS CANDY BAR—IN THE BEST WAY IMAGINABLE.

ASHLAND AMBER
CALDERA BREWING COMPANY
ABV: 5.4%

IN THIS ERA OF EXCESSIVELY HOPPED ALES, IT'S NICE TO KICK BACK WITH A BREW THAT WON'T KICK YOUR BUTT. THAT'S WHAT MAKES THIS OREGON OUTFIT'S ASHLAND AMBER SUCH A DELIGHT. ASHLAND POURS A VIBRANT AUBURN, SHOWCASING FAMILIAR FLAVORS OF CARAMEL AND FRESH-BAKED BREAD. THE TASTE FOLLOWS A STRAIGHTFORWARD SCRIPT, WITH A BALANCED BILL OF CITRIC HOPS AND BISCUIT MALT. IT'S A SIMPLE, SNAPPY REFRESHMENT, AN ACHIEVEMENT WORTH A TOAST.

PIKELAND PILS
SLY FOX BREWING COMPANY
ABV: 4.9%

WHENEVER I SPEND A DAY BY WATER, I LIKE TO BRING A SLY FOX SIXER. THE PENNSYLVANIA BREWERY MAKES CLASSIC, DRINKABLE CANNED BEERS, SUCH AS THE FRUITY ROYAL WEISSE ALE, THE PROFUSELY HOPPED 113 IPA, OR, BETTER YET, THE PIKELAND PILS. THE PITCH-PERFECT GERMAN PILSNER IS AS GOLDEN AS A SUNRISE AND AS CLEAR AS THE CARIBBEAN, WITH BUBBLES RACING BREAKNECK TO THE SURFACE. DRY, LIGHT, AND EASY, IT'S A GULPER THAT FINISHES WITH A SPLASH OF SPICY BITTERNESS.

PINE BELT PALE ALE
SOUTHERN STAR BREWING COMPANY
ABV: 6.3%

EVERYTHING'S BIGGER IN TEXAS, INCLUDING THIS BREWERY'S BEERS—THEY'RE SOLD BY THE SIXTEEN-OUNCE CAN. DOES BIGGER MEAN BETTER? NOT ALWAYS, BUT YOU'LL BE PLENTY PLEASED WHEN OPENING THIS PALE ALE. YOU COULD DRINK IT STRAIGHT OUT OF THE CAN, BUT I PREFER POURING THE HAZY, ORANGE-AMBER ELIXIR INTO A MUG. THAT WAY, I CAN SAVOR THE NOSE OF PINE RESIN AND TROPICAL FRUIT, PLUS THE CARAMEL AND CREAMY MALT CHARACTER.

BUFFALO SWEAT
TALLGRASS BREWING CO.
ABV: 5%

DO BUFFALOS SWEAT? DARNED IF I KNOW. BUT I DO KNOW THAT THIS KANSAS BREWERY'S BUFFALO SWEAT IS A KNOCKOUT MILK STOUT. OODLES OF ROASTED BARLEY IMBUE BUFFALO

WITH A DEEP BROWN HUE, WHILE THE
UNUSUAL ADDITION OF CREAM SUGAR
MAKES THE STOUT SMOOTH, RICH,
AND OH SO DRINKABLE. IT TASTES

A LITTLE LIKE COFFEE WITH A
DOLLOP OF WHOLE MILK AND COCOA
SPRINKLED ON TOP.

Primal Growler

When departing my Brooklyn apartment every morn, I throw a couple of critical items into my bag. First, due to my knee-knocking fear of dehydration, I pack a plastic Nalgene bottle brimming with water. Second, I carry a book to make my subway commute tolerable. Last, and most important for this suds geek, I bring a clean growler. I'm no morning drunk; rather, I never miss a chance to buy great beer.

Increasingly, bars, beer shops, and breweries are selling draft beer by the growler. It's a reusable 64-ounce glass jug—often emblazoned with the logo of a brewery, pub, or brew shop—that can retain the crispness of keg-fresh brew for around a week (after opening, about 36 hours). Not that I wait that long. Heck, it takes Herculean self-restraint to not immediately guzzle the elixir, like a parched man in the desert passed a bottle of Poland Spring.

Here's why I get schoolgirl excited: Typically, beer sold by the growler is never bottled, meaning it's imbibed only at a brewery or a pub. However, bars can be cost prohibitive, and I'm not always flush enough to fork over $5 or $6 a pint. (New York City can bankrupt a beer lover.) However, I can usually grab a growler for anywhere from $10 to $15, netting four pints. That's some thirst-quenching math.

However, growlers weren't invented solely for modern-day skinflints such as myself. The concept dates back more than a century, when beer was transported from pubs to homes in a lidded tin pail. According to lore, the sloshing beer rumbled as carbon dioxide escaped—hence, growler. An alternate history: Growlers were buckets of beer given to famished factory workers, rescuing "growling" stomachs.

However, by the 1960s, growlers had pulled a dodo and disappeared. Their resurgence is due to Grand Teton Brewing, formerly the Otto Brothers' Brewing Company, in Jackson Hole, Wyoming. When the brewery opened in 1988, it was draft-only. The brothers wanted to sell takeaway beer, but a bottling line was cost prohibitive. Wise old dad suggested a blast from his past: the growler. Bingo. But instead of tin, the brothers settled on glass jugs, which they silk-screened with the company logo. In 1989, growlers were born. And my bag will never be light again.

Part of my ever-growing collection of growlers. I need a bigger apartment.

Share and Share Alike

Despite the temptation, I don't recommend treating a growler like a Big Gulp of beer. The glass jug is the perfect size for sharing with fellow suds lovers. During dinner parties, or perhaps when a football game is on TV, I like bringing a growler of beer to pass around as if it were a jug of Carlo Rossi wine, that rotgut grape juice of my youth. Other times, I'll invite friends to my apartment for a growler sampling session. Everyone is instructed to buy a different beer, and the growlers are opened one at a time, ensuring that the beer remains fizzy and fresh. But if you decide to drink the growler by yourself, I won't judge. Sometimes a beer is so good, you have to be selfish.

Keep It Clean

I loathe washing dishes as much as the next man or woman, but I'll gladly give myself dishpan hands in order to keep my growler clean. If the jug is not washed out shortly after it's emptied, it can become a breeding ground for mold and other fungi—and not the kind reserved for sour beer. Thoroughly rinsing out the growler with hot water and scrubbing the cap should suffice, but if mold takes hold, don't be afraid to add a bit of bleach mixed with dish soap and scalding water. Cap the growler, shake, empty, rinse. Then rinse again. Soapy residue will adversely affect the beer's head, and you certainly don't want to swallow a mouthful of bleach.

EiGHT

BRINGING IT HOME:

In Basements, in Bedroom Closets, and on the Dinner Table, Beer Is Taking Over New Territory

USED TO BE BEER KNEW ITS PLACE, STICKING TO dark bars and bright supermarkets' refrigerated confines. Beer didn't linger in your basement, slowly maturing, patiently waiting for a special occasion to be sipped. Beer didn't dare show its sudsy head at dinnertime, unless it was invited to the party by pizza or a greasy burger. But today, beer is no longer content to be typecast.

Today's craft beer, with its kaleidoscopic flavor profiles, can match any dish at your favorite restaurant or your dinner table—from Thai curries to spaghetti or caviar, if that catches your fancy. Beer is no longer an instant pleasure, as certain kinds of rich, robust brews gain newfound nuances and complexities after a stint in your cellar. More than ever, home is where the craft beer is.

Of a Certain Age

In spring 2010, Indianapolis's Grant Curlow posted a YouTube clip
that could make even the most casual beer fan drool.

In his prosaically titled *Beer Cellar Video*, Curlow spends
6 minutes and 48 seconds slowly and nearly wordlessly panning
over a concrete basement where, arranged in stacks and racks
and scattered across the plywood floor, there are more than 700
bottles of coveted brews, such as Firestone Walker's barrel-aged
XII, Bell's Batch 9,000 strong ale, and Three Floyds' wax-capped
Dark Lord Russian imperial stout. Then there's his Belgian
bounty, including Trappist ales and sour lambics, some of which
are older than Curlow's 24 years—and only going to grow older
and, hopefully, better. "I've got lambics down there I'm waiting
for twenty years to try," says Curlow, who started collecting
during college and recently parlayed his passion into a job as the
craft-beer specialist for Monarch Beverage Company. "I'm in no
rush to open them."

Welcome to the new world of old beer. Like wine, beer has
the capacity to age, evolve, and develop complex new aromas and
flavors. Think that Sierra Nevada Bigfoot Barleywine is a rich treat
right now? Try it in ten years, when it has mellowed into a smooth
elixir worthy of a snifter and a cigar. Time, combined with yeast and
bacteria, can buff a beer's rough edges and unlock its full potential—
or, given a few months too many, create a liquid best sent down
the drain.

Aging beer isn't an exact science. Still, you can use tricks and
tactics to tilt the sands of time in your favor. By creating an ideal
climate, selecting the right beers to put to bed, and following storage
protocols, you can start a cellar of your own, even if you live in a
skyscraping apartment.

The Air Down There

After committing to build a beer collection, the first step is creating a safe, cozy environment in which the brews can slumber undisturbed—the cart before the horse. Some of the best advice on building a cellar can be found in Lovell, Maine, a tiny town near White Mountain National Forest that's home to Ebenezer's Pub. Despite its rural digs, Ebenezer's is a world-class Belgian bar and possibly the country's foremost repository for vintage beer. "I'm trying

The bar at Ebenezer's Pub.

The legendary cellar at Ebenezer's Pub.

to build a time machine," says co-owner Chris Lively of his climate-monitored cellar. It features a security system to guard his thousand-plus bottles that span more than a century of brewing. Like a liquid Library of Congress, "I want to have these beers here a hundred, two hundred, or three hundred years from now. We cellar beers for the interest of the beer world."

For *your* interests, Lively suggests a cellar, or a basement, where the temperature will remain relatively low (about 55 degrees Fahrenheit is ideal, give or take five degrees), with narrow temperature fluctuation; a range of more than 20 degrees will wreak havoc. This also holds true for wine, which you can cellar alongside beer. (Red wine is typically stored at 50 to 55 degrees, and white wine is best aged at 45 degrees.)

Unlike wine, which rests on its side to keep the cork (if it has one) moist, beer should be stored upright, even if it has a cork, says Alan Sprints, founder of Portland, Oregon's Hair of the Dog Brewing Company. "That way, sediment remains in the bottom. Store bottles on their side, and sediment kicks up when you pour." Using a shelf system, or a fridge, will help prevent accidentally sending an upright bottle crashing to the ground.

The next step: block sunlight. Beer is photosensitive. Glass bottles let in UV rays, which cause chemicals called isohumulones (they help make beer bitter) to decompose and create compounds found in skunks' spray. Voila! Skunked beer.

Another cellaring enemy is humidity. "If there's not enough humidity, the corks will dry out," Liveley says. "If there's too much humidity, it could damage beer and invite black mold," which can enter through the cork or a loose crown cap. Lively likens black mold to a silent, deadly assassin. "Your beers will die a slow death," he says. Keep them safe with an air purifier, while using a humidifier or a dehumidifier to calibrate the climate. The optimum atmosphere has "the kind of humidity you have in fall or spring" on the East Coast, Lively notes. (An ideal humidity range is about 50 to 70 percent.) What you *don't* want is to walk into your cellar and feel a warm dampness, which indicates you've got a perfect breeding ground for bacteria. If you're going to cellar beer, Lively recommends having a mold analysis done every two years. "It's literally a bacterial war in the cellar."

Though underground storage is ideal because temperatures tend to stay steady, it's not imperative. If that's not an option, opt for

Beer-cellaring expert Bill Sysak.

an inexpensive wine fridge or, if that's cost prohibitive, "look toward a bedroom in the middle of your house"—the temperature should be more stable—"and use the closet," suggests Bill Sysak, the beverage supervisor and certified cicerone (sort of a beer sommelier) at Stone World Bistro and Gardens. "Buy a two-dollar thermometer and check the closet over a couple seasons. If you don't have extreme temperature fluctuations, you know you have a place that's safe for beer." (He also recommends running a humidifier.)

Before starting at Stone Brewing, Sysak spent more than 30 years amassing one of California's—if not the country's—finest collections of cellared beers. At one point, he had accumulated more than 2,500 bottles, which he stored everywhere, from a three-door cooler in the garage (the convenience-store relic is not turned on, yet it maintains temperatures between 62 and 65 degrees) to a cabinet under the bathroom sink. "I also have three smaller wine coolers and bottles stuck under the house," Sysak says. "The point is, a lot of my beer isn't refrigerated." But what if you live

Cellaring expert Bill Sysak's collection of aged beers—well, part of it.

in Las Vegas or another scorching city? No worries, says Sysak. "If you don't have a beer refrigerator or a cellar, and your average temperature is in the high sixties or seventies, you can insulate bottles with [polystyrenefoam] wine shipping crates," Sysak says. "Craft beer is much more durable than people think."

Brews to Choose

Now that your cellar, fridge, or closet is secured, the fun part is filling it. However, not every beer should be allowed to age. Most are best as soon as they're bottled, especially hop-forward pale ales and IPAs. Hops are most pungent and aromatic when fresh, and even a few months will dull their character. (For example, the label on Russian River's amped-up IPA Pliny the Elder reads DOES NOT IMPROVE WITH AGE! HOPPY BEERS ARE NOT MEANT TO BE AGED!)

When selecting beers for aging, Sysak suggests following general guidelines. First, it's beneficial if a beer is 8 percent ABV or stronger, since an elevated alcohol profile will typically become smoother, mellower, and more agreeable with time. Another rule of thumb is to select a darker, maltier beer, because the sweet, residual sugars tend to soften. Above all, ensure that the beer is bottle-conditioned, wherein live yeasts lurk inside the bottle.

"Though the yeast doesn't continue to ferment, it helps the beer age," explains Hair of the Dog's Alan Sprints, who always finishes his beers with fermenting yeast. "All of our beers are meant to age," he says of creations such as Dave, an English-style barley wine brewed more than fifteen years ago and boasting 29 percent ABV. "It's so much better now than it ever was. That shows the patience it takes to hang on to a beer for an extended period of time."

So which beer styles are worth the wait? Sysak recommends Belgian strong ales, barley wines, imperial stouts, and, bucking the high-alcohol guideline, sour Belgians, such as lambics and Flanders red ales. With aging beer, there are always exceptions to the rule, Sysak says. "I have tripels, saisons, and blonde ales that are ten or fifteen years old and beautiful."

Other outliers include ales inoculated with wild yeasts such as *Brettanomyces*. They're often unstable, since the yeast rapidly works through a beer and alters its character. One month it's sublime, the next it's undrinkable. However, Brett-dosed beers such as Orval, made by Trappist monks at the Abbey Notre-Dame d'Orval in Belgium, and Sanctification, from Russian River Brewing, respond well to cellaring. "They don't age into the ten- to twenty-year range, but they do grow complex and amazing," Sysak says. (Additionally, Sysak says, beers boasting multiple strains of yeasts and bacteria, such as *Lactobacillus*, hold up better.)

If you can swing it, purchase at least two bottles of each brew—or more. That way, you can crack open a bottle and taste how the beer is aging. Plus, you'll have spares in the event you want more of a good thing, or need to replace a bottle ruined by a bad seal. "Historically, I buy large quantities," Sysak says. "If you have a beer that you enjoy and it has a proven track record, it's nice to get a case, whether that's twelve bottles or twenty-four," Sysak says.

However, you don't want to overdo it on a single beer. While you may be crazy for Founders' Kentucky Breakfast Stout, "you never know how your taste buds will evolve," says Curlow, who started out collecting strong stouts before focusing on Belgian lambics and Trappist ales. "Keep your cellar varied." Since Curlow started saving beer as a college freshman, it's a wonder he resisted the temptation to dip into his stock. "You buy more than you can drink," he says. "That still holds true today."

A Matter of Taste

Pouring and sampling is a critical way to determine how a beer is developing before it ends up past its prime. Though an expiration date isn't stamped on the bottle like a carton of milk, beer does have a limited life span. "I have beers that are fifty years old, but for beers that can be aged, the average life span ranges from a couple years to eight to ten years," Sysak says. Taste. Evaluate. Wait. But don't wait too long. "At five years, many beers begin to show signs of deterioration," Sysak says. Typically, higher-gravity barley wines, imperial stouts, and old ales (a dark, malty English ale that's usually as complex as it is strong) have the longest shelf life. "There are rare bottles of English ales out there that are over a hundred years old," Sysak says. "Of course, they are a crapshoot, just like old wine. You can pay an exorbitant amount for nectar or vinegar."

Settling on the ideal aging time takes trial and error. "Try it fresh, then anywhere from a month to six months to a year apart to see how the beer ages," Sysak says. "There's always that time when you wonder, 'Should I wait one more year? I like how that flavor is developing.' Then you try it and go, 'Shoot, it's past its prime.'"

When aging beers, clunkers come with the territory. "I know there are going to be some duds, but we just have to suck it up when it happens," says Dave Blanchard, cofounder of Brick Store Pub in Decatur, Georgia, where vintage beers are stored in an adjoining, underground bank vault. In 2005, the bar began acquiring close to 500 varieties of age-worthy beer, refusing to release them until fall 2010. "It was a big gamble, because I know some of the vintage beer won't be as good after aging," Blanchard says. "It's a big leap of faith."

To make that leap of faith less daunting, Sysak suggests turning to resources such as RateBeer.com and BeerAdvocate.com, which have active forums dedicated to aging. "If you post, 'I have a 2003 AleSmith Speedway Stout. Has anyone opened it lately?,' sure enough, a dozen people will respond."

Combining sensory analysis with crowd-sourced wisdom will allow you to make minute adjustments. If your beer is close to peaking, transfer it to a cooler environment to slow aging. If you'd like the beer to age faster, slightly elevate its environment's temperature. "I've taken imperial stouts that have a hot, fusil note"—that is, alcohol—"and increased the cellaring temperatures into the mid-sixties," Sysak says. This slightly oxidizes the beer, creating a sweet, sherry-like nuance. "Brewers will never say to do this," he says, underscoring a simple point: When it comes to aging, you can create the rules as you go along.

Pop Your Tops

After creating, stocking, and maintaining a cellar, it's easy to imagine that you've just built a beer museum. But remember, one of the pleasures of building an enviable collection is reaping the fruits of your labor.

For Sysak, savoring and sharing aged beer is part of the fun. He once cohosted (with Tom Nickel, of San Diego's O'Brien's American Pub) a vertical tasting of Thomas Hardy's ales (a classic English beer that's no longer brewed) from the first release, in 1968, to 2004. Even crazier, for ten years he hosted a party on his birthday dubbed "the largest, most extreme private beer party in the world." Every ten minutes for twelve hours, Sysak opened two rare beers—say, a Drie Fonteinen Kriek or a Pizza Port Cuvee de Tomme—along with up to twenty kegs of beer, "in case you got thirsty in between the nine minutes of beer pours," Sysak says of the event, which sometimes swelled to 250 people.

Of course, opening an aged beer doesn't require a blowout. "One thing I'm most proud of is that people use my beers to celebrate special occasions," such as birthdays or anniversaries, says Hair of the Dog's Sprints. But even that's too formal a reason for Curlow to crack a treasure. "You don't need a reason to open a cellared bottle," he says. "I love bringing friends over and popping something unusual. Whether it's a random Thursday or Sunday, when you pop open the bottle, it'll be the celebration."

TEN TO CELLAR

TRAPPISTES ROCHEFORT 10
BRASSERIE DE ROCHEFORT
ABV: 11.3%

POURING AN INTENSE LEATHER BROWN, THIS BELGIAN MONK-MADE QUADRUPLE SMELLS OF LICORICE AND DARK FRUIT THAT'S SPENT SEVERAL MONTHS BAKING IN THE SUN. DESPITE THE ALCOHOL WALLOP, 10 REMAINS AS CREAMY AND QUAFFABLE AS CAFÉ AU LAIT. THE CHRISTMAS-FRIENDLY FLAVORS OF CARAMEL, FIGS, AND SPICE CAKE WILL BECOME MORE COMPLEX WITH TIME.

ADAM
HAIR OF THE DOG BREWING COMPANY
ABV: 10%

THIS NEARLY TAR-BLACK, GERMAN-STYLE STRONG ALE IS LIKE FORMER CHILD ACTOR JOSEPH GORDON-LEVITT: EVEN BETTER WITH AGE. BUT EVEN YOUNG ADAM IS DIVINE, WITH THE AROMAS OF BROWNIES AND DARK, WRINKLY FRUITS. ADAM IS DENSE YET SMOOTH AND CRAMMED WITH OPULENT FLAVORS OF DATES, CARAMEL, ROASTED MALT, AND A HINT OF SMOKE. ADAM BATCHES HAVE AGED FOR MORE THAN SIXTEEN YEARS—AND COUNTING.

BLACK CHOCOLATE STOUT
BROOKLYN BREWERY
ABV: 10.1%

THIS IMPERIAL STOUT POURS AS DARK AS A NEW YORK CITY BLACKOUT, TOPPED BY A TAN HEAD BOASTING A BOUQUET OF DARK-ROASTED MALTS, ESPRESSO, MOLASSES, AND CHOCOLATE. FLAVORS FOLLOW SUIT, BACKED BY A THICK, FULL-BODIED MOUTHFEEL AND ALCOHOL ON THE BACK END. IN SEVERAL YEARS, BCS SHOULD BE SMOOTHER, WITH MORE VIBRANT CHOCOLATE FLAVORS.

EXPEDITION STOUT
BELL'S BREWERY
ABV: 10.5%

A CELLARING FAVE, BELL'S BURLY WINTER SEASONAL DECANTS THE COLOR OF A DARK, MOONLESS NIGHT. EXPEDITION'S SWEET AROMA IS COMPOSED OF UNSWEETENED CHOCOLATE, AS WELL AS ROASTED

AND TOASTED MALTS AND JAVA. EXPEDITION SLIDES OVER YOUR TONGUE, SLICK AND CREAMY, WITH FLAVORS DARTING FROM MOLASSES TO COCOA TO COFFEE; THE BITTERNESS COMES QUICKLY AND UNEXPECTEDLY, LIKE A MULE KICK. GIVE EXPEDITION TIME, AND THE ALCOHOL BURN WILL MELLOW LIKE A CALIFORNIA SURFER.

GUEUZE 100% LAMBIC

BRASSERIE CANTILLON
ABV: 5%

THIS BELGIAN CLASSIC IS MADE BY BLENDING ONE-, TWO-, AND THREE-YEAR-OLD BATCHES OF OAK-AGED, SPONTANEOUSLY FERMENTED LAMBIC. EACH YEAR'S RELEASE IS UNIQUE, BUT EXPECT A FUNKY, CITRUSY, SOUR AROMA. GUEUZE DRINKS AS TART AND CRISP AS FRESH-SQUEEZED LEMONADE, WITH NOTES OF HAY AND MELON. IT'S DOWNRIGHT REFRESHING ON A SWELTERING SUMMER AFTERNOON. CELLARING WILL HELP THE SOURNESS SOFTEN.

XS OLD CRUSTACEAN BARLEY WINE

ROGUE ALES
ABV: 11.5%

THIS GNARLY BARLEY WINE ISSUES FORTH RUBY RED, A SHADE DARKER THAN DOROTHY'S SLIPPERS, PACKING A PERFUME OF CARAMEL AND HEADY, CITRIC HOPS TO THE TUNE OF 110 IBUS. THERE'S AN ABUNDANCE OF BITTERNESS ON THE PALATE, AS WELL AS RAISINS AND BROWN SUGAR. WHEN AGED, THE HOP PROFILE WILL BECOME SUBDUED YET OMNIPRESENT, LIKE A LOYAL POOCH NEVER LEAVING HIS MASTER'S SIDE.

THE ABYSS

DESCHUTES BREWERY
ABV: 11%

EVERY FALL, DESCHUTES RELEASES THIS DECADENT STOUT THE COLOR OF COAL AS PART OF ITS RESERVE SERIES. ABYSSIS IS BREWED WITH A MEASURE OF LICORICE AND MOLASSES, THEN A THIRD OF THE BEER IS DUMPED INTO OAK

AND BOURBON BARRELS TO SOAK UP THE FLAVORS OF SPIRITS AND WOOD. THE BLENDED OUTCOME IS RICH, BEGUILING BLISS: BITTER COFFEE AND CHOCOLATE, VANILLA, ROASTED MALTS, CHARRED OAK. TIME WILL DEEPEN THE PROFILE.

OLD RASPUTIN RUSSIAN IMPERIAL STOUT

NORTH COAST BREWING COMPANY
ABV: 9%
DESPITE ITS RELATIVELY LOW COST AND UBIQUITY, OLD RASPUTIN IS A RARE CREATURE. THE CALIFORNIA BREWERY'S IMPERIAL STOUT POURS HONEY THICK, RELEASING A BLOOM OF CHOCOLATE-DIPPED RAISINS, ESPRESSO, AND BREAD YANKED HOT FROM THE OVEN. IT'S AS RICH AS A LOTTERY WINNER, BUT THOSE 75 BITTER IBUS PERFORM A NICE BALANCING ACT. KEEP OLD RASPUTIN FOR FIVE OR TEN YEARS, AND THIS BARGAIN BEER (A CASE OFTEN COSTS LESS THAN $50) WILL BECOME A PRICELESS LUXURY.

SPEEDWAY STOUT
ALESMITH BREWING COMPANY
ABV: 12%
SAN DIEGO'S ALESMITH WILL REV YOUR ENGINES WITH SPEEDWAY, A COFFEE-CHARGED IMPERIAL STOUT THE APPROXIMATE COLOR AND VISCOSITY OF MOTOR OIL AFTER A MONTHLONG ROAD TRIP. SPEEDWAY SMELLS AND TASTES OF GROUND COFFEE AND DARK CHOCOLATE, MAMMOTH FLAVORS THAT TANGO ON YOUR TONGUE ALONGSIDE MOLASSES AND SUN-RIPENED FRUIT. MOUTHFEEL? AS SILKY AS VICTORIA'S SECRET SKIVVIES. SPEEDWAY IS SPLENDID NOW. AFTER FIVE YEARS, IT'S PROFOUND AND MAGICAL.

VINTAGE HARVEST ALE
J.W. LEES & CO.
ABV: 11.5%
MARK YOUR CALENDARS FOR DECEMBER 1. THAT'S THE DATE THAT BRITAIN'S J.W. LEES RELEASES ITS ONCE-A-YEAR HARVEST ALE, A LIQUID CELEBRATION MADE OF THAT SEASON'S HOPS AND BARLEY YIELD. LIKE A SAVILE ROW SUIT, THIS ENGLISH BARLEY WINE IS TAILOR-MADE FOR CELLARING. SILKEN HARVEST TASTES SOMEWHAT LIKE MAPLE SYRUP MIXED WITH WHISKEY, TOFFEE, AND BROWN SUGAR. AFTER TEN YEARS, HARVEST ALE WILL BECOME AS INTRICATE AS HIGHER-ORDER ALGEBRA.

What a Pair: Beer and Food

It's a howling-wind fall evening in Brooklyn, New York, vicious weather that keeps people homebound and heating up cans of soup. But instead of hunkering inside, tonight dozens of thirsty, hungry Brooklynites have braved the cold to visit Beer Table.

Tables would be more accurate, with three long, communal perches crammed inside the diminutive woodsy tavern. It's decorated with rough brick walls and shelves bursting with bottled suds and enough pickled vegetables to rival your granny's root cellar. Tacked above the bar is paper scrawled with the evening's draft beers—including Kiuchi Brewery's Hitachino Nest Espresso Stout and cask-poured New England Brewing's Sea Hag IPA—which are dispensed from taps topped with disassembled meat-grinder parts.

The blend of food and beer goes beyond simple bar paraphernalia, as I discover when a lanky, bearded server delivers a menu. It lists a snack-food smorgasbord of dehydrated watermelon chips, pickled eggs sprinkled with jalapeño powder, and a three-course dinner of smoked trout, rich pot-au-feu, and spiced carrot cake. Most impressively, each flavorful dish is matched to an equally flavorful beer. "We're trying to go beyond burgers and steak and pair nontraditional food with beer," says Beer Table co-owner Justin Philips of his nightly dinners. "Wine should not rule the dinner table."

Welcome to the Table

These are good days to be a craft beer. After decades of being dwarfed by macrobrews, microbreweries are filling taps nationwide. While that counts big at the bar, the dinner table is a different tale. At most restaurants, the drinks program remains dominated by wine. Filet mignon? Allow us to recommend a cabernet sauvignon.

And madam, for your pan-seared scallops, a viognier? It's true, red and white have their place —but what about brown? It's coming to a dinner table near you.

Home cooks and restaurant chefs are discovering that beer's flavor spectrum—from bitter IPAs to chocolaty stouts—combined with its low acidity and palate-cleansing carbonation makes it a perfect mate for food. They're using brews as both an ingredient and an accompaniment, creating multicourse beer-pairing dinners of surprising depth and complexity that go far beyond mozzarella sticks with a pint of pilsner.

In San Francisco, Bar Crudo hosts a dinner series coupling fresh-caught seafood with microbrews and Belgian ales, while Monk's Kettle's monthly event highlights a single brewery's beers served with each course (for instance, a Dogfish Head dinner included Mediterranean-style lamb meatballs paired with their ancient Finnish-style rye ale Sah'tea). Up the coast in Astoria, Oregon, the Fort George Brewery & Public House features monthly multicourse dinners that have included an oyster-centric feast accompanied by an array of roasty stouts. Meanwhile, pairing dinners at Philadelphia's Latin-Asian–leaning Chifa have featured octopus ceviche with purple olives and avocado served with local Victory Brewing's Brett-injected Wild Devil Belgian ale.

"We're using beer as a culinary tool," says Jerry Hartley, owner of the J. Clyde, in Birmingham, Alabama, which hosts a monthly beer-pairing dinner. Since launching his series in August 2007, Hartley has seen crowds swell to 35 or 40. Dishes like crawfish gumbo opposite Abita Turbodog draw them in. "There's no better way to educate people about beer and change its image than to pair it with food," he says.

While restaurants and bars host numerous food-pairing events, there are plenty of private dinners, too. In New York, beer-industry veteran Samuel Merritt's Civilization of Beer creates pairing dinners for private and corporate clients, while San Francisco–based "beer chef" Bruce Paton curates beer banquets at the local Cathedral Hill Hotel. Want to create a beer-food feast at home? Follow Garrett Oliver's book *The Brewmaster's Table* and learn to pair barley wines with cheddar cheese.

Still, few enthusiasts treat beer as reverentially as Sean Z. Paxton, of Sonoma, California, aka the "Homebrew Chef." Since the mid-1990s, Paxton, a trained chef and photographer, has spread his gastronomic gospel with evangelical fervor. Whereas most beer-pairing zealots mimic sommeliers, matching a meal's flavor to a particular brew, Paxton goes a step further.

"Beer is an ingredient," he says. "And there are thousands of flavors to choose from." Paxton uses beer with deft, painterly strokes, in inventive dishes that make beer-can chicken seem like caveman grub. At San Francisco's divey, sticker-strewn Toronado Pub, he

Paxton's cauliflower salad is made with curry-scented cauliflower, golden raisins soaked in Russian River's Damnation golden ale, toasted almonds, mache, hemp seeds, and a dressing of organic yogurt mixed with Cantillon Gueuze.

Menu

AUTHENTIC · BELGIAN

EBENEZER'S PUB

ANNO 2010

BELGIAN BEER FEAST

19 AUGUST — LOVELL, MAINE

RECEPTION BEERS
Fantôme Pissenlit and Allagash Blonde

BIÈRE GELÉE
Cambridge Brewing Co. Arquebus gelee layered with local blueberries pickled in bay leaf, clove and Saechuan peppercorns

CHARCUTERIE DE FLANDRES
Lardo, orange & fennel salami, Belgian style 'Spam' a complied served with De Ranke Guldenberg sweet mustard, gherkins, Petrus Oud Bruin jelly, artisanal crackers and breads
Russian River Brewing Co. - Temptation 9 liter (Batch 4)

CREPINETTE
Belgian candi sugar, orange peel and coriander cured Berkshire pork belly with chanterelles, leeks, De Dolle Oerbier Reserva 2005, caramelized fennel, dates and thyme, wrapped in pork caul fat and drizzled with B&S bourbon barrel aged maple syrup, arugula salad, burnt orange peel essences
Wild Pauwepel - De Struise Brouwers

CROQUETTE WITH A TWIST
Purple potatoes, garbanzo beans, duck hearts sous-vide in Ichtegm's Flemish Red Ale, blended together and served with a Belgian styled 'naan' bread, herbed black quinoa salad tossed with house-made organic goat butter poached baby leeks, Boon Geuze sheep's milk yoghurt sauce and a few Belgian five spiced powered duck chicharones, just because...
Brabantse Trots - Geuze tegen de Grote Dorst

SONOMA FOIE GRAS POACHED MAINE LOBSTER
Cantillon Grand Cru Bruocsella/chamomile tea/blood orange gastrique, Tripel Karmeliet braised Belgian endive, chervil purée garnished with house cured lobster roe, saffron infused sea salt
Cantillon Crianza Helena

HAIR OF THE HARE
Braised rabbit with roasted shallots, Boccalone Guanciale, thyme, sour cherries, rabbit stock and Hair of the Dog Cherry Adam 2009 on a bed of cedar smoked rutabaga purée, a few drops of Blis Double Solera Sherry Vinegar, deep fried rabbit ears
Dirty Horse 1981 on tap - De Struise Brouwers

LOBSTER WATERZOOI
Maine lobster, crawfish, P.E.I mussels, lobster De Dolle Dulle Teve stock in local organic cream, white asparagus, lobster mushrooms, black garlic, baby purple carrots, fennel bulb and fingerling potatoes
Pretty Things Beer & Ale Project - D'Or Mouse

'SPECIAL' WOOD BARREL SMOKED DUCK BREASTS
Bison bone marrow Allagash Bière Vinegash Gastrique, Westvleteren 8 Foam, leek/shallot/celery root purée, black truffle infused salt

POMMES FRITES
Dusted with Espelette seasonings and served with a Chimay Red aioli
Allagash Brewery Co. - First Release of Victor Francenstein

ROASTED CAULIFLOWER SALAD
House blended Belgian curry scented purple cauliflower, Westmalle Tripel soaked dried apricots, orange tea smoked pistachios, maché greens and toasted hemp seeds tossed in a house-made local goat milk yoghurt Cantillon Gueuze dressing
Girardin Gueuze 1882 with a splash of Peach Vanilla Bean Allagash Tripel Elixir

CHEESE SELECTION
"Cremont" VT Butter & Cheese Creamery ♥ "Cave-Aged Beer Cheese" Harpersfield Cheese
"Le Fêtardé" Fromagerie Le Champ des Meules ♥ "Drunk Monk" Cato Corner Farm
House-made Russian River Supplication sour cherry paste, 3 Fonteinen Oude Geuze infused 30 year old honey, apricot Cantillon Cuvée des Champions purée celery hop salt, artisanal crackers and breads
Cambridge Brewing Co. Heather Ale ♥ Orval

SMOUTEBOLLEN
Belgian donuts made with t'Smisje Catherine the Great, served with a warm Belgian chocolate Brasserie Dieu Du Ciel Aphrodisiaque fondue
Rochefort 8

BELGIAN DARK CHOCOLATE TRUFFLE
Filled with a Rochefort 10 fig cocoa TCHO nib caramel

BLACK ALBERT TOFFEE
Topped with Kabert infused Belgian chocolate

DE STRUISE TSJEESES RESERVA JELLIES coated with wild blueberry sugar

HANSSENS EXPERIMENTAL RASPBERRY JELLIES coated with a clove sugar
Collaboration Project between Portsmouth Brewing Co & De Struise Brouwers - Kabert

---

AFTER PARTY BEERS
*De Dolle Bruinmel 1982, Eylenbosch Gueuze 1984, Chimay Grande Reserve 1987,
Vertical of Fantôme Efreeje 1994, 1996 & 1999, 3 Fonteinen Oude Geuze 2004 Mugmans*

PROPRIETOR: CHRISTOPHER LIVELY — EXECUTIVE CHEF: SEAN Z. PAXTON

Bringing It Home

Left: For this dish, Paxton brined duck breasts in New Belgium's Transatlantique Kriek, seared them medium rare, and created a reduction of New Belgium's Dark Kriek. The duck is plated alongside pearl-barley risotto made with seasonal vegetables.

Below: This decadent plate is composed of Paxton's homemade duck-liver pâté infused with Lost Abbey's Ten Commandments ale; pork rillettes saturated with Petrus Oud Bruin–soaked figs and prunes; cornichons; heirloom radishes; and mustard made with Corsendonk Christmas Ale. Wow.

produces an annual Belgian beer dinner with ten-plus courses, such as hop shoots blanched in Delirium Tremens strong pale ale and Flemish red ale–marinated foie gras torchon topped with Duchesse de Bourgogne foam. Paxton has also taken this concept to its most lavish, delicious

extreme at Ebenezer's Pub in Lovell, Maine, where past Belgian-beer dinners have clocked in at an epic *six hours*.

For the 2010 marathon meal, Paxton debuted more than a dozen mouth-dropping pairings. If you were lucky enough to nab a $295 seat, you would've devoured Hair of the Hare, encompassing braised rabbit (the hare) with a stock shot through with Hair of the Dog's Cherry Adam from the Wood, which was served alongside sour, circa 1981 De Struise Dirty Horse. Pomme frites came with Chimay Red aioli and Allagash Brewing's tart wild ale Victor Francenstein, which was aged with Cabernet Franc grapes. For dessert? Toffee incorporating intense Russian imperial stout Black Albert from De Struise Brouwers topped with Belgian chocolate infused with Kabert—a ludicrously rare blend of Black Albert and Portsmouth Brewery's revered Kate the Great imperial stout.

"To be considered a beer dinner, you should cook with beer, which is the best ingredient and half the fun," enthuses Paxton. "We've been cooking with wine for hundreds of years, but to me there's nothing better than a nice beef stew with a Scotch ale. It blows wine out of the water."

TIPS FOR PLANNING A BEER-PAIRING DINNER

HOMEBREW CHEF SEAN Z. PAXTON OFFERS HIS TOP TIPS.

1. **BEER IS AN INGREDIENT.** "YOU CAN USE BEER JUST LIKE YOU WOULD OREGANO OR THYME, TO ADD FLAVOR," PAXTON SAYS. "BITTER IPAS AND SWEET BARLEY WINES CAN BE VITAL TO ANY RECIPE."

2. **TWEAK THE STANDARDS.** "SAKE AND SUSHI IS AN AMAZING COMBINATION, BUT SO IS SUSHI WITH A CRISP PILSNER OR LAGER," PAXTON SAYS. "DON'T BE AFRAID TO DEVIATE FROM THE NORM."

3. **STICK TO BEERS YOU LIKE.** "TRUST YOUR TASTE BUDS. IF YOU DON'T LIKE A SOUR, COMPLEX LAMBIC, DON'T PUT IT ON THE MENU."

4. **EAT AND DRINK SEASONALLY.** "USE SEASONAL INGREDIENTS AND MATCH THEM TO SEASONAL BEERS," PAXTON URGES. "DARK, RICH BEERS WORK WELL WITH STEWS AND BRAISED MEATS FOR A REASON."

5. **COMPLEMENT AND CONTRAST.** "WITH BEER PAIRINGS, YOU EITHER WANT TO COMPLEMENT THE FLAVOR (LIKE A MANGO SALSA OVER FISH WITH HEFEWEIZEN) OR CONTRAST IT BY SERVING A SUPER-HOPPY IPA WITH SPICY THAI."

6. **MAKE A SCENE.** "WHEN YOU DESIGN A DINNER, THINK ABOUT HOW YOU CAN MAKE IT INTERESTING," PAXTON SAYS. "MAKE A QUIRKY APPETIZER OR USE COOL STEMWARE OR KEEP THE MENU SECRET. THE POINT OF THE DINNER IS TO LEARN, HAVE FUN, AND INSPIRE PEOPLE."

7. **THE MORE THE MERRIER.** INVITE AS MANY PEOPLE AS YOU CAN FEED, PAXTON SUGGESTS. "OUR SOCIETY HAS GOTTEN SO USED TO EATING IN FRONT OF A TV. A BEER-PAIRING DINNER IS AN ORGANIC WAY TO GATHER A LIKE-MINDED COMMUNITY."

8. **BEGIN MILD, END BIG.** "START WITH LIGHTER, SIMPLER BEERS AND MOVE UP TO STRONGER, MORE COMPLEX BEERS," PAXTON SAYS. "IF YOU KICK OFF DINNER WITH AN IMPERIAL STOUT, YOU'LL BLOW OUT PEOPLE'S PALATES."

9. **HAVE A THEME.** "ORGANIZE YOUR BEER DINNER AROUND A SINGLE BREWERY OR PERHAPS A COUNTRY. IT SERVES AS A UNIFYING PRINCIPLE YOU CAN BUILD AROUND."

10. **STEADY THE COURSE.** "A THREE-COURSE DINNER CAN BE JUST AS REWARDING AS A TEN-COURSE DINNER," PAXTON SAYS. "DON'T BITE OFF MORE THAN YOU CAN CHEW, AND FEEL FREE TO KEEP THE RECIPES SIMPLE."

11. **POUR LIGHTLY.** "RESIST THE URGE TO SERVE AN ENTIRE BEER FOR EACH COURSE. FOUR OR FIVE OUNCES WILL DO. YOU DON'T WANT PEOPLE TO DRINK TOO MUCH, TOO QUICKLY."

A broken-down meat grinder doubles as taps at Brooklyn's Beer Table.

Dinner Is Served

When Justin Philips, a former beer importer, and his wife, Tricia, opened Beer Table in February 2008, they wanted to place equal emphasis on food and beer. In addition to quirky pickled veggies and butter beans with country ham, there's a Bavarian-style brunch consisting of crispy, fruit-topped Belgian-style waffles served with plump weisswurst and light, wheaty Schneider-Weisse. But a sausage-beer brunch is kid's play compared to dinner.

Chefs take to a tiled kitchen smaller than a mop closet and, armed with a couple of pots and one burner, devise dishes rooted in locally sourced New American cuisine. One night, there's roasted beets with arugula and pickled baby fennel. The next, stewed chicken with wheatberries, or caramelized bacon with roasted fingerling potatoes and chives. Each dish is custom paired to one of Beer Table's assiduously sourced global brews.

To test Beer Table's talent, I take a seat one Tuesday night for dinner. While couples chatter and the sound system hums with gentle jazz, Justin and Tricia attend to customers, delivering pints of

The dinnertime scene at Beer Table.

froth-capped Smuttynose Farmhouse and reciting dinner details. "I can't believe you cook in there," says one patron, motioning toward the chef furiously working the Lilliputian kitchen.

After taking my order, Justin—who often shares waiter duties with Tricia—delivers crisp bread crowned with shriveled, pickled oysters. The crunch balances the oysters' slippery brininess and primes my palate for the first course: a tangle of tangy, crunchy julienned celeriac and Empire apples studded with pinkish smoked trout and vivid-green parsley. "That trout was smoked by the Eel Man," he says. Wait—the Eel Man?

"His name's Ray Turner, and he catches eel, trout, and other fish and smokes them," Justin says of Turner's Hancock, New York, operation, Delaware Delicacies Smoke House. Locally sourced, indeed. Justin then presents Germany's Aecht Schlenkerla Rauchbier Helles. The brewery that crafted this light lager specializes in rauchbier (smoke beer), made using smoked malt. The crisp, sparkling Schlenkerla evokes campfires in aroma and taste, an ideal companion for the trout salad. The snappy apples and celery root provide a pleasing contrast and temper the trout's woodsy blast, further accentuated by the lager's gentle, smoky essence. "It's like the beer was brewed for this dish," says a nearby guest, forking up trout and taking a long drink.

After I clean my plate, Justin delivers the classic boiled French pot-au-feu. It's presented with fall-apart beef chunks, a rich marrowbone, and tender potatoes and carrots. On the side, there's salt, horseradish, and coarse-ground mustard for dipping and a double-walled glass brimming with savory beef broth.

"You can either pour it on top or drink it," Justin explains. He pours me a wineglass full of ambrosial Cuvée des Fleurs, which Long Island brewery Southampton makes with edible flowers. I sip the rich, savory broth, then the hazy, amber beer—like a liquid scalpel, Cuvée's spicy sweetness cuts through the broth, tempting me to kick it back

Diners savoring suds and sustenance at Beer Table.

like a bolt of bourbon. Instead, I dribble broth on the pot-au-feu and then follow the lead of several boisterous Australians, who are ravenously scooping out bone marrow. I follow suit, spreading a dab of gelatinous marrow on a spud. On its own, the marrow is much too rich. But Cuvée's alchemic magic scales back the decadence.

"I take it you liked dinner," Justin says, scooping up my empty plate and glass. "Mm-hmmm," I mumble, mentally scheming to sneak into the kitchen and steal an armful of marrowbones and a Cuvée bottle.

"Ready for dessert?"

I have the world's smallest sweet tooth, preferring a warming, post-dinner bourbon. But this dessert is too tempting to pass up: carrot cake spackled with ginger-spiked cream cheese, the plate painted with blood-orange sauce. Justin fills a wide-mouthed snifter with Dansk Mjød Old Danish Braggot, a malty beer blended with sweet mead. "Wow, this cakes melts into the beer," gushes a woman with curly brown ringlets. I fork up some cake, then sip Braggot. She's right. The beer's candy sweetness is a perfect match for the cake.

"It was a perfect ending to a hearty meal," says Bec Death, a member of that boisterous Aussie party. She typically favors beer over wine but had never tried a beer dinner. Curiosity took her to tonight's meal, which left her pleasantly surprised and hankering for another. "Each course built up to the next," she says. "The pairings always complemented, not overwhelmed, the food."

One of her dining companions, eco-friendly clothing company owner Billie Paris, was equally impressed. "We tend to have beer with snacks like wasabi peas and chips, but we hadn't thought to experiment with beer-and-meal matching," says Paris, who's eager to sample another pairing meal and switch up her usual dinner protocol: beer when perusing the menu, then wine to accompany the food. And she's excited by beer's myriad matching capabilities. "Who would have known that there was a dessert-type beer?"

And that's what it comes down to. Pint by pint, entrée after entrée, bars and restaurants are deviating from decades of standard operating procedure, and Beer Table is happy to join that march. "Many people see us as more of a drinking place," Justin says, clearing my empty plate. "But we're really a tasting spot where people happen to drink."

A CHEAT SHEET TO TEN COMMON BREW-AND-CHEW PAIRINGS

PIZZA: GO FOR A CRISP, SUBTLY SWEET AND HOPPY VIENNA LAGER, SUCH AS BROOKLYN BREWERY'S BROOKLYN LAGER OR GREAT LAKES BREWING COMPANY'S ELIOTT NESS.

OYSTERS: A CREAMY, ROASTY DRY IRISH STOUT, SUCH AS GUINNESS OR AVERY BREWING COMPANY'S OUT OF BOUNDS STOUT, HELPS BRING OUT THE BRINY OCEANIC TANG.

HAMBURGERS: TO CUT THROUGH THE RICHNESS, TRY A LIGHTLY HOPPED PALE ALE LIKE STONE BREWING CO.'S PALE ALE OR BOULDER BEER'S HAZED & INFUSED.

THAI: TO STAND UP TO CURRIES' LIP-SEARING HEAT, SELECT A SPICY, BOLDLY HOPPED IPA—MAYBE BEAR REPUBLIC BREWING CO.'S RACER 5 OR FOUNDERS BREWING COMPANY'S CENTENNIAL IPA.

CHOCOLATE: PAIR THE SWEET WITH A DARK, CHOCOLATE-KISSED IMPERIAL STOUT SUCH AS ALESMITH BREWING COMPANY'S SPEEDWAY OR GREAT DIVIDE'S YETI.

SUSHI: RAW FISH WORKS WONDERFULLY WITH LIGHT, DELICATE HEFEWEIZEN (TRY WEIHENSTEPHANER HEFEWEISSBIER) OR PERHAPS A WITBIER, SUCH AS ALLAGASH BREWING COMPANY'S WHITE.

FRIED CHICKEN: FOR CRUNCHY, GREASY FRIED CHICKEN, GO WITH A STRONG, HOP-TINGED MAIBOCK, SUCH AS ROGUE BREWERY'S DEAD GUY ALE OR ABITA BREWING CO.'S ANDYGATOR.

SALADS: IF THE SALAD HAS A CREAM DRESSING, TRY A BRIGHT PILSNER SUCH AS VICTORY BREWING COMPANY'S PRIMA PILS; A VINAIGRETTE OR ACIDIC DRESSING REQUIRES A COMPLEMENTARY FLAVOR, SUCH AS THE DUCK-RABBIT CRAFT BREWERY'S HOPPY DUCK-RABBIT BROWN ALE.

STEAK: CHARRED MEAT MAKES NICE WITH A RICH, MALTY BELGIAN DUBBEL, SUCH AS A CHIMAY PREMIÈRE OR BROUWERIJ ST. BERNARDUS'S ST. BERNARDUS PRIOR 8.

SALMON: THE GRILLED FISH WOULD GO GREAT WITH A SAISON, SUCH AS GOOSE ISLAND BEER CO.'S SOFIE, OR A WHEAT BEER LIKE TWO BROTHERS BREWING COMPANY'S EBEL'S WEISS.

EVER SINCE DENVER'S GREAT AMERICAN BEER FESTIVAL appeared on the scene in 1982, beer fests have been instrumental in spreading the gospel of craft beer. For curious drinkers, the events offer an educational smorgasbord of breweries and beer styles. But when the festival ends, so does the craft-beer education. Where else in town can drinkers purchase a pint of that IPA they adored?

At Philly Beer Week, "Ben Franklin" gets ready to swing the Hammer of Glory—the festival's official keg-tapping mallet.

"Festivals are a great introduction to beer, not a beer scene," says Josh Schaffner. He's the director of New York Craft Beer Week, one of dozens of beer-centric "weeks" in North America. These collaborative, community-rooted celebrations bring together a city or region's taverns, restaurants, brewers, and beer lovers, who curate craft beer–focused events such as beer-pairing dinners, double IPA fests, pub crawls, and canoe trips to breweries.

Sure, microbrew meccas such as Philadelphia, Chicago, and Seattle stage their expected revelries, but there are also festivities in lesser-known beer cities such as Syracuse, Baltimore, and Cleveland. "There's even an Alabama Beer Week," notes beer writer Jay Brooks, who helps run San Francisco Beer Week, "and there's not a lot of craft beer in Alabama." Yet.

Craft Beer Weeks

The dates for the beer weeks may change. Contact organizers for current info.

AMERICAN CRAFT BEER WEEK, MAY

craftbeer.com

The Brewers Association's national craft beer week grew out of the longer-running craft-beer month.

Alabama

ALABAMA BEER WEEK, JUNE

alabamabeerweek.com

Launched in 2010, events were held in Huntsville, Mobile, Tuscaloosa, Mobile, and Birmingham, home to the Magic City Brewfest at the historic Sloss Furnaces.

Alaska

ALASKA BEER WEEK, JANUARY

brewersguildofalaska.org

The festivities have included Belgian-beer dinners, vintage tastings of Alaskan Brewing Company's lauded Smoked Porter, and, in Anchorage, the Great Alaska Beer & Barley Wine Festival.

Arizona

ARIZONA BEER WEEK, FEBRUARY

arizonabeerweek.com

Begun in 2011, the statewide blowout included a canned-brew festival at Phoenix's Mad Chef Gastropub, beer brunches, and an official beer for the week.

California

SACRAMENTO CRAFT BEER WEEK, FEBRUARY
sacramentobeerweek.com
Find beer-centric scavenger hunts, Belgian-beer tastings, and a locally brewed IPA fest.

SAN DIEGO BEER WEEK, NOVEMBER
sdbw.org
The SoCal city pulls out all the stops with a rare-beer *breakfast*, lunches with brewmasters, and festivals at local breweries such as Green Flash.

SAN FRANCISCO BEER WEEK, FEBRUARY
sfbeerweek.org
The Bay Area offers strong beer paired with strong sausages, group bike rides, and a double IPA festival.

Colorado

DENVER BEER FEST, SEPTEMBER

denver.org/denverbeerfest/default.aspx

Dovetailing with the GABF, the week's events include rare-beer tastings, the Colorado Beer Ice Cream Festival, and bus tours of local breweries.

Georgia

ATLANTA BEER WEEK, MAY

s93573.gridserver.com

For its kickoff in 2010, the week featured beer-pairing dinners, Dogfish Head–sponsored bocce ball tournaments, and a Belgian beer fest.

Illinois

CHICAGO CRAFT BEER WEEK, MAY

chibeerweek.com

For its first year in 2010, the organizers offered specially brewed beers, canoe trips complete with brewery pit stops, and a road race that finished with a tour of Half Acre Beer Company.

Indiana

INDIANA BEER WEEK, JULY

brewersofindianaguild.com/beerweek.html

The highlight of the week is Indianapolis's Indiana Microbrewers Festival, which features dozens of the state's—and the nation's—best brewers.

Kentucky

LOUISVILLE CRAFT BEER WEEK, SEPTEMBER/OCTOBER

louisvillecraftbeerweek.com

During the inaugural 2010 week, events included a cask-ale fest, beer brunch, and Volksfest, featuring barrel-aged brews and a homebrew competition.

Maryland

BALTIMORE BEER WEEK, OCTOBER

bbweek.com

Homebrew tastings, Maryland Oktoberfest (enter the beer-belly competition!), and blind taste tests set Baltimore's celebration apart.

Massachusetts

BOSTON BEER WEEK, MAY/JUNE

beeradvocate.com/bbw

Produced by the website Beer Advocate, the week is anchored by the East Coast's largest beer bash, the American Craft Beer Fest.

Michigan

DETROIT BEER WEEK, OCTOBER

facebook.com/detroitbeerweek

Take a bike tour of the Motor City's historic and current breweries, go on a pub crawl, or hit the Detroit Fall Beer Festival.

Minnesota

MINNESOTA AMERICAN CRAFT BEER WEEK, MAY

mncraftbeerweek.com

Founded in 2010, the week includes brewery tours, special-release beers, and brewer-run tastings.

Mississippi

MISSISSIPPI CRAFT BEER WEEK, JULY

facebook.com/raiseyourpints

The must-hit event is Jackson's Top of the Hops Beer Fest, featuring 150-plus beers and educational seminars.

Missouri

ST. LOUIS CRAFT BEER WEEK, APRIL/MAY

stlbeerweek.com

Attend symposiums on brewing, play beer bingo, and explore the St. Louis Microfest, the city's largest craft-beer tasting event.

New Hampshire

PORTSMOUTH BEER WEEKEND, MARCH

smuttynose.com

The celebration of New Hampshire brews is headlined by tastings of rare Smuttynose vintages and the annual release of Portsmouth Brewery's Kate the Great imperial stout.

New York

BUFFALO BEER WEEK, MAY

buffalobeerweek.com

Past events have included extreme-beer tastings, homemade sausage and craft-beer pairings, and brewery showcases.

NEW YORK CRAFT BEER WEEK, SEPTEMBER/ OCTOBER

nycbeerweek.com

The Big Apple goes all out with cask-ale festivals, IPA tastings aboard yachts, and bashes inside four-star restaurants.

SYRACUSE BEER WEEK, NOVEMBER

greatbrewers.com/festival/syracuse-beer-week

The city features sampling sessions from upstate breweries such as Middle Ages and Empire, along with the Uber Beer Festival.

North Carolina

CHARLOTTE CRAFT BEER WEEK, MARCH

charlottecraftbeerweek.org

The Hop-a-Palooza IPA event, rare cask-ale tasting, and bars dedicating their taps to North Carolina's terrific beers help Charlotte shine.

RALEIGH BEER WEEK, AUGUST/SEPTEMBER

raleighbeerweek.blogspot.com

Launched in 2010, the inaugural week offered rare cask ales, beer cocktails, and a forum featuring brewers from Brooklyn Brewery and Terrapin Beer Co.

Ohio

CLEVELAND BEER WEEK, OCTOBER

clevelandbeerweek.org

Enjoy one-off collaborative brews, the Son of Brewzilla Homebrew Competition, and a fall-beer festival.

OHIO BREW WEEK, JULY

ohiobrewweek.com

The Athens-based week features the Brew BBQ Cook-off Competition, meatball-eating contest, and, oh yeah, lots of great Ohio beers.

Oregon

OREGON CRAFT BEER MONTH, JULY

oregoncraftbeermonth.com

Launched as a week in 2005, the bash mushroomed into a

monthlong celebration the ensuing year. Expect gobs of special beer releases, dinners, and fests, including Portland's legendary Oregon Brewers Festival.

Pennsylvania

PHILLY BEER WEEK, JULY

phillybeerweek.org

From pig roasts to beer-pairing seminars, festivals, and meet-the-brewer pub crawls, Philly offers it all.

Rhode Island

PROVIDENCE CRAFT BEER WEEK, OCTOBER

facebook.com/profile.php?id=100001547380154

Beer dinners and brewer visits culminate in the enormous Beervana Fest, hosted at the historic Rhodes-on-the-Pawtuxet, in nearby Cranston.

Texas

AUSTIN CRAFT BEER WEEK, OCTOBER

austinbeerweek.com

The Texas bash has featured collaborative beers, unusual cask ales, and special vertical tastings of Saint Arnold Brewing Company's Divine Reserve beers.

SAN ANTONIO BEER WEEK, MAY

sanantoniobeerweek.com

Beer-pairing dinners, pro-am brewing competition, and a bus pub crawl highlighted the first bash in 2011.

Virginia

RICHMOND BEER WEEK, NOVEMBER

richmondbeerweek.com

Craft-beer release parties, beer-themed movie screenings, and Belgian-beer dinners rounded out the city's first week, in 2010.

Washington

SEATTLE BEER WEEK, FEBRUARY

seattlebeerweek.com

Past events have included the Tour de Pints bike ride, Iron Brewer competition, and a brunch featuring *Brettanomyces*-soured beers.

SNOHOMISH COUNTY BEER WEEK, AUGUST

snohomishcountybeerweek.com

Area breweries, such as Diamond Knot and Big E brew special beers for the week.

Washington, D.C.

D.C. BEER WEEK, AUGUST

dcbeerweek.com

Organized by chef Teddy Folkman and beer distributor Jeff Wells, this week's events have included a craft-beer cruise down the Potomac River and an oyster fest with Rogue Ales.

DC CRAFT BEER WEEK, MAY

ontaponline.com

On Tap magazine orchestrates this event, featuring beer dinners and meet and greets with brewers.

Wisconsin

MADISON CRAFT BEER WEEK, APRIL/MAY

madbeerweek.com

The inaugural 2011-event offered a cask-ale festival and loads of exotic ales from New Glarus Brewing.

MILWAUKEE BEER WEEK, SEPTEMBER

milwaukeebeerweek.com

The famous brewing city's events have included Oktoberfest bashes and a beer-sampling session at the Harley-Davidson Museum.

Canada

ONTARIO CRAFT BEER WEEK, JUNE

ontariocraftbrewers.com/craftbeerweek/index.php

Past highlights have included a "field to firkin" farm tour, a tasting event of Ontario's canned craft beer, and tapas paired with beer.

TORONTO BEER WEEK, SEPTEMBER

torontobeerweek.com

Pub crawls, meet-the-brewer nights, and beer dinners were featured during the first week, in 2010.

VANCOUVER CRAFT BEER WEEK, MAY

vancouvercraftbeerweek.com

The 2010 launch featured a multivenue beer-dinner "crawl," a homebrew competition, and the Hoppapalooza bitter-beer event.

GLOSSARY

Adjunct Fermentable substances that are substituted for the cereal grains (chiefly barley) that constitute beer. Adjuncts, such as rice and corn, are used for several reasons. First, they're cheaper than barley. Second, they can lighten a beer's body. That's why Coors Light is the color of watered-down urine. That said, *adjunct* may seem like an evil word, but deployed judiciously, adjuncts can create delicious beer.

Alcohol This mood-brightening by-product of fermentation occurs when yeasts devour sugars in the wort. Alcohol is measured in two categories: alcohol by volume (ABV) and alcohol by weight (ABW). In craft brewing, ABV is the standard measurement, but here's a quick tip on how to convert ABW to ABV: multiply by 1.25. Alcohol is about 80 percent the weight of water, making a 6 percent ABV beer about 4.8 percent ABW.

Ale One of two big families of beer, the other being lager. Like my great-aunt in Florida, ale yeasts favor warmer temperatures, hanging out at the top of a fermentation tank. An ale's flavors and aromas are typically a touch estery—that is, fruity—and can be sweeter and fuller-bodied than lagers. Ales encompass an enormous grab bag of styles, from ambers to IPAs to Belgian strong ales.

Alternating proprietorship Arrangement by which brewers and winemakers may make their preferred potions at wineries and breweries they don't own. It's a relationship favored by nomadic brewers.

Aroma hops Hops that are used later in the boil for their bouquet, not their bitterness.

Astringent A drying, puckering taste. It can be negative or positive, depending on your taste buds.

Barley The predominant cereal grain used to make beer. Besides water, it's the biggest ingredient in brewing.

Barrel The standard term of measurement for brewing. A barrel equals 31 gallons. A half barrel, which is the standard keg you toted to parties in college, holds 15.5 gallons.

Beer engine A manually operated pump used to dispense cask ale.

Berliner weisse This ghostly pale, low-alcohol German wheat beer gets its sour, acidic tang from warm-fermenting yeasts and *Lactobacillus* bacteria. Drink it straight, or add a shot of sweet syrup (*mit Schuss*) and slurp it through a straw.

Bittering hops Used early in the boil to add bitterness, not aroma.

Bock A strong German lager with a hearty malt character and dark hue. Look for a beer with a goat on the label. A nearly syrupy, wine-strength eisbock is created by freezing the beer and removing the ice, thus creating a supercharged brew.

Boil This is the stage in beer making where the wort is boiled in order to kill bacteria and yeast, as well as to cause proteins to coagulate. Hops are added during this stage.

Bottle-conditioned Beer that's naturally carbonated by live yeast lurking within the bottle.

Brewers Association Based in Boulder, Colorado, this trade organization is the country's preeminent craft-beer advocate. It curates Denver's annual Great American Beer Festival.

Brew kettle The vessel in which the wort is boiled with hops.

California Common A rootin'-tootin', all-American lager fermented with a special lager yeast that functions better at toastier temperatures. The amber-hued brews are characterized by a bit of malt, fruit, and light bitterness.

Cascadian dark ale The name that brewers in the Pacific Northwest want to confer to dark, hoppy ales. Myself, I prefer the moniker *black IPA*, while the Brewers Association recommends American-Style Black Ale.

Cask A wooden, metal, or plastic vessel used to mature or ferment beer.

Cask ale Also called *real ale*, cask ale is unfiltered, naturally carbonated beer that's best served at 55 degrees Fahrenheit, which plays up its subtler flavors and aromas.

Cask-conditioned Beer that's fermented in a cask by a secondary dose of yeast.

Cicerone A beer sommelier who passes the Cicerone Certification Program.

Craft brewer A nebulous, controversial, confusing term that, according to the Brewers Association, describes a brewery that's small and independent and produces annually less than six million barrels of traditional beer. To me, craft brewers are any breweries that make flavorful, unique beer that you'll never see advertised during the Super Bowl. Since many microbreweries are no longer micro, *craft brewery* is the preferred descriptor.

Doppelbock A maltier, more potent bock. It's so rich, it's almost like drinking your dinner.

Dry-hopping The process when hops are added to beer that has finished fermenting or is conditioning. This step is what creates those intense, fragrant aromatic brews that make hops lovers swoon.

Dubbel This Trappist-style Belgian ale is a tour de force of rich malt and caramel flavors, with dark fruit and a whisper of bitterness to boot.

Extreme beers Extra flavor, extra alcohol, extra *everything*. These are brawny, beefy beers that'll knock you for a loop. Extreme beers include double IPAs, triple IPAs, Russian imperial stouts—in fact, anything with the word *imperial* on it.

Fermentation The metabolic process during which yeasts devour the sugars in the wort like Pac-Man, creating alcohol and carbon dioxide.

Filtration The removal of all the floating proteins and yeasts, creating a clearer, more stable—and sometimes less flavorful—beer.

Firkin A wooden, plastic, or, more commonly, metal keg that holds 10.8 gallons. You can also call it a cask.

Gluten It's the protein present in many grains, including barley. Sufferers of celiac disease can't drink beers that contain gluten— sadly, most of 'em.

Gose A specialty of Leipzig, Germany, this cloudy yellow wheat beer is dry and refreshing, with some coriander spicing and salt, which adds a sharp complexity. *Lactobacillus* bacteria or a dose of lactic acid gives gose a sour profile.

Gravity Scientifically speaking, it's the weight of a liquid in relation to the weight of an equal amount of water. To determine a beer's alcohol percentage, brewers measure the gravity before fermentation (original gravity) and after fermentation (final gravity). The higher the gravity, the stronger the beer.

Great American Beer Festival Since 1982, this has been the Super Bowl of American brewing. Annually, more than 400 brewers show up in hopes of garnering a bronze, silver, or gold medal in one of nearly 80 categories. Winning could alter a brewery's fortunes forever. Attending the festival leaves you (well, me) drunk for days.

Gueuze This traditional Belgian beer is made by blending one-, two-, and three-year-old lambics, then letting the mixture age and continue fermenting in the bottle. The result is a dry, fruity elixir with a lip-pursing sourness.

Hefeweizen A beer style from southern Germany made with 50 percent wheat or higher. It's a twangy, refreshing beer with notes of bananas and cloves, thanks to the yeast strain. Some folks like to squeeze in lemons. As far as I'm concerned, it's as unnecessary as nipples on men. Bonus trivia: *Hefe* means *with yeast*.

Hopback A sealed, hops-stuffed vessel through which the wort circulates, snatching up heady aromas and flavors.

Hops The creeping bine (a bine climbs by wrapping its stem around a support, as compared to a vine, which climbs with tendrils or suckers) *Humulus lupulus*'s female flowers (called cones), which flavor beers and provide bitterness. Each variety has its own unique flavor profile (*see page* 4). Hop resins possess two primary acids, alpha and beta. Beta acids contribute to a beer's bouquet. Alpha acids serve as a preservative and contribute bitterness early in the boil, flavor later in the boil, and aroma in the last minutes of a boil. Oh, and you might ask: Why do some hops smell like marijuana? The plants are related.

India pale ale (IPA) A super-bitter style of beer that, according to lore, was created when British brewers highly hopped ales to preserve them during long ocean voyages. This may be poppycock, but it's a fun tale to tell when bending elbows at a bar. An imperial, or double IPA, increases the hops and malt, creating a more bitter, boozier beer.

International bitterness unit (IBU) A scientific scale that measures bitterness in beer. A low IBU (Budweiser is around 11) means the beer isn't hoppy; when an IBU tops triple digits, you're in for a mouth-scrunching ride.

Kölsch This pale, elegant German ale receives its fruity, biscuity flavors from a warmer fermentation, before it is lagered at cooler temperatures to smooth out the sweet malts.

Lager The second main style of beer. Like penguins, bottom-fermenting lager yeasts prefer cooler temperatures. They also take longer to ferment, hence the term *lager*; *lagern* means *to rest* in German. Lagers are typically crisp, delicate, and as refreshing as a dip in a lake in August.

Lambic Made with wheat, this traditional Belgian beer is spontaneously fermented with wild yeasts, resulting in a sour, tart, barnyard-leaning profile. Lambics can be broken down into three general classes: those made with fruit such as cherries (kriek), raspberries (framboise), or black currants (cassis); gueuze, which is a blend of young and old lambics; and faro, a lambic sweetened with candi or brown sugar.

Macrobrewery MillerCoors, Anheuser-Busch InBev, and the other behemoths that rule American brewing. Contrary to common belief, macrobreweries do not make bad beer. Their brewing protocols are among the industry's most rigid. Rather, the problem is that they make lowest-common-denominator beer.

Maibock A lighter-hued, somewhat hoppier bock lager.

Malt To create malt, cereal grains are bathed in water. This jump-starts germination, allowing the grain to create the enzymes required to convert starches and proteins into fermentable sugars. The process is arrested when maltsters—the men who make malt—heat and dry the grain. Like coffee, grain can be roasted to create different flavors.

Märzen Since hot weather can muck up fermentation, this robust, full-bodied lager is brewed in early spring—*März* is the German word for *March*—then lagered into the fall, when it is traditionally served during Oktoberfest.

Mash The initial step in brewing. Crushed grain is steeped in a big ol' pot of boiling water, transforming starches to sugars.

Mash tun The vessel in which brewers boil their mash.

Mouthfeel How the beer feels when you drink it—a combination of body, texture, carbonation, and flavor. Mouthfeel is as subjective as a movie review.

Nanobrewery A wee brewery that, in my book, brews on a three-barrel system or smaller. Care to convince me otherwise? I'm all ears: josh.bernstein@gmail.com.

Nitrogen tap A draft-beer system that sends nitrogen coursing through beers such as stouts, augmenting its creamy mouthfeel.

Noble hops European hop varieties that are aromatic and less bitter. That's not necessarily negative. These hops, including Hallertauer, Tettnanger, Spalt, and Saaz, impart a spicy, herbal, zesty character. Commonly found in pilsners and European lagers.

Pasteurization Murdering yeast through a serious application of heat. Unpasteurized beers retain their yeast, which means the beer will continue to evolve over time.

Pilsner In the 1840s, this beer style was born in the Czech Republic town of Plzen, aka Pilsen. The straw-gold brew is see-through and packs plenty of spicy floral notes and zingy bitterness—the trademark of noble hops.

Pitch Adding yeast to the cooled-down wort.

Porter The style originated in Britain as a strong, dark brew made from a blend of sour or stale, mild and new ales. Though that style fell out of practice, porters still endure. They include the potent, dark brown Baltic (originally shipped across the North Sea) and innovative American riffs that can incorporate smoked malts, vanilla, or a mountain of hops.

Priming Dosing a fermented beer with priming sugar after it has been bottled or kegged, spurring on increased carbonation and flavor creation.

Rauchbier This German beer is made with malts that have been smoked over a roaring beech-wood fire, imbuing the malt with a smokiness. (*Rauch* is German for *smoke.*) It's a bit like drinking a liquefied ham or hunk of Texas BBQ.

Reinheitsgebot The German Purity Law dates back to 1516, when William IV, Duke of Bavaria, decreed that beer could be made from only hops, water, and grain—predating the discovery of yeast, which has since been added to the list. Unlike American brewers' anything-in-the-kettle attitude, German brewers are somewhat handicapped when it comes to exploring styles of beer because of this law.

Roggenbier While closely related to hefeweizen (the two beer styles use the same yeast strain that creates clove- and banana-like flavors), roggenbier trades wheat for rye. (*Roggen* is German for *rye.*) They're crisp and drying, with a bit of a spicy jolt.

Saison Originally brewed to slake the summertime thirst of Belgian farmhands, earthy, spicy saisons inhabit a wide stylistic range: Some are fruity, while others are desert-dry, peppery, and aromatic. Also called a farmhouse ale.

Session beer Beer low in alcohol, not in flavor. Best for sipping during a long-haul drinking session.

Skunked When UV light strikes beer, it causes isohumulones— chemicals released when hops are boiled—to break down, creating chemical compounds identical to those found in skunk spray. Never buy bottled beer that's been sunning in a store's window like a teenager at the beach.

Sorghum An African grass with a high sugar content that, when turned into a syrup, is used to craft gluten-free beer. Sorghum is the salvation of beer-loving sufferers of celiac disease.

Sour beer See *Wild ale*.

Sparging Removing the grains from the mash, leaving behind hot, watery wort.

Steam beer See *California Common*.

Stout This dark ale originally developed in Ireland and Britain and can be creamy, bitter, or coffee-like. Styles include the strong, full-bodied *imperial;* the sweet *milk stout* (made with lactose); the burly, roasty *Russian imperial*, which was originally brewed for that country's czars; the silky *oatmeal stout;* and the drinkable *Irish dry stout*, which includes Guinness.

Terroir The unique characteristics that soil, climate, and people give agricultural products. It was once reserved for wine and coffee, but beer is making a grab for the term.

Tripel This Trappist-style Belgian ale is a burly belly warmer, oftentimes boasting a double-digit ABV. The pale golden ale boasts a big ol' creamy head, complex flavors of fruit and spice, and a sticky-sweet finish.

Wet-hopping Using fresh, sticky, undried hops to make fresh-hopped beer. It's fall's fleeting delicacy.

Wild ale A catchall category of funky-tasting, offbeat sour beers dosed with wild yeasts such as *Brettanomyces* and bacterias like *Lactobacillus* (*see page 50*).

Witbier An unfiltered Belgian wheat beer that's amply spiced with orange peel, coriander, and whatever herbs catch the brewer's fancy. They're crisp and lively, and aces on an 80-degree afternoon. Drink it with a lemon if you must, but doing so is a little like coating filet mignon in ketchup.

Wort The hot soup that's extracted from the mash. It's like an all-you-can-eat buffet for the yeasts that create beer.

Yeast The microscopic critters that ferment your favorite beverage and make 5 p.m. the best hour of the day. Grains and hops notwithstanding, yeast drives about 90 percent of a beer's flavor profile. Each strain provides a different flavor profile, and breweries often develop their own idiosyncratic yeast strains. The main yeast strains used to create beer are from the *Saccharomyces* genus.

Photo Credits

À l'abri de la Tempête 172; Allagash Brewing Company 52, 108; Bard's Tale Beer Company 39; Barrier Brewing Co. 202; Bear Republic Brewery 34 (top); Bernt Rostad 243; Bill Russell/Just Beer 149; BrewDog 64; Brewery Ommegang 157; Brouwerij St. Bernardus 154 (left); Caldera Brewing Company 229 (left); Cascade Brewing 49; Chris Lohring 72; Chuck Cook 206; Cigar City Brewing 69 (top); Clipper City Brewing Company 185 (top); Denver Beer Fest 263; Deschutes Brewery 244 (right); Dieu du Ciel! 83, 84, 85, 86; Dogfish Head Craft Brewery 8, 102; Elizabeth Street Brewery 190; Elysian Brewing Company 165, 167, 168 (right); Epic Brewing Company/Luke Nicholas 23; Firestone Walker Brewing Company 106, 107; Flow Media & Graphics 113, 114; Foggy Noggin 200; Founders Brewing Company 117; Full Sail Brewing 90, 91; Goose Island Beer Co. 54, 110, 111; Great Divide Brewing Co. 163; Harviestoun Brewery 78, 109; Jason Kaplan 182, 183; Jeff Gill 220, 229 (right); Jenene Chesbrough 37, 195, 228 (left), 231; John Holzer 238; Josh Hallett 192, 193 (top); Joshua M. Bernstein 202; Julie Barnard 181; Karl Strauss Brewing 14; Kiuchi Brewery 154 (right); Kyle Roth/Clevelandhops.com IX, 10, 137 (left); Lakefront Brewery 147(left); Laurelwood Public House and Brewery 132; Lazy Magnolia Brewing Company 215, 217; Lesley Louden/Blameitonthefood.com 235, 236; Lew Bryson 74; Lost Abbey/ Port Brewing Company 50; Maui Brewing Co. 228 (right); Michael Harlan Turkell 253, 254, 256, 257; Mike Cadoux/Peak Organic Brewery 130, 135; Mike McCune 216; Mikkeller 35, 209; Mother Earth Brewing 159; © 2010 Nathan Arnone/Southern Tier Brewing Company 168 (left); Natian Brewery 205; New Planet Gluten Free Beer 44; North Carolina Brewers Guild 61; North Coast Brewing Company 245; Notch Brewing Company 79; NY Craft Beer Week 259, 265; Oakshire Brewing 22; Odell Brewing Company 112, 118; Oskar Blues Brewery 222, 223, 227; Philly Beer Week 260; Portsmouth Brewery 59 ; Powers & Crewe Photography 125 ; Pretty Things Beer and Ale Project 208, 212 ; Rogue Ales 139, 144, 147 (right) 193, (bottom); Schmaltz Brewing Company 34 (bottom); Sean Z. Paxton 248, 249, 250; SF Beer Week 262; Shelton Brothers 174, 176, 244 (left); Shimone Samuel 138; Shipyard Brewing Company 12; Shirley Wilson/Indie Hops 3; Sierra Nevada Brewing Co. 141, 143, 148; Sisterhood of the Suds 214; Stillwater Artisanal Ales 213 ; Stone Brewing Co. 20; StudioSchulz 69 (bottom), 164 ; Suemedha Sood 180 ; Surly Brewing Co. 71 ; The Alchemist Pub and Brewery 41; The Boston Beer Company 185 (bottom), 186 ; The Bruery 66, 95 ; Tim LaBarge 137 (right); Tim Stahl 203 ; Uinta Brewing Company 16 ; Upright Brewing 99; Worth Brewing 198 ; Yards Brewing Company 77, 104

shutterstock:

Collection of coffee splashes used throughout: © Shutterstock/Kess
Hand-drawn arrow doodles used throughout: © Shutterstock/aggressor
Torn Masking Tape used throughout: © Shutterstock/ Studio DMM Photography,
    Designs & Art
Grunge red wine glass stains used throughout: © Shutterstock/alekup
Collection of old note paper paper on white background used throughout:
    © Shutterstock/Picsfive
Sheet from notebook on white background used throughout: © Shutterstock/Skyline
Ancient vintage book used throughout: © Shutterstock/Andrey Burmakin
Collection of different stripes of masking tape used throughout:
    © Shutterstock/Jules_Kitano
Vector hand drawn comic elements used throughout: © Shutterstock/Yayayoyo
A page ripped off from the notebook used throughout: © Shutterstock/ vovan
Scribble beer mugs used throughout: © Shutterstock/advent
Watercolor blot background, raster illustration used throughout: © Shutterstock/
    Color Symphony
Food doodles used throughout: © Shutterstock/Canicula
Textured paper notes with red clip used throughout: © Shutterstock/vesna cvorovic
Abstract hand drawn watercolor blot, raster illustration used throughout:
    © Shutterstock/Color Symphony
Big collection of hand drawn food used throughout: © Shutterstock/ Canicula
Torn and cut tape strips used throughout: © Shutterstock/ixer
Aged instant photo with masking tape used throughout: © Shutterstock/samantha
    grandy
Picture of an instant photo front isolated on white used throughout: © Shutterstock/
    Christoph Weihs

ii, iii: © Shutterstock/Beata Becla; xii: © Shutterstock/Artex67; 4: © Shutterstock/
Tamara Kulikova; 9: © Shutterstock/Artex67; 21: © Shutterstock/Jita; 25: ©
Shutterstock/huyangshu; 46: © Shutterstock/lineartestpilot; 56. © Shutterstock/
Kochergin; 68: © Shutterstock/Artex67; 88bl: © Shutterstock/Doris Rich;
88br: © Shutterstock/IgorGolovniov; 105: © Shutterstock/Artex67; 116: ©
Shutterstock/iralu; 119: © Shutterstock/Harper; 128: © Shutterstock/Artex67; 129:
© Shutterstock/blue67sign; 13, 124: © Shutterstock/advent; 150: © Shutterstock/
Amid; 156: © Shutterstock/Artex67; 162: © Shutterstock/Madlen; 232: © Shutterstock/
Artex67; 259: © Shutterstock/photostudio 7; 81, 242: © Shutterstock/Artex67

INDEX

Note: Page numbers in *italics* indicate brews to try.

C

Cadoux, Jon, 187
Cadoux, Mike, 130, 133, 134, 136
Calagione, Sam, 81, 101
Caldera Brewing Company, *228–229*
California Common, 92–*94*
Canada
  beer weeks, 269
  Dieu du Ciel!, 83–86
Canned beer, 219–229
  advantages of cans, 220–221, 222
  bars serving, 225–226
  bottled beer vs., 220, 221–222
  brews to try, *226–229*
  growth of, 221, 225–226
  hand-canning system, 222–224
  image issues, 224–225
  recycling advantages, 219–221
  tinny taste and, 222
  volume and cost issues, 222
Cantwell, Dick, 166–168
Cape Ann Brewing Company, 15, *16*
Captain Lawrence Brewing Company,
    55
Caradonna, Tony, 30
Cascade Brewing, 48–49, *55*, *100*
Cascade hops, 2, 4, 11, *22*, *92*, *94*, *136*,
    148, *149*, *163*, 170
Cask ales, 119–128
  Alex Hall and, 120, 121, 122–123,
    126, 127
  beer engines for, 119–120, 122,
    126–127, 128
  cask breathers and, 126, 127
  cleanliness and, 126–127
  creating, 119–120
  earning place at pub, 123–126
  festivals and, 121–123
  firkins for, 119–120, 123, 125–126,
    127, 128
  quality and flavor enhancers,
    126–127
  return to, 120–121
  sparklers and, 127–128
  tips for sussing out proper pints,
    127–128
Cathedral Hill Hotel, 248
CDAs, 21, *22*

Celiac disease, beer and. *See* Gluten-free
    beer
Celia Framboise, 41, *43*
Celia IPA, 41–42
Celis, Pierre, 152–153, *154*
Cellar Door American Farmhouse Ale, *213*
Cellars. *See* Aging beer
Centennial hops, 4, *10*, 19, *22*, *92*, *137*,
    148, *163*, *164*, 226
Central City Brewing Company, *226*
Challenger hops, 4
Charlotte Craft Beer Week, 266
Chasing Tail Golden Ale, *217*
Chateau Jiahu, 101, *103*
Chatoe Rogue Series, 145, 146, *147*
Chicago Craft Beer Week, 263
Chinook hops, 4, *19*, 133, *164*
Chocolate Stout, *137*. *See also* Black
    Chocolate Stout
ChurchKey, 124–126
Cilurzo, Vinnie, 46–47, 54
Citra Blonde Summer Ale, *19*
Citra hops, 3, 4, 18–*19*, *22*, *33*, *213*
Civilization of Beer, 247–248
Cleveland Beer Week, 266
Clipper City Brewing Company, 120, 182,
    184, 188
Coconut Porter, 184, *227*
Cold Smoke Scotch Ale, *149*
Collaborations, 178–*179*, 187–188
Collaborator Stout, 188
Columbus (Tomahawk) hops, 4, 226
Competitions, 180–183, 184–186, 188–189
Corn, about, 27
Cornett, Tonya, 215, *216*
Corps Mort, *172*
Craft Brewing Company, *204*
Craftsman Brewing Company, 90–91
Crystal hops, 5
Crystal (or caramel) malts, 26
Cucapá Brewing Company, 113–115
Cummings, Charlie, 11

D

Daisy Cutter Pale Ale, 225, *226*
Daniels, Ray, 224
Dark Lord Day, 60, 61
Dark Lord Russian-Style Imperial Stout,
    65, *70*, 234